PALLADIO'S VILLAS

PALLADIO'S VILLAS
Life in the Renaissance Countryside

Paul Holberton

JOHN MURRAY

For Daniel and Jonathan Heaf

© Paul Holberton 1990
First published 1990
by John Murray (Publishers) Ltd
50 Albemarle Street, London w1x 4bd

British Library Cataloguing in Publication Data
Holberton, Paul
Palladio's villas: life in the Renaissance countryside
1. Italy. Architectural design. Palladio, Andrea, 1508–1580
I. Title
720'.92'4

ISBN 0–7195–4782–2

Printed and bound in Great Britain by
Butler & Tanner Ltd, Frome and London

Contents

Preface

This book is for anyone who has visited or will visit Palladio's villas and who knows or loves Italy. It is a kind of act of conservation, attempting to preserve not the physical monuments but their cultural environment. Either read it straight through, Part 1 to Part 4, or turn immediately to Part 2 or 3 (which corresponds most closely to the subtitle) or 4.

The Bibliography will suggest how much booty I have carried off from other scholars, though I have not raided as far and wide as I would have done, if I could have settled longer in this lush territory. One of the book's merits, however, should be to have made available for the first time in English the fruits of a mass of recent Italian and also German research. There has not been available in English anything like the profiles I have given in the second part of the book of Palladio's mentors Giangiorgio Trissino, Alvise Cornaro and Daniele Barbaro, such as I know I was once frustrated not to find. Much the same is true for the main section of the book, in which I have culled comments and quotations in Italian or Latin which have seldom been translated.

It is a general book, and it was not written for academics I know or do not know, although they may let their students read it. They may be irritated not to find the original Italian or footnotes and references, but really they should be able to track down everything by deductive use of the Bibliography; if that fails they can write to me or consult the eventual Italian edition. I owe special thanks to Clare Robertson for reading the text and to François Quiviger for pointing out to me several books and articles I would not otherwise have found. In Vicenza Mirella Furlanello even lent me her car.

My own photographs were taken with a Nikon F501; credits for the others are listed in the Acknowledgements. Most of the villas reproduced are privately owned, and I, and I hope my readers, appreciate the generosity of their proprietors in permitting me both to visit them and to take photographs. I owe special thanks to donna Diamante Luling Buschetti of the villa Barbaro, Maser, and to conte Giangiacomo di Thiene of the

Castello Porto, Thiene; I count among my friends dott. Vincenzo barone Ciani-Bassetti and his wife Ilaria of the Castello, Roncade.

A few words on some peculiarities of the text. Since I have Italian, it comes naturally to use Italian terms (once they have been translated or approximated). This may seem to non-Italian speakers pretentious, but I hope that most readers will be susceptible to the idea, though any linguist would reject it, that if one uses their terms one is somehow closer in spirit to those who employed them. In quotations (in single inverted commas) I have sometimes rendered individual words (after due explanation) into a forced English equivalent in double inverted commas – for instance, 'This villa "discovers" [*scopre*] the countryside around it'.

The English tend naturally to stress most Italian words and names correctly – Palládio, Vittória, Cornáro. Those, however, that defy English expectations, such as Véneto, Lépanto, Tríssino or Masér, I have marked for the benefit of the reader, on their first appearance and in the index, with an accent. It is anyway Italian convention to mark the stress when it falls on a final vowel (*civiltà*). Those who have no Italian at all may also read this book, but I would hate them not to know that *c* and *g* are soft (= ch, j) before *i* and *e*, except if an *h* is inserted: *ch* and *gh* are always hard (= k, gh). *Sc* + *i* or *e* makes the sound sh.

It should be borne in mind that the name of a villa is simply the name of its proprietor. Many are known instead by the names of previous proprietors (not necessarily their Renaissance ones), for instance the villa Capri, ora (= now) Valmarana (often also called the Rotonda), or the villa Barbaro, now Luling Buschetti (often also called Maser after its locality). Sometimes the villa is known by two successive owners yoked together, for example Porto-Colleoni. In this book I have always named villas after the first owner. There is further possible confusion in the fact that the names of the Italian nobility usually derive from place-names, but already by the Renaissance period many families no longer inhabited their ilk: some did, such as Giácomo Angarano in Angarano, Bonifazio Pojana in Pojana, but the Porto, and no longer the Thiene, lived in the small town of Thiene (the *h* is not pronounced).

References to Palladio's treatise on architecture *I Quattro Libri dell'Architettura* (*Four Books of Architecture*), henceforth abbreviated to *Quattro Libri* or *Four Books*, are given in brackets as follows: (QL II, i) stands for chapter i of the second of the four books.

Introduction

Perhaps Michelangelo had greater fame and influence; perhaps other architects, from Bramante to Sanmicheli or Ligorio, were equally ingenious; but no architect better than Palladio (Plate 1) represents the triumph of reason and civilization during the period called the Renaissance. As Palladio declared in his *Four Books of Architecture* (*I Quattro Libri dell'Architettura*) which will stand as the clearest, simplest and best organized textbook on the subject ever written — we know the heroes of antiquity to have been heroic not only by report of what they did, but by the stupendous remains of their buildings: similarly, Palladio's architecture epitomizes the qualities that enabled his contemporaries to deprecate foreigners or their forebears as ignorant and barbarous, and to congratulate themselves on their own perfected 'imitation of nature'.

No other artist or architect achieved such a tight and tidy synthesis or such a workable and logical grammar as Palladio's. Palladio has, however, too long been seen in exclusively abstract terms. His buildings are often regarded as an exercise in pure form — rather like models of themselves, real-life versions of the wooden scale models that were made and exhibited in the early 1970s, translating the woodcuts of the *Four Books* into three dimensions. If Palladio has been cited by architects or artists in this century (for example, by Le Corbusier) it has been to support a modernist or conceptual theory or system, as an exemplary idealist. His architecture already seemed idealist, at the beginning of this century, for De Chirico, whose 'infinitely nostalgic' cityscapes were partly inspired by the woodcuts in Palladio's *Four Books*; not only the empty squares and porticoes in the paintings, but even the little flags that hang out straight in the windless stillness recall those of Palladio's woodcuts.

The interest of architectural historians has also been, predominantly, in Palladio's form, although especially since the 1960s they have extended the scope of their enquiry, not content only to date, catalogue and attribute Palladio's buildings and drawings. However, architectural historians have been trained and continue to train students chiefly in the observation and

Plate 1
Portrait of Palladio, now hanging – appropriately enough, since that is the
building represented beside him – in the villa Rotonda. The villa Rotonda has
been described as 'almost the symbol of all Palladio's architecture'.

analysis of the visual and material. This book takes the quality and the formal felicities of Palladio's architecture rather more for granted. It is concerned instead with the uses of the buildings, with attitudes to them, and with their owners, who, for all that some of them were (by Palladio's own admission) 'very well studied in this art', were not technicians.

Further, this book demonstrates considerable scepticism about Palladio's famous proportions. I confess that my case against the importance that is generally given to the mathematical relationships between the parts of Palladio's buildings is not deeply argued: I merely state my alternative opinions in Chapter 19 of Part 4, 'Architecture'. Any detailed argument is likely to become excessively minute and ultimately circular. I would suggest rather that any reader who feels strongly on the subject go back to Rudolf Wittkower's *Architectural Principles in the Age of Humanism*, which pamphleted the notion, and pry at the cracks between his particular evidence and his general conclusions. They will find that he has a good point about churches, but churches are by definition symbolic buildings in a way villas are not.

I am also dissatisfied with the reaction that there has already been against the excessive abstraction in approaching Palladio. It is stressed that Palladio's villas were really, as he says they were, working farms – but then it is admitted that he nonetheless contrived, almost despite their owners, to build dreamer's architecture. The Palladio exhibition in London in 1975 featured, beside the models, a little cache of agricultural implements, of the kind no doubt that Palladio's porticoes (as he says in the *Four Books*) should have kept dry. It would be a mistake to think that any client of Palladio's ever handled such implements. I shall argue in some detail in this book that Palladio's villas were *not* glorified farmhouses. Farming, or rather an interest in *agricoltura,* a term which is not quite equivalent to modern 'agriculture', was fashionable among landowners who commissioned villas from Palladio, but it was not the motivation for building them; nor could any single farm ever have paid for the villa that rose (or that was meant to rise) majestically upon it.

The point is rather that the clients, too, wanted buildings of a certain visible quality – if not exactly for the sake of pure form. The final cause of Palladio's secular buildings was to provide a suitable environment or to be suitable possessions of gentlemen. Palladio was a courtier, in salary and status virtually an artisan, in the service of a pyramidal society – a society almost as static as a pyramid and, at the apex, as dynastic as that of the pyramids' builders. His buildings fulfilled and embodied the ideal of the 'magnificence' appropriate to those on the upper steps of society, gentlemen, noblemen, aristocrats – *gentiluómini, nóbili, cavalieri.* The all-important quality in the terms of their day to which Palladio's buildings were to conform was *civiltà*, a term connoting privilege and power as well as politeness.

Is it not also the case that the 'gentlemanliness' implicit in Palladio's architecture, and not just its formal qualities, caused the success of Palladianism in England? In the same way that Van Dyck turned to Titian's portraiture to learn how to project a 'civil' image, so Inigo Jones studied Palladio, and together, by their parallel assimilation of Venetian models, these two artists at the court of Charles I founded the dominant strand in the fine arts of the English-speaking world, until the Renaissance tradition foundered in the nineteenth century.

This book is, if you like, more about the illusion than the reality – if you will grant that illusions are also the stuff of history. It is about context, though it dwells more on vanished picnics than on political vicissitudes. It attempts to resuscitate around these now evacuated monuments of Renaissance architecture something of the joy and sweet air their owners consciously inhaled, more usually than not in gardens that no longer accompany the villas. The sixteenth-century vogue for *agricoltura* encompassed gardening, or was virtually an extension of gardening to the orchards and the fields. The dairy installed by Lorenzo the Magnificent at his villa of Poggio a Caiano near Florence in the late fifteenth century was an important precedent for Palladio's clients' activity; a successor was Marie-Antoinette's dairy-farm beside the Trianon. No owner of a Palladian villa would have remained unaffected by Sannazaro's pastoral classic, *L'Arcadia*. Almost all were in some sense living out a fantasy, as the statues and paintings with which they adorned their villas and gardens testify. In Palladio's time there was great enthusiasm, a craze exceeding the sober facts, for an ideal of life specific to the villa: Anton Francesco Doni wrote of his *smanio*, or feverish passion, for villas – villas such as he could never own, but loved to visit, temporary paradises on earth.

This book cannot hope to bring alive the generally bare rooms of Palladio's villas open to the public as if it were an historically authentic version of Joseph Losey's film of Mozart's *Don Giovanni* (in which the villa Rotonda was a set). It is not possible, and perhaps not even worthwhile, to make a waxworks, children's museum reconstruction of daily life in Palladio's buildings – to discover what his patrons ate for breakfast, how often they beat their wives, what they did in this room on Wednesdays. Certainly, the occasional crumb of information that is spared from the daily bread of history is worth a nibble, but the book is not about life in Palladio's villas as a daily routine or a backstage humdrum. It is about the villas in so far as they reflect a style of life pursued, whether attained or not – the image and convention of what life should be, known in Italian as *rappresentanza* or *figura*.

The occupants of Palladio's and other such houses were not concerned in their letters or other records to dwell on the personal and individual, but tended to reduce or elevate their ordinary experience to the general and universal. In the Renaissance, philosophy had dreamt of everything: particular events were examples or demonstrations of established platitudes, the new was part of the old. Therefore what is important in Palladio's villas and the way of life they sheltered and embodied was the normal and standard, not the odd or peculiar. They all, in different degrees or combinations, follow common ideals, some of them newly fashionable, many unchanged for centuries. Palladio's houses represent a paradigm of gentlemanly life, and do so, in so far as architecture can, almost didactically.

One can only see Palladio's villas, and their occupants, in perspective. It is a perfectly valid and satisfying mode of vision. There are clearly traditions within which Palladio's villas belong and for which Palladio evolved satisfactory forms. Even if these attitudes were not overwhelmingly interesting, the excellence of the architecture of the villas would make their study worthwhile, for knowledge of them increases appreciation of the monuments.

PART 1
Palladio's Career and Clientele

1

State, Sea and Land

It has been many times remarked and echoed that 'Palladio's birth in Padua in 1508 was perfectly timed and placed'. It was not in fact quite perfectly placed, since as soon as he could he removed himself to Vicenza, but both Palladio's built architecture and his even more influential book, *I Quattro Libri dell'Architettura*, were peculiarly products of their time. Their season was Janus-headed. Looking back, it paraded the triumph and final conquest of the High Renaissance, the irreversible transformation and amelioration of life, with all the arts in full flourish, with human curiosity aroused and unquenchably alive; looking forward, the flourishing arts and letters and even the spirit of enquiry could be seen as an irrelevance and a distraction, diverting from a decline.

Italy's decadence during the sixteenth century was not in origin spiritual or moral, but political and economic; it was not internal or natural, but the imposed consequence of external defeat. The country had been defeated nationally and severally in the 'Wars of Italy', which began with French invasions at the end of the fifteenth century and were concluded only by 1530. The Wars crippled the political and perhaps even the mercantile ambition and expansionism characteristic of the numerous states of Italy in the fifteenth century, even in Venice, which had survived the Wars better than any other local power. However, even during the Wars and for some time after them Italian culture was affirmed, enjoyed and developed with great enthusiasm. Palladio's career began in this second sense on an upswing which on a graph might look like that of the 1920s or the 1960s after the First and Second World Wars; but there were hard limits to the possible growth.

At many turns one finds a striking escapism in Italian culture during the peaceful years of the sixteenth century — one testimony that has often been called is the aversion of Venetian aristocrats away from the perils of the sea towards the land, on which Palladio built them splendid villas. However, it is a little too easy to blame on escapism the eventual stagnation to which the Renaissance succumbed. The real limits were not set by

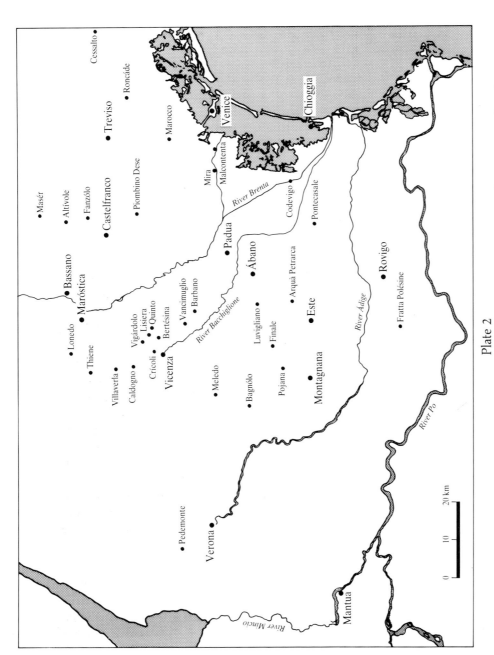

Plate 2

Northern Italy: major towns and rivers, and the small towns and hamlets with villas mentioned in the text.

individual or collective decisions. The escapism, though undeniable, was an effect and not a cause: the cause was the situation, one of individual and political stiflement, for which the Wars were responsible. Because the Wars did not interrupt the progress and production of fine arts throughout Italy, their importance may not seem so central, but, next after the cultural watershed of the Renaissance itself, they were perhaps the single most important factor determining the course of Palladio's career and the nature of his opportunities.

The Wars as a whole date from the French invasion of Italy in 1494, of limited effect, but followed by another in 1499, to which Milan fell. Even Milan was incidental to the struggle for the control of the southern kingdom of Naples, which Ferdinand II of Spain attained for himself in 1504. Also interested was the Holy Roman Emperor Maximilian Hapsburg, desirous to reclaim territory that had once been Charlemagne's. The Italian states, including of course papal Rome, attempted to play these powers as much against other Italian states as against each other. Palladio was born, on 8 November 1508, one month before all, or almost all, combined against Venice. Louis XII of France moved from Milan; Maximilian came down from the Alps and the Dolomites; Ferdinand II moved from the south, the Venetians having opportunistically, while the kingdom was disputed, taken possession of cities belonging to Naples on the Adriatic seaboard. Of the Italians Francesco Gonzaga, Duke of Mantua in southern Lombardy, was now a commander for the French, though previously he had led the Venetian army: the Venetians reckoned his wife Isabella d'Este had swayed him, for her brother Alfonso d'Este, Duke of Ferrara, and his subjects had bitter grievances at Venetian incursion into the Polésine, the land, or marsh, round the mouth of the Po to the south of the lagoon. (Ferrara and Venice had already been at war over the Polesine in the early 1480s. Venice eventually had the best of it: hence, *inter alia*, Palladio's villa in the 1550s for the Venetian Badoér at Fratta Polesine.) Last, and the real villain of the piece in Venetian eyes, was Pope Julius II, driven indeflectibly by a new vision of real papal power, and no longer tolerant of a long tradition of nominal 'fiefdom' in the Romagna, where Venice had again insinuated her beneficent protection. Pope Julius joined the League (known as the League of Cambrai after the town in northern France where the agreement was made) only in April 1509, just a few days before Venice offered to restore, too late, the disputed cities of Faenza and Rímini.

In fact, this menacing combination of so many powers was not unstoppable and was certainly unstable. The Venetians had already trounced Maximilian acting alone in 1508, but they were thrown into panic and despair by the heavy defeat of their army by the French at Agnadello (by the river Adda, 20 miles east of Milan) in 1509, in a battle which should have been evenly matched. The mainland garrisons were small and the citadels were seldom defensible in this age when cannon for the first time realized its potential. As a result of the defeat the Véneto was immediately overrun and even Padua, a day's journey from Venice, was taken. However, the lagoon was not threatened; Padua was retaken; the Venetians drew together another army, the League wavered, and by 1511 the Venetians were fighting with Julius II against Ferrara and the French. However, in 1512 the French won another victory at Ravenna. By 1513 the Venetians were in alliance with the French, but in the same year were defeated by the Germans at the Battle of Motta di Livenza. During this time, although Padua had quickly been retaken and successfully defended, the Venetians were expelled for a second or third time from other cities they had reoccupied, such as Palladio's own adopted town to be, Vicenza, which they regained from Maximilian in 1509, then lost to the French in 1510, regained, then lost again in 1511, then finally regained. Verona was not retaken until 1517. By that date, within ten years of Agnadello, the Venetians had recuperated all their major possessions on the mainland or 'Terraferma', but shakily and with considerable difficulty; they had lost beyond hope their more adventurous or recent subjections, for instance those down the Italian Adriatic coast. Further, they had kept or regained what they had only by dint of a series of compromises and cessions of principle and advantage, notably to the Pope. The cost in money of the war had been simply enormous. Before the war the Venetians had not seen limits, and they had been consistently undaunted and aggressive; now the Lion had lost its appetite. Having once been proud and greedy, they had been humbled and demoralised. They had been badly frightened, and then worn down. They were ready to be content – a profound change of spirit and attitude.

They could not yet be content, however, since the political situation remained uncertain and volatile until the end of the 1520s, and in the aftermath of a highly destructive war there long continued slump, plague and famine. In the economies of the day, which remained local and land-based though supplemented by trade, any one of these three implicated the others, and their spiral was locked by a fall in population. The population figures give a ready measure of the damage and the pain of recovery. In the city of Verona, for which there are precise figures, there had been nearly 50,000 inhabitants before the outbreak of war; in 1518, the year after its recapture by the Venetians, it had just over 25,000. But the city did not regain the numbers it once had had until the 1550s. Thus in 1529 there were still only 27,000 inhabitants. In 1541 there were only 32,000. The graph does not accelerate until the 1540s: in 1545 the figure was approaching 40,000; the next figure comes in 1555, when the population had reached 45,000, and only in 1558, two generations after the outbreak, was the population again just under 50,000. The economy, trade and levels of general prosperity would have conformed, given some variation, however, due to the harvests. Introduced by the memorable vintage of 1540, there were signs everywhere of a burgeoning in the 1540s, and in the 1550s there was a sunny spell of affluence, which continued, although there was a succession of bad harvests at the end of the 1550s. There was also trouble germinating: for the Venetians, difficulties in placing goods in the markets of the eastern Mediterranean, and in the second half of the 1560s Turkish belligerence stirring beyond appeasement. In 1570 there came war, the pyrrhic victory of the Battle of Lépanto and the loss despite it of Cyprus; the failures of two of the three Venetian merchant banks, which were not replaced; in 1576 a devastating plague. Much of the trouble was sheer ill fortune, and in another age and other circumstances might have been remedied by good; in fact Venice's capital base irreversibly declined.

To this pattern Palladio's activity in building villas and palaces for private patrons very neatly conforms: his first independent jobs came in the later 1530s, numerous commissions in and around Vicenza followed in the 1540s and into the 1550s, including, in 1549, the anchor of his career, the Basilica at Vicenza; in the 1550s and 1560s his practice spread to Venice and his reputation grew; in 1570 he moved, for the remaining ten years of his life, to Venice, where his last work was the Redentore church, a thanks-offering for the cessation of the plague that was itself a factor in Venice's decline.

The Venetians, when compared with the rest of Italy, had many good reasons to be content. It used to be said that the High Renaissance continued uninterrupted in Venice, while the rest of Italy, in travail, succumbed to Mannerism. In fact the Wars of Italy were a disaster for all, but the Venetians had not, like the Milanese, Genoese and Neapolitans, passed under the direct control of foreign powers. They had not, like the Florentines, been forced to accept a governor, even if the governor was native, a Médici. Nor had their city been sacked, a horror which even in 1509 had never quite become thinkable, but which in 1527 befell Rome traumatically: the Pope's own palace was looted, the Sistine Chapel stripped. For the Venetians, the damage, though great, was reparable; for other Italians the way of life of the past was beyond recapture. Venice's eastern front, and her 'empire by sea', had remained intact throughout the Wars, since the King of Hungary, who threatened Venetian ports in modern Yugoslavia and Albania, had refused to enter the League of Cambrai; also the Turks had ignored their new opportunity, although in 1499 they had for the first time defeated a Venetian fleet, and a large one,

at the Battle of Zónchio (in the southern Peloponnese). It says much for
the change of Venetian perspective that the commander of the fleet at
Zonchio, Antonio Grimani, who had been clapped in irons on his return
from the battle in 1499, was in 1521 elected Doge.

The change of perspective included the 'switch to the land', the abandonment, as it is sometimes represented, by Venice of her traditional
source of wealth, trade across the sea, for a land-bound existence — a shift
held responsible for the outcrop of Palladio's villas in the strata of history.
Trade across the sea had been the motor of Venetian power, though it
was of course much less significant for the cities of the Terraferma. During
the Wars it had been severely dented by the loss of western markets; but
it recovered, and during the sixteenth century did not suddenly decline.
In 1501, when the news had broken that the Portuguese had returned with
cargoes from the Indies, there had been lamentation in Venice; however,
as it transpired, the overland spice-route, exiting in Syria, was neither
superseded nor even effectually undercut during the sixteenth century.
There were changes in the pattern of trade: for instance, the state-organized
annual *mude* or convoys that had set off and returned regularly and
profitably during the fifteenth century became infrequent while the eastern
Mediterranean markets become more competitive and volatile, and for the
individual trader the seas became more dangerous. It became not so easy
'to make two ducats out of one' in the old way, simply by ferrying goods
from one port to another — although the import seems not to have been
so problematic as the export: Venetians would all too often find that for
the goods they were carrying out (very often wool, kerseys) the outlet
was overstocked or their prices undercut. There is the recorded case of
Nicolò Donà, who as a young man in 1561 gave up trading in disgust at
the humiliation of arriving at Aleppo with outbound goods both inferior
and overpriced. Disasters had always been frequent, but in the fifteenth
century no one would have voiced such a sentiment as this in a letter
home from Syria in 1555: 'It is less bad to keep capital at home than to
put it into circulation with so many risks and without profit'.

On the other hand the colossal losses sustained by the Venetians in the
war of 1570 reveal that by comparison these were only hiccoughs in
the hum of their trade. The difficulties arising beforehand undoubtedly
contributed to the Venetian failure to recover after 1570, but that later
failure should not be read back into the earlier period, the period of the
construction of Palladio's villas. Although Nicolò Donà had renounced a
merchant's life in 1561, his brother Andrea had continued in trade, but
lost his life at Lepanto. After 1570 one Giuseppe Dolfín declared himself
virtually destitute, because in the 1560s he had invested 200,000 ducats
in coral, which he had then lost altogether in the war, and he had also had

to sell land and a timber-yard in order to ransom two sons. For many the loss of Cyprus was similarly ruinous — not counting the large sums contributed to its vain defence by both wealthy and not so wealthy patricians (for instance, Palladio's patron Daniele Bárbaro, 800 ducats), which they never saw again. Before 1570 Cyprus had been highly profitable, particularly for its sugar-crop — a Venetian Caribbean. During Palladio's career industry expanded, and some sectors, such as woollens, became significant as they had not been in northern Italy in the fifteenth century. Notably, in Vicenza the silk industry prospered. Above all Venice was unshaken as a metropolis and a financial capital, where it was possible, Whittington-like, to make a fortune: for instance, Bartolomeo Bontempelli, from unknown origins in Bergamo, had come to Venice in 1552 at the age of thirteen; ten years later he partly owned one shop; another sixteen years later he fully owned another; another nine years on he owned both, with money invested elsewhere. On his death in 1616 he left farms, houses, a share in a copper mine, money in government stocks and in loans, and a large amount of cash.

The discovery of the New World, or the rise of the port of Antwerp, factors such as these could not alter the geographical logic that made Venice an entrepôt between the eastern Mediterranean and Germany, and predicated profit. When Venetian trade eventually declined, the reasons for it were less that Venice was now inconveniently situated for Atlantic-borne trade, more that other ships, English above all, began to work its routes in the place of Venetian carriers. Flemish merchants transferred to Venice by preference after the sack of Antwerp in 1576 and the blockade of the Scheldt in 1585. The full effect of the loss both of too many ships and of too many patricians who could sail them at Lepanto, the failure to hold Cyprus, the devastating plague of 1575–6, the failure of the last merchant bank in 1584, did not appear until right at the end of the century. Palladio before his death in 1580 would hardly have felt even a nip of the chill. Although the Venetians murmured at their allies, who had sailed off rather than following up after the battle, Lepanto was cause at the time for magnificatory celebration which registered no disquiet: there is none in the stucco trophies recording the battle applied to Palladio's Loggia del Capitanio in Vicenza. For Palladio the plague was marked by an invitation to build virtually the church of his dreams, generously budgeted, the Redentore, his crowning masterpiece.

In reality there was no conflict between investment in land and in trade: one did not cause money to flow out of the other. Daniele Barbaro's successor as official historian of Venice, Paolo Paruta, argued that Venice had more ships in the late sixteenth century than at the end of the fourteenth, and that the land empire had largely paid for them. It was of course at the end of the fourteenth and the beginning of the fifteenth century, and not at the end of the fifteenth and the beginning of the sixteenth, that Venice acquired her mainland dominion. Even before she did so, many Venetians already had interests vested in the mainland; in fact they had always been farmers as well as fishermen and sailors. When she did so, the main reason was actually to assist trade – to guarantee the safe onward shipment of merchandise imported from the east, to subvent taxes and impediments along its necessary routes (many of which were still by water).

Naturally the intrinsic value of the land empire had been appreciated already in the fifteenth century: those taxes formerly paid to others and levies on the subject cities now boosted the revenue of the Venetian government, hence Paruta's argument. Perhaps particularly in the second half of the fifteenth century more and more Venetians invested in land: the Venetian proprietors of several Palladian villas had inherited a previous house on the site from their grandfathers. The fact that the Wars of Cambrai did not after all turn the Venetians away from the land, as one might have expected, proves that its attraction had already bonded in the fifteenth century. It is interesting that a diarist reports in the year of disaster 1509 that many regarded land, despite its occupation by the enemy, as a better investment than the traditional gilt-edge, government stock, for government bonds, which fell through the floor, were mere paper and ink. Land was real, and eventually, once the war was over, recoverable. Certainly after the Wars the rise in land prices that had started in the late fifteenth century was sustained. However, it looks as though the Venetians bought land not with money switched from trade – not with their adventure capital – but with their secure money, their savings, their provision for daughters' dowries; not to make money, but to hold safe a patrimony.

A crucial point, I believe, and I will argue it later, is that returns on land *never* matched returns from trade, even if what one could get from trade was no longer as good as two ducats for one. Returns from land do not seem to have been as high as the interest on moneylending or on government stock. That does not mean, however, that the Venetians (like the mainland nobility) did not try to get more out of their land, once they had it. Certainly they did: they took up *agricoltura*, they went out to their farms themselves instead of leasing them or leaving their management to factors. Furthermore, they knew from before the Wars that the import of grain to non-self-sufficient Venice was highly profitable; then after the Wars its price rose and it became more difficult to procure. In such circumstances improvement of home-based agricultural yields was prudent and desirable; in many cases the asset, land, already existed, and in any outcome it was a safe investment. In this way one arrives at some explanation for Palladio's villas: partly because they had hopes of achieving better yields from them, both the Venetians and the wealthy of the mainland cities began to spend more time on their mainland possessions. They could no longer camp in the country, but needed a decent house. That is only part of the explanation, but it encourages a correct perspective on the 'switch to the land', which was not at the expense of trade, although it took place in a worsening trade climate. Three phases may be distinguished: purchase of the land, exploitation of the land and then, after the period in which Palladio built villas, loss of the sea. It was only at the very end of the sixteenth century that the Venetians managed, as the phrase went, 'to lose their trousers' — *spantalonarsi*.

Another crucial point, involving a quite different perspective, is that Palladio built most of his villas not indeed for Venetian patrons but for the mainland nobility. Although, excluding the villa Rotonda, his most famous and largest completed villas were for Venetians, he had already evolved their distinctive and essential characteristics in his work for local, Vicentine barons. The Venetians did not simply 'switch to the land' as it were to virgin territory, but turned to doing something the mainland nobility were already doing. One such mainland activity then fashionable was to employ Palladio to build or rebuild villas. Significantly, Venetians commissioned Palladio almost exclusively to build villas during the 1550s, but when by 1570 he had extended his range and had become a Venetian architect, living in Venice, he was employed on everything else except villas. Villas, however, went on being built — by Vincenzo Scamozzi of Vicenza, for instance, until he eventually also transferred to Venice. The Venetians, who generally had more money, built grander villas, but the Terraferma nobility had already set the style. Of course they, too, had been ready to be content, accepting after the Wars that there was no alternative to Venetian dominion.

It has been said that Venice declined because she 'stood still in a changing world', but the decisions that led to her eventual ossification were as sensible, flexible and ruthless as those of her formative period. Always for good reason, sometimes with success, the state attempted to manipulate or mitigate economic trends by taxation and policy. Even the lack of ships that became acute after Lepanto hardly resulted from Venetian negligence, but from chronic and intractable problems with shipbuilding and manning with which the government had wrestled. There was no failure of good sense or shrewd argument. On the other hand there was a new mood, in so far as the Venetians felt they had to be content; in common with the rest of Italy, they recognized, as their Early Renaissance forebears had not, that men cannot control events.

Venetians of the sixteenth century would not have forgotten, as we may, the greater difficulties and worse crises of their earlier history. Venice had once controlled Constantinople – one could say that ever since the city had been in decline. The loss of Ragusa (in present Yugoslavia) had been still closer to home and haemorrhaged Venetian control of the Adriatic. In the late fourteenth century the Genoese had been at Chióggia, in the lagoon itself, posing a worse danger to the city than any since. The earlier history of Venice had not been one of triumph. The city had always been subject to some adversity, as the Venetians saw it – it was almost a mentality. Therefore, at the end of the century it did not seem that the sixteenth century had been a period of deterioration: on the contrary it seemed almost the kind of breathing space Fortune had never before vouchsafed.

As Doge Nicolò Contarini wrote looking back to the way things stood in the 1590s: 'At that time there was manifestly trust between the State of the Republic and all the crowned heads of Europe; with everyone, one could say, there was open friendship. Besides that the State abounded with all the riches that, under ordered government, a fertile countryside, an industrious populace and a favourable geography can produce.' With little doubt his next sentence includes in its reference time passed in villas like those built by Palladio: 'The only thing lacking to her complete happiness was the charge that a necessary consequence of it was idleness and idleness's companions luxury and vice, which in principle have always been detested as the cause of the ruin of cities but in practice have been loved, once men had become used to them.'

However, Contarini continues: 'Lest anyone should be under the illusion that the said repose of the city had been totally slothful, it is a fact that up to that time Venetian ships furrowed the whole Mediterranean sea, bearing the richest cargoes, which none could rival, and even carried their navigation beyond it, in certain regions. Whence mercantile commerce flourished and increased marvellously, with public benefit beyond reckoning. In addition the rivers and waters which had been doing damage with their currents to the lagoon – that unique and miraculous God-given, not human-built, bulwark of the city – were with incomparable skill and expense diverted away from it; and those which were harmful to agriculture were embanked and enclosed by strong dykes. For which reason the city did not lose the singular precedence bestowed by Heaven on her alone; and those fields that had been the lowest of marshes, deep lakes and ponds, were now transformed by ingenuity, effort and expense into the most fertile terrain, pleasant meadows and charming gardens, adorned with many rich and proud mansions; forests and hills were subjected not only to the axe but to the plough, and produced as much, if not more, than the arable countryside, to such an extent that the grain that in earlier times had to be procured from distant countries, and almost begged from enemies, was now abundant at home, and it looked as though shortly Venice would be supplementing the supplies of others.'

The Venetians had little choice except to be content. Their fifteenth-century or earlier imperialism had been nourished in a context of small states, smaller than Venice (only Naples was a larger city during the Renaissance, with a population reaching 200,000; Venice had once also reached the figure, but never regained it after the fourteenth-century decimations by plague); now the arena was held by 'the greater powers', as Venice had recognized them to be long since. Once she had recovered her major losses, and her pride, once the portions into which Italy had been carved had been more stably allocated, Venice accepted what she had as her lot, with virtually the same passivity as was shown by the conquered states of Italy. After the Wars, Venetian efforts turned not simply to reparation but to defensive provision against the disaster's recurrence (cities such as Padua and Verona were fortified; the more aggressive principle of a counter-attacking mobile army was abandoned). The Venetians looked to keep and develop what they had, not to seek more. Venice became the champion of peace, and of the virtues associated with it. Palladio's villas were one of the fruits of the peace — and also more profoundly of the change of heart, of the 'idleness' consequent upon peace.

In the years during which Venice had acquired her mainland dominions, the first of them Treviso in 1389, there had been something old-time Spartan about the solidarity of her patriciate and their dedication to political duty above all else. There was little room for a broader culture or for personal interests except within or beside a public career. In this sense the Renaissance had been slow to touch Venice: compared to Florence she had been backward almost till the end of the fifteenth century. However, bumps of individual self-preference were appearing in the second half of the century, and in the altered climate of the sixteenth century, literary, artistic, scientific and religious interests blossomed. One can see it at a glance in the differences in the careers of the leading talents of the successive generations, often of the same family. For instance Leonardo Giustinián, born 1388, pupil of the famed humanist school in Ferrara of Guarino Guarini, correspondent of leading intellectuals all over Italy, held high State office from the age of forty. He was author of the most exquisite songs and music, but the music is entirely lost and the songs are preserved only in a few manuscripts. All of them were amorous, serenades and ballads, entirely subsidiary, a mere pastime, of no account then — but this realm of things is the very soul of sixteenth-century culture, and it is superabundant. Leonardo's brother was Lorenzo, later St Lorenzo Giustinian, who could not avoid, once his spiritual eminence had been recognized, election to the bishopric of Venice, which involved him for the rest of his life in numerous political affairs. The career of Blessed Tommaso Giustiniani, of the same family, in the first half of the sixteenth century, was by contrast completely unpublic, though he was an advocate of Church reform (one of those many in Italy who felt the same need for change as Luther or Calvin): he held no office even within the retiring Camaldolese order which he had joined, but became an ever stricter hermit. Over the turn of the sixteenth century the contrast between Bernardo and Pietro Bembo, father and son, is equally sharp. While Bernardo was bound by many ties to Florentine intellectuals in the circle of Lorenzo the Magnificent, he spent most of his career as Venetian ambassador to Italy's several courts; Pietro, however, broke free of the State, making his career as a courtier on the mainland, then as a papal secretary and eventually as a cardinal (at which point he had to take minor orders), but essentially as a man of letters. Pietro Bembo eventually became official historian of the Republic he had never served. In Venice in the fifteenth century there had been no equivalent of a man like Gabriel Vendramín in the sixteenth century, a Doge's first cousin, but who absolutely declined a political career; however, he knew Titian as a friend, and was widely recognized as a patron and connoisseur. In the fifteenth century the books with which to make a public library had been bequeathed to Venice, but no St Mark's Library, no physical sign of the new 'Athenian' Venice and statement of cultural hegemony, had been constructed: the erection began in 1537 of the interloper beside the religious and government buildings of the Piazza.

In so far as they were merchants, the Venetians revelled in peace. They were perhaps impotent to expand; but they successfully publicized a positive policy of peace, emphasizing peace as the external face of their 'well ordered government' – the so-called 'myth of Venice' as an ideal constitution. Palladio's villas are an extension of the myth, which worked as a myth not just grossly in the sense of a propaganda lie, but subtly as an element of self-esteem, as a myth believed, a faith unquestioned. The escapism that the villas embody was not seen rudely as escapism, but also as the worthy cultivation of the human spirit. In order to give his heart and mind not to the cheap or expensive but to things of value, a gentleman had to have ease. Ease derived from the successful imposition of serene order. Ease is a possible translation of the quality Palladio in the *Four Books* called *comodità*; Isaac Ware, in his translation of Palladio dedicated to Lord Burlington, rendered it 'conveniency'. To *comodità*, says Palladio (QL II, i), the second of the *Four Books*, the one containing his plans for town and country houses, is 'principally directed'.

2

Palladio's Early Career

Would Palladio in later life have remembered the heady days during his infancy of the recapture and fraught defence of Padua, when, in the absence of troops, Venetian nobles themselves guarded the walls; when mills were established in the streets to ensure the supply of bread, and whole suburbs, outside the walls, were razed lest the enemy find cover in them? In the drastic transformation exacted by war the city's famous University had closed, its professors fled (one or two had been hanged for treason when the Venetians retook the city), its students debarred. It was not until 1517 that the boy Andrea della Góndola could have seen and heard around him the normal pace of the city picking up; that was when he would have seen for the first time the students' different 'nations' in the porticoed streets and heard of their riots; violence had broken out at Carnival-time before the University had been open a month, and continued to recur thereafter. The wisdom of reopening was questioned, since so many of the students, whose privilege it was to bear arms, came from elsewhere, particularly from Germany, and the truce which had been agreed with the Holy Roman Emperor was fragile. However, there was a desire to see the prestigious University functioning again. In the later fifteenth century it had become pre-eminent in Italy in law and philosophy, partly thanks to Venetian efforts; after its annexation of the city in 1405 the Venetian state paid the professors' salaries, and had been prepared to offer escalating sums to attract the best qualified. After the Cambrai wars it attempted to follow the same policy, and at first exorbitant demands by the top professors were swallowed, but the money with which to pay salaries was no longer so easily available. After an attempt to extract a contribution from the local clergy had failed, the authorities, unable to match a salary offered elsewhere, watched professors leave. The restoration of what was now perceived as 'the good time' and of the student numbers of yesteryear was achieved gradually.

It was the same story in almost every aspect of life during Andrea's adolescence. A report of 1521, the year in which Andrea, aged thirteen,

15

started an apprenticeship, states that the colleges in Padua had no funds from their endowments 'because of the wars and the enemies' raids and the soldiers' destruction by fire of estates and houses in every part of Paduan territory'. Similar reports said as much of Treviso, Vicenza and Verona. In Padua, it was not until the early 1530s that new provision was finally made for the colleges, and the number of students again attained its earlier level. Although hostilities had ceased, famine and plague made conditions almost as calamitous in the country in the later years of the third decade as they had been just under twenty years before. Though they struck the richer classes less hard, famine and plague severely inhibited the urban economy, where money was short except among speculators – who included, it would seem, Alvise (= Luigi) Cornaro, destined to be a vital influence on Palladio during the later 1530s, but with whom he probably had no contact at this time.

Andrea was the son of an artisan, or in today's terms a technician, a *berettarius*, one skilled in the preparation and instalment of mill-stones (not a hatmaker, as the term has been translated). His father was called Pietro, and had no established surname, but Andrea inherited the nickname 'della Gondola', 'of the boat', which derived presumably from the mode in which the stones were delivered to their destinations. The boy was apprenticed to one Bartolomeo Cavazza, a journeyman stonemason from Vicenza but working in Padua, of whom little is known. He would have worked as a member of a team to the designs and terms of others, employed on small-scale repairs and modernizations, and he was not involved in the few more significant projects being undertaken in Padua in the 1520s – the rebuilding of the enormous church of Santa Giustina and the creation by Giovanni Maria Falconetto of a small loggia for Alvise Cornaro. Andrea came to Cavazza probably through his godfather, Vincenzo Grandi, also a stonemason of Vicentine origin. Vincenzo Grandi was perhaps an important figure in Palladio's early life, and in any case a more significant one than Cavazza: more is known of him, and he was working at the time of Palladio's apprenticeship on the tomb of the prominent intellectual Antonio Trombetta in the Santo (the church of Sant'Antonio), carrying out a design by the still more considerable figure Andrea Riccio, the leading master of small-scale bronzework of his time in Italy. But university life cannot have been much then to Andrea, son of Pietro the boatman or the mill-stone man, whose culture was no greater than what the local parish priest had taught him. One may doubt that he then knew even who 'Palladius' was or what the word meant.

Having fulfilled only three years of his apprenticeship, Andrea left Cavazza and Padua for Vicenza and some alternative position, though it is not known what it was. It is not known, either, why he left Cavazza, except that it was not the headstrong straining of a great talent at petty bonds, since he was accompanied to Vicenza by his father, with whom, during his time with Cavazza, he had continued to lodge. Impulsiveness, and the 'bizarre' behaviour due to the excess of melancholy typical of artists (as it was diagnosed at the time), were anyway never Palladio's style. According to the deposition made by Cavazza when he sued for breach of contract, Andrea fled; but Vicenza was the nearest town, it was not like running off to sea. A possible explanation is that Andrea and his father came to consider the six years' apprenticeship stipulated by the guild in Padua unfavourably long, knowing that the guild in Vicenza had no such rule. At first Cavazza's suit was successful, and in 1524 Andrea returned to his service, but within the year he left for Vicenza again, where he now remained, as an assistant in the shop of the sculptors Giovanni da Porlezza and Girólamo Pittoni. Since Giovanni da Porlezza was guarantor in 1524 for his inscription in the masons' guild, Cavazza was unable to claim him back this time around for the further two years he was still due.

Only ties of kin and friendship can have taken Pietro and Andrea to Vicenza rather than elsewhere: they can hardly have reckoned Vicenza to present greater opportunities than Padua. Padua was the larger and more important town, where indeed much more building went on from the 1520s to the 1540s than in Vicenza; in the later 1520s and early 1530s Falconetto designed and built gateways and the surviving clock-tower in the Piazza delle Frutta; at the end of the 1530s new projects to improve and extend government and University buildings were put under way, culminating in the refurbishment in 1545 of the main University building, the palazzo del Bò, 'with dignity and ornament'. In Vicenza at the same time there were minor repairs, frames for altarpieces, new doorways, and no more than the discussion of a rebuilding of the Town Hall, the Basilica as it would be, with which Palladio eventually dignified and ornamented his adopted city. The Vicentines had even successfully resisted the work of fortification that had transformed Padua and, notably, Verona in the aftermath of the Wars, since it would have meant, as had happened perforce in Padua, the destruction of tracts of their property in the suburbs: the present walls of the town date from the 1630s. Vicenza would number about 20,000 inhabitants by the middle of the century; the population of Padua was half as large again. However, the less distinguished town had certain advantages compared to Padua: sheltered among the first foothills of the Alps rather than wholly in the plain, it had better land, less marshy and less prone to flood, and capable of supporting pasture, vines and fruit as well as the grain and rice to which most of the Padovano was suited. Vicenza's agricultural prosperity is indicated by the comparatively large proportion of its overall population residing in the countryside, and its prosperity in general by tax assessments which approach those of larger towns. Most important, since formerly, though rather briefly, it had been a self-governing commune, Vicenza was the equal of other greater cities in the Venetian 'empire' in retaining its own laws, institutions and local aristocracy, whose leading members, generally speaking, were richer, more active and more independent than those of Padua, where the Venetians maintained more direct and strict control.

For the rest of the 1520s and for most even of the 1530s very little is heard of Palladio. He worked as a junior partner in Giovanni da Porlezza and Girolamo Pittoni's shop in the *contrà* or street of Pedemuro in Vicenza, and not only worked but lived in their building, even immediately after his marriage in 1534. He must gradually have become a more important presence in the joint enterprise, but his early work, as a mason and a sculptor, was all performed within the shop and in the name of the shop. He probably undertook his first villas, during the later 1530s, in his own right, but his plans for the Basilica, the mainstay of his career, were presented, in 1545, jointly with Giovanni da Porlezza, whose was the first of the two names. Palladio's was a slow maturation. There is no sign even that he had ambition. The story instead, though it is a little too fairytale, is that he was 'spotted' in the late 1530s by the Vicentine nobleman Giangiorgio Tríssino, given an education, taken to Rome to see the monuments, and launched on his career.

Undoubtedly Trissino took Palladio up; however, though by virtue of his literary and critical writing Trissino was the most distinguished citizen of Vicenza, he was often away, and when at home not necessarily the most influential figure in local society. While he had much to teach Palladio, and his connections further afield were surely valuable to his protégé, one may doubt that within Vicenza he was capable of making Palladio's career. His being Trissino's man might even have compromised Palladio, for Trissino certainly had personal and family enemies as well as friends. It seems more likely that Palladio, patiently, also made his own way, insinuating himself with the natural courteousness for which he is later praised into the consciousness and dependence of the Vicentine nobility.

The evidence for this is circumstantial but cumulatively persuasive. By the late 1530s, when it seems he first met Trissino, though Trissino had been resident in the city intermittently from 1532 or earlier, Palladio was nearly thirty, and, having married, had probably just set up on his own and in his own house. His wife, Allegradonna, the daughter of a carpenter, had probably entered service about the same age as Palladio had begun his apprenticeship, receiving in lieu of wages her eventual dowry, as was usual; her dowry, it is known, was provided by the noblewoman Angela Pojana, whose maid therefore she had probably been, and the Pojana might have arranged the marriage itself. Angela's husband, Bonifazio, would later commission the villa and the palazzo Pojana. Other commissions came from previous clients of the Pedemuro workshop by a process resembling capillary attraction, spreading through the branches of family trees as one relative recommended him to another. For instance, in 1531 the Pedemuro workshop had undertaken a doorway to the Servite church, Santa Maria dei Servi, for the parishioner Francesco Godi, whose coat of arms still adorns its pediment. Next year another member of the same family, Enrico Antonio Godi, employed the workshop to decorate a chapel in the church of San Michele (now gone). Then about five years later Enrico Antonio Godi's son Girolamo turned to Palladio to build him a villa at Lonedo outside Vicenza — apparently Palladio's first opportunity to build a villa, while the document in which Girolamo recorded how much he paid him is the first in which he is named as *architetto*. The Pedemuro workshop, the most prominent in the town, also won official commissions, for instance the repair of the Loggia del Capitaniato (wholly rebuilt many years later by Palladio at the peak of his career); probably, more than a decade before he received the contract for the new town hall or Basilica, Palladio had already installed a doorway leading from the old building to the adjoining 'Constable's house', which is dated 1536. He would have obtained that work if not within the Pedemuro workshop at least thanks to it. The doorway bears the arms of the Venetian *podestà* Nicolò Tagliapietra, with whom Palladio had no further contact, but his first commission from a Venetian patron was a villa for Vettor Pisani, son and heir of Giovanni Pisani, who had been governor of Vicenza in 1525 and had employed the Pedemuro workshop in 1528.

How much did Palladio learn in the Pedemuro workshop? Obviously he learnt through and through the stonemason's trade, from the physical skill of carving to the logistics of the procurement of materials and the running of a yard. Inigo Jones was told that Palladio himself carved a capital on the façade of palazzo Thiene in Vicenza. He was paid (with another man) for carving the masks on the keystones of the Basilica, and at least one carved well-head is attributable to him. He is most unlikely to have had anything to do with human figures, which appear in his drawings only as the statues seen from a distance atop parapets or attics or in niches. But carving involved to a greater or lesser degree formwork or design, and the early biographer who brings in Trissino rather like a magical godmother says that Palladio was already 'much inclined to mathematical sciences'. His bent as an architectural draughtsman might have been the first sign of his talents, and may explain more plausibly why Trissino decided to take him to Rome, to record and measure the monuments. One more potentially significant influence may be mentioned. A family name of the engineer and architect Michele Sanmicheli of Verona was again da Porlezza, and when Sanmicheli came from Verona in 1541 to advise on the Town Hall, he stayed in *contrà* Pedemuro with Giovanni da Porlezza, who was probably his relative. In that case Palladio would have been well placed to learn from the work of this exceedingly proficient and travelled architect, before he met Trissino.

The most prestigious commission the Pedemuro workshop received while Palladio was part of it was to create a new high altar for the Cathedral in Vicenza, in 1534. In most respects the surviving monument better illustrates what Palladio moved away from than any germ of his forming style, even though it has four splendid, if slight, columns free-standing under a forward-jutting entablature, a classicism never seen before the Wars. Its dominant effect, however, is determined by 'all the porphyry, serpentine, jasper, alabaster, marble and fine figured stones of every sort ... pieces both large and small, round balls and of every sort' that the donor, Aurelio dell'Acqua, provided. They typify the approach of the fifteenth century, an approach of which the greatest monument is the façade of the Certosa (Charterhouse) of Pavía, but which is evident also in several Early Renaissance palace façades in Venice, and in Vicenza itself in the enormous, multi-coloured frame constructed in 1502 to house Giovanni Bellini's *Baptism of Christ* in the church of Santa Corona. The intention was to make a fine, indeed 'sumptuous' show, an aim which, it is true, would also characterize Palladio's own building, in so far as it was expensive and magnificent; but in the interim there was to be a marked change in the means by which the effect was produced. The change was due chiefly to trends of fashion prevailing in Italy as a whole, those of the Roman High Renaissance, with which Palladio became acquainted thanks to the aid and commitment of Trissino.

When, in the palpably increasing prosperity and more confident climate of the 1540s and 1550s, the Vicentine nobility required an architect, they turned to Palladio both because they knew him, and because they knew that he knew the Roman monuments and could build in a style sanctioned by authority. Naturally, like so many successful Renaissance artists (Raphael, Titian), Palladio also had the necessary grace and manners. But, unlike Jacopo Sansovino or Giulio Romano, who came from Rome and arrived with a reputation, Palladio was a homebred creature of the Vicentine aristocracy, from whom he was then passed up to the Venetians: that, incidentally, is why he was never paid the kind of sums received by Giulio or Sansovino, and he never, unlike Titian, who painted for Charles V, achieved the rank of gentleman.

Palladio had some schoolboy Latin, at the least, learnt from the canon in Padua, and he must have kept it in being during his years of apprenticeship and early mastership. He informs us in the *Four Books* (QL III, vii) that 'in his youth' he read Caesar's history of his conquest of Gaul, and attempted a reconstruction of the bridge Caesar describes building over the Rhine. Would he not at the same time or soon after also have tackled Vitruvius's treatise on architecture, the sole surviving from antiquity? He called Vitruvius his 'guide and master', whom he had studied 'in his first years', as soon as he felt himself drawn towards architecture (QL, I, proem). According to later writers, however, he was introduced to Vitruvius by Giangiorgio Trissino. As I have said, Palladio's adoption by Trissino has the air of a fairy story, and later writers, because Trissino was a nobleman and had written books, may have given him a greater share of the credit and motivation than is due. Although Vitruvius's treatise was notoriously difficult to understand, that was not because of its ideas or syntax, which are straightforward and unpretentious, but because of its technical material and terminology.

Giangiorgio Trissino, rather, was able to read Vitruvius beside him and to introduce him to the circles in which it was most hotly discussed. Further, he gave Palladio his name, and with it a new identity, a new rôle and a new status. He was no longer a craftsman, to be known only by his own and his father's Christian names, 'Andrea di Pietro', but on the way to becoming a humanist 'architect' (at that time still something of a learned term) who breathed and was nourished by the same air, the ennobling vapour of antiquity, as the highest society. It was usual enough at the time for artists, or entertainers in general, to adopt sobriquets, 'Antico' or by contrast 'Moderno', even 'Pyrgoteles' after the Greek sculptor; 'Ruzante', 'Fedra', 'Cherea' after the characters they had played on the stage; the singer Serafino; 'l'Único Aretino', the unique Aretine, or 'il Divino' Aretino or Michelangelo. The choice of the name Palladio, which undoubtably was Trissino's, was peculiarly felicitous — antique-sounding, and having the etymological meaning of Minervine, that is, prudent and skilled. Possibly it had other associations as well, for instance with the Roman writer Palladius, who had written on agriculture (including a few remarks on architecture) in the fourth century AD, but it is difficult to believe that, as a stonemason or architect (even of farm buildings), Palladio wished to be regarded as a new Palladius. It is probable anyway that Trissino meant by it only the moral quality. He used the name again, for an angel, in the epic poem *Italia Liberata da' Gotthi* (Italy Liberated from the Goths) he was writing at the time, and the angel Palladio is paired with another called Sofronio, which means the same thing, 'prudent', in Greek. The thirty-year-old must have earned the epithet as much from his bearing as from his talents: everything suggests that he was in all things sensible, level-headed, clear, informed and adroit.

3

Several Gentlemen of Vicenza . . .

It was true that in the early fifteenth century Venice had not conquered the towns of the Terraferma by force of arms: the towns, one after another but each independently, had voluntarily voted themselves under Venetian rule. But it was a polite truth. Previously, and for several generations, these towns had been subject to despots, the Scaliger (or Della Scala) of Verona, the Carrara of Padua, and then at the end of the fourteenth century Giangaleazzo Visconti of Milan. Visconti had allied with the Carrara to oust the Scaliger, and with Venice to oust the Carrara, and then, in 1402, had died suddenly, leaving a son, Gianmaria, incapable of filling his rôle. Venice had taken her opportunity, proferring moderation in the place of tyranny, honourable terms and a protection that proved worth paying for in the round of wars that continued more or less incessantly until the Peace of Lodi of 1454. The fact disguised was that little had changed, except that Venetian bottoms changing at yearly or two-yearly intervals had taken the place of those of the despot and his agents on the seat of government. Perhaps their justice was sometimes fairer, but their rule was actually more stifling, for where there was a court there was often room for individual advancement, but entry into the ranks of the Venetian nobility was absolutely precluded; or, as Machiavelli pointed out, despots die and change, but the republic was perpetual.

The crux of the terms on which these towns surrendered – though all were slightly different – was that, while being overlorded by Venice, they should preserve their own 'laws and customs', that is, their own internal justice and fiscal and other administration. In every respect, however, they were accountable in theory or in practice directly or on appeal to the Venetian 'rectors' (*rettori*), as they were collectively known. (They were known individually by a variety of local terms, and the larger the town the greater the number of them who served together, dividing different functions and offices between them; the main division was between the civic governor (*podestà*) and the military (*capitano* or *capitanio*), but the military arm had overlapping responsibilities, notably fiscal, and it did

happen that the civic and military appointees disagreed and wrote strenu-
ously home to blame one another.) It was also the usual practice of the
leading citizens of a subject town to appeal in any important matter over
the heads of the rectors directly to Venice, whither they would send, with
a fine feeling for their status, an 'embassy'. Indeed the united will of the
leading men of a subject town often had its way, particularly when they
were resisting change; and both the Venetian court of appeal and its
overriding special body of the Council of Ten had a similar bias to maintain
any previous state of affairs, however inefficient or unfair, rather than
permit or pursue reform. This invisible balance tended to check and
eventually immobilized any political movement.

The key that turned on the deadlock was the internal constitution of
the subject towns themselves. According to the standard medieval pattern,
the independent communes had been ruled by a parliament, or Great
Council, which deputed justice and the executive to various committees
or courts. The great halls that had arisen in the thirteenth century to house
the councils and courts still stand, the grandest of them in Padua, echoed
on a smaller scale by the hall in Vicenza which Palladio transformed into
the Basilica. But the Great Councils themselves had atrophied, especially
during the years of autocratic or imposed rule, until they were somewhat
arbitrarily revived in the fifteenth century in order to license the changeover
to Venetian control and to provide its means of local administration. The
system remained that of a pool which elected the magistrates and smaller
councils, but membership of the Great Council or pool was now limited
to men of the richest and most prestigious families, at first only in practice,
but from the end of the fifteenth century also constitutionally. Eligibility
to membership became hereditary, the Council became an effective and
then a rigid aristocracy, jealously guarding its perquisites.

Although in Venice the Great Council had also long since been 'closed',
the operation of government there was very different. In Venice the offices
to be filled and councils to be constituted were much more numerous and
various, not to say demanding, and the Great Council was much larger.
In the Terraferma the Great Councils came to consist of a hundred or so
men or often (in actual attendance) fewer who were drawn to fill the same
small number of offices time and again, often altering or disregarding
the laws of 'contumacy' which forbade their continuous occupation, and
contriving as far as they could perpetually to re-elect themselves. For these
offices they drew salaries and 'utilities', and by them were enabled above
all to machinate justice to their advantage and to divert on to others the
burdens of taxes; by contrast, for most Venetian aristocrats, certainly
the more powerful ones, the direct perquisites of office were much less
significant. Whatever the shortcomings of the Venetian aristocracy, and

there were often complaints, they were at least checked or stretched by political realities; by comparison it mattered little what the Terraferma nobles got up to on their own patch. The Terraferma nobility was protected, even if indirectly, by the Venetian overlordship from any consequences of their actions, or inactions, that might lead to upset. Broadly, Venetian policy was to avoid scandal, seldom interfering with chronic abuse of wealth and patronage and intervening decisively only in order to preserve public order. Occasional initiatives towards reform by individual rectors received little support from the central government.

Therefore right from the beginning of the Venetian occupation there was a tendency among the Terraferma aristocracy to the vices that ensue upon privilege without responsibility. These included a more or less harmless, if parasitic, idleness: the fact that Bréscia was the first of the Terraferma towns under Venetian domination to 'close' its council (in 1488) might be correlated with the ill reputation of its nobility, described in the report of the Venetian *podestà* in 1553 as 'soft and devoted to leisure, and [they] do not frequent the public squares, but the greater part of the time stay at home in their ground-floor rooms with their doors open, and visit one another, and indulge in gaming'. Nobles such as these would claim that they could do nothing else, since trade or 'work of the hands' was incompatible with their status. They would be galvanized only by a threat to their leisured existence, such as a diminution in the revenues which supported it: so one finds noblemen bitterly decrying any concession to the lower orders lest it take 'the bread from our mouths'.

However, Brescia seems to have been prematurely comatose. Elsewhere, the ideology of nobility was not yet dead or empty. The 'contract' of the nobleman's entitlement to live from his land and others' work upon it was his consequent freedom to devote himself to arms and letters: many still did so. The practice of arms was real even though the age of chivalry had now passed (thanks to the gun, according to Ariosto in his *Orlando Furioso*). The problem, rather, in other towns in the sixteenth century was that the nobility did frequent the public squares, where they would quarrel loudly and violently, resorting to the arms they were proud to carry and knew how to use. There were several complaints of that from the Venetian rectors of Vicenza, and the Vicentine nobility was undoubtedly turbulent and spirited, perhaps more than most. Generally speaking the stranglehold of Venetian power seems to have been less deadening in Vicenza; for this there are several likely reasons.

Vicenza had apparently greater freedom in self-administration than any other city in the Terraferma — certainly much greater than Padua, where there was virtually direct Venetian government. It is significant that the Vicentines still believed it possible in the mid-sixteenth century to expand their influence within the Venetian state, witness the long campaign on which they embarked in the 1530s to win the administration of Maróstica and Lonigo, towns in Vicentine territory but overseen directly by a Venetian rector. Within the city, there seems in Palladio's time to have been no clear internal hierarchy, and the various devices by which power was clung to were new or still to be introduced. The Vicentine nobility more than others kept up their connections with foreign courts, chiefly that of the Emperor, but also with the courts of Spain and France, as well as with the aristocracy of other Italian cities outside the Venetian state. They also had trading connections (by overland routes) abroad, and not infrequently they served in arms abroad (by contrast they served in the Venetian forces rather seldom) and they would send their sons to Italian courts to complete their moral education. As for their intellectual education, the city boasted a higher proportion of degrees or 'doctorates' among its nobility during the sixteenth century than any other in the Terraferma, degrees which were mostly obtained, moreover, elsewhere than in Padua, the Venetian state university. Perhaps the most significant indicator of the liveliness and independent-mindedness of the city was its notorious openness to heresy, to Lutheranism in general and Anabaptism and Socinianism in particular. Several noblemen, including Palladio's patron and landlord Odoardo Thiene, who became a citizen of Calvin's Geneva, were forced into exile after their beliefs had become scandalous.

Since 'the city is very arms-bearing and full of valiant youth', wrote a contemporary in 1509, it had been 'inclined, rather than not', towards the Emperor when the Wars of the League of Cambrai had begun; certain families, and the writer lists the Nogarola, Thiene, Trissino, Loschi and Trento, had even left with Maximilian's troops. Ties undoubtably existed and continued to exist between those families – Giangiorgio Trissino, for instance, had Marco Thiene as a son-in-law, and his sister had married a Loschi – and antagonisms between them and others such as the pro-Venetian Porto. Although by the late 1530s there was little heat left in any quarrel for or against Venice or the Emperor, the Porto enjoyed a pre-eminence partly achieved as a result of their fidelity to Venice – also because of their wealth. In 1532 Francesco da Porto had been made Collaterale (Paymaster-General), a great and unusual honour since, involving the provision of the mainland army, the post directly touched the security of the State. For whatever reason, there were numerous factions and antagonisms dividing the families of Vicenza; some of them certainly repeated traditional alliances and hatreds, although a family could divide against itself – for instance, after his second marriage Giangiorgio Trissino quarrelled both with his son by his first marriage, Giulio, and with Giulio's mother's relatives, the Loschi.

Several indications of the family factions of Vicentine society survive in the reports of the Venetian rectors, for instance in 1539: 'Although up to now [December] in this city entrusted to me the people have lived in peace and tranquillity, now that the nobles have come in from outside in the country to live in the town, one sees nothing except weapons ...'. Again in 1548: 'Winter is approaching, when with the long nights many in this city, as is their custom, begin to go about in armed bands ... for no other purpose, but that of ... disturbing peaceful and quiet living'. There was obviously a seasonal rhythm to these bouts of Jacobean drama; if the Venetian *podestà* could see no purpose in them, that might be regarded as typical of the Venetian administration, which preferred to reduce what might be called 'social problems' to a mere innate human propensity to evil. Further, although as yet in sixteenth-century Vicenza it might lack the polish of later ritual, this was the dawn in Europe of the age of duelling, universally condemned by the authorities as wasteful and pointless. In fact the essence of pride and honour lay in these personal and gang confrontations. In the Renaissance power consisted in physical dominance and was expressed primarily by being personally overbearing. On the obverse it was a nobleman's ancestral right to bear arms; on the reverse it was only force that obtained submission.

It is difficult to discover what any particular quarrel was about. Perhaps the most illuminating account, though it still leaves a modern reader very much in the dark, is one that Giangiorgio Trissino wrote in the early 1530s analysing the antagonisms by which the city to which he had newly returned was convulsed. He notes in no particular order: 'Origin of the discords of Vicenza. General greed to have more goods and more honours, one more than another, by means licit or illicit. Then the direction of the Council at the whim of its officers, and the rule that two of the outgoing deputies should continue in office for another [term of] two months. Again, the evil and intolerable nature [typical] of the Genoese [i.e. avarice]. Again, the same evil nature of the Sienese [prodigality]. The privileges of the Porto; the annulment [by Venice] of [certain] titles of "count" [granted presumably by the Emperor]; the partiality of certain judges. Quarrels old and new and being born: the Salo and the Traverso; the Porto and the Thiene with Giovanni da Trissino; Thiene with Capra; the Godi with the Roma; the Porto with Il Toso; the Bologna with the Sanzuani; Davide Loschi with Francesco Capra; Marcantonio Thiene with Verlato; Marco da Thiene [of an earlier generation than Giangiorgio's son-in-law] with Angarano; Branzo with Monza; Branzo with Branzo, that is Agostino Branzo with Branzo Branzo.'

It is also interesting to review his suggestions for their resolution: 'Remedies. That the Council of X [in Venice] decide on the restoration of the Great Council to what it was fifteen years ago or more; but to oversee its decisions and not to let them elect themselves . . . Again, make marriage alliances: Marcantonio da Thiene with Zuan Trissino; the Collaterale [Francesco da Porto] with Giambattista da Trissino through the daughter of Gerolamo [his brother]. Also with Verlato through the daughter of Alessandro his brother.' Evidently the entrenchment of certain elements of the nobility in the executive and judiciary chafed hard on the sores of old quarrels: by preventing the perpetuation of the established composition of the Council Trissino intended to achieve a wider distribution of the offices. Trissino was against the general trend, which was towards a tighter and more settled oligarchy, as probably also suited the Council of Ten, who did not follow his advice if it ever reached them. Nor did he achieve his marriage alliances, although some bridge between the Porto and the Thiene was achieved by the marriage of Girolamo da Porto's son Iseppo (= Giuseppe) to Marcantonio Thiene's sister Livia (whom Giangiorgio had presumably destined for a Trissino husband). (Both Marcantonio Thiene and Iseppo Porto were early patrons of Palladio.) Marriage, the most important ingredient of his medicine — amounting to an exchange of goods in a kind of mutual investment, realized in the eventual children — was a remedy as rhythmic and ritual as the disease it wished to cure, although the actual match involved calculation, if it were to achieve the balance of power which would effectively extend peace downwards from the greater figures to the lesser ones. Perhaps one may see in Trissino's mind the Vicentine nobility gathered in some vast banquet like those painted by Veronese, conspicuously displaying in mutual harmony the tokens of the wealth and influence over which they had fought.

At any rate, the individual dissensions of Vicentine society did not work to prevent the nobility uniting to present a joint front or public face to the outside world — rather the opposite. With the same pride or vainglory that inspired their 'discords' they vied with one another in the service and representation of their city: the same vigour animated both public and private display. The ways in which the Vicentine aristocracy set out to prove its 'magnificence' were on the whole, and necessarily, conventional, but they were rendered comparatively successful despite the town's small size and lack of political importance by the will with which they were carried out and the real wealth that lay behind it. When suitable occasions arrived, such as Bishop Ridolfi's entry in 1543, they achieved a splendid turn-out. No doubt they would also have responded more than adequately if the Council of Trent, as it was to be, had been held in Vicenza, as was mooted, but the city was rejected with little doubt because heresy was so prevalent there. As it was, political visits (not counting those of Venetians; the new rectors every two years had an entry, but it did not excite the same enthusiasm) were not so frequent, and the Vicentines — like the inhabitants of many other cities — also organized 'cultural' events. It was usual everywhere to lay on festivities for Carnival, and also as celebrated and fiery a preacher as possible for Lent, in order to attract and impress visitors; also in the milder time of the year tournaments, for which there was a long local tradition (at Treviso or Marostica, for instance), and races such as the *palio* of Ferrara or the one which is still run in Siena.

Carnival in the Renaissance often involved the performance of a play, one in suitable spirit of course, therefore a 'comedy', accompanied invariably by interval performances (*intermezzi*) usually of still greater verve. For Carnival 1539 in Vicenza there was organized a 'most sumptuous comedy', staged on a set built by the famed architect Sebastiano Serlio, at the house of the Collaterale Francesco da Porto. According to a pamphlet issued largely in order to celebrate the occasion, one could admire 'the richness of the decorations, the banquets, the very great expense, the velvet, the silver, the gold, the pearls, the necklaces, the nobility and the beauty of the magnificent and splendid city of Vicenza'. 'Very many foreigners came from different places to hear it,' the pamphlet adds. The tradition was continued, come the middle of the century, by the newly founded 'academies', those in Padua and Vicenza being particularly devoted to the organization of theatrical events. In 1562, though it had been mooted for several years previously, the Accademia Olimpica of Vicenza finally produced Trissino's *Sophonisba*, during Carnival, in an upper room of the still rebuilding Basilica. Then in 1579 the same Accademia undertook to produce a new play, for which they obtained the use of the old city prison and then a design for a theatre within it by Palladio, executed after his death — the present Teatro Olimpico (Plate 3). The fact that these productions were by no means annual is a sign that they were expensive and very special occasions.

The common denominator between these temporary displays and architecture proper is obvious enough, but one more link that has largely vanished once made them still closer. Throughout the first half of the sixteenth century the practice that had become widespread in the fifteenth century of painting house façades continued unabated; it was only in the second half of the sixteenth century that it began to fall away (partly at least under the criticism that it interfered with the Architecture). By the end of the fifteenth century houses in towns everywhere, great and little, were adorned with friezes and trophies and antique-looking objects and figures of all kinds, usually in the brightest colours, though including stone-coloured figures. (Rows of these decorated façades even survive today, though they are very much faded and recently much corroded as well: one fine example is the main street of the old town of Serravalle in Vittorio

Plate 3
Teatro Olimpico, Vicenza. Its first play, Sophocles's *Oedipus Rex*, was staged in
1585. It opened with a sudden fragrance, the sound of trumpets and drums, and
then music and voices. The heads of the statues are portraits of members of the
Accademia Olimpica.

Véneto.) These decorations might be undertaken both in the ordinary
course of events and, often, on some particular occasion: for instance, the
façade dated 1492 of the house of the Bonamico family survives in the
town of Bassano, and may have been painted on the occasion of a marriage,
since it has a frieze animated by a series of little episodes which might
well derive from a play of amorous subject put on at the time. Again,
when the Emperor Charles V entered the town of Trent in 1530, we
learn that the houses along the processional route were newly painted,
undoubtedly with classicizing decoration. Although the houses on the
street along which he passed have now been replaced, the survival in other
parts of the town of several splendid painted Renaissance façades proves
the fact that these decorations remained, untouched and for a long time
unfaded, on permanent holiday.

Inscriptions on Renaissance house façades, painted or carved, declaring
them 'for the honour [or "ornament"] of myself, my family and my city'

or something similar are remarkably common, all over northern Italy. What was unusual about the Vicentines was only that they employed architecture for their personal, dynastic and city esteem so consciously and single-mindedly and grandly, and that they not merely employed but in effect selected and trained Palladio for the purpose. It was already recognized that the employment of a learned expert superior to a mere craftsman enhanced the building's value — witness an inscription dated 1485 on a house in the little town of Serravalle already mentioned, that adds to the standard 'PATRIAE ORNAMENTO SIBI ET SUIS' the name of Pisano of Treviso 'ARCHITECTO'. The name of Pisano of Treviso is and always will be obscure, but so might Palladio's have been if he had not been given the opportunity to build grandly, repeatedly and conspicuously, and if he had not been in effect the 'court' architect to the Vicentine nobility, who therefore employed him and him only for their public and private 'representance', (*rappresentanza*) or 'state'.

4

The Public Worth of Private Houses

In sum, the idea prevailed everywhere – it was the essence of nobility – that private contribution to the common weal increased individual prestige; but in Vicenza the oligarchy was unusually active, wealthy and competitive. The idea underwrote both their villas and their town houses, or, as it might be better put, their palaces both in Vicenza and outside it.

When in 1532 Charles V came to visit Vicenza, the honour of being the Emperor's host went to Stefano Gualdo, who had been aide-de-camp to the commander of the papal forces, Pompeo Colonna. He entertained him at his private villa in the Vicentine hills, although almost the entire Vicentine aristocracy went out for the occasion. There was a hunt, the Emperor dispensed honours, and later the whole event was commemorated in verse. Not long afterwards, Gualdo's friend Giangiorgio Trissino, though he had been in Venice on that occasion, decided to rebuild a house he owned at Crícoli, a short distance outside Vicenza (now almost engulfed in its suburbs), evidently with a similar occasion in mind. However, among the attractions of the house was that of its 'Architecture' (Trissino's capital A), essentially its façade copied from an elevation of Raphael's villa Madama in Rome (undertaken from about 1517 for Leo X and the future Clement VII, and also intended as a kind of reception hostel). It is significant that Trissino replaced a recent enough Early Renaissance loggia in coloured marble with a façade declaring its classicism: it includes a proper sequence of correctly composed orders, Corinthian above Ionic, also pedimental window-heads (alternating round with triangular) and niches with statues in them (see Plate 26 on p. 77). However, not only its Architecture but also its delightful site and gardens (for which, after he had trouble with the privets, he obtained the services of a gardener from Isabella d'Este in Mantua) were to attract eminent persons to stay there.

Up to a point Trissino was successful: he entertained, and his new house and garden attracted a buzz of comment. It was in this context of prestigious 'representation' that Trissino took up Palladio. On the other hand the next comparable event in the Vicentine calendar, in 1539, took place not at Cricoli but at the house of Francesco da Porto at Thiene, to the north of the Vicenza. At the time Trissino was again away, in Padua or Venice, but on a subsequent occasion he was outdone by the Porto in stated contest: there is a letter of 1549 in which he does not conceal his disappointment that the Cardinal of Augsburg had not come to Cricoli, despite its Architecture, but had gone to Thiene.

The Porto house at Thiene (Plate 4), though perhaps less elegant, was much grander, and probably had better gardens, also newly laid out. (Though no longer what they were, the gardens still belong to the villa, enclosed by its wall, and the grotto survives (see Plate 42).) There is not much doubt that the Porto had also been built for the sake of 'representance', although the house is strikingly early: it was going up from about 1441 to 1453. It was therefore one of the first great houses built in the Terraferma anywhere. It was undertaken by Francesco da Porto's grandfather Francesco, who had inherited both from his father and from his uncle and was conspicuously the richest man in Vicenza in his day: he

Plate 4
Villa Porto (known usually as the Castello Porto-Colleoni), Thiene, Vicenza. The house, within its park, still occupies the centre of Thiene, and the town's thriving stall market encamps along its battlemented walls. For views of the grotto in the garden behind the house and of the interior see Plates 42 and 59a and b. There is a plan of the house at Plate 54.

owned about 3,500 acres. In the oration delivered at his funeral in 1478 it was observed: 'And his character could be perceived in his many and outstanding works, but in nothing was it more manifest than in the very beautiful and admirable villa in Thiene; when I went over to visit it last summer I did not believe I was looking at a private house but plainly at a royal edifice'. Shortly afterwards the forty-room mansion was com-memorated in a poem, in terms deriving from descriptions of pavilions in Virgil, as 'a huge seat with a soaring roof; though a private house, the richest in fields of any in the Veneto, and the best kept in rich cultivation. Its twin towers reach to the stars; between them the inner rooms and chambers, spacious and with high ceilings, run long distances in great luxury: the country gods can glory in no more comfortable porticoes or hall'. In the funeral oration it was said further that 'every time the citizens of Vicenza assembled to elect their magistrates, he came first in every vote, and obtained the most honourable offices; not only from natives of Vicenza but also from the nobles of the towns of its territory he received agreement and trust'; also, 'he did not fail to travel to Venice, to appear before that severe and most wise Senate, every time that the gravity of events required it, nor did he resent the effort, as so many do, but went quickly and gladly'. His architecture was piece of a piece with his rôle as pillar of his country.

Perhaps even more interestingly, when in the second half of the sixteenth century the Porto inheritance was the subject of a lawsuit, witnesses and judges contemporary to Palladio gave their own ideas of Francesco da Porto's motives for building more than a century before — *viva voce*, therefore rather ungrammatically: 'It should be added, that Lord Francesco did not have the incentive to acquire and heap up wealth because he was already very rich; but he looked to spending his money in honourable fashion, even though one might presume, when a man could afford it, that — because, the nature of the first man being corrupted, one presumes [human nature] more inclined to desires and pleasures and the satisfaction of want than to effort and hard work — [that he would use his money to enjoy himself; but he did not]; and this is shown by the royal palace he built in Thiene with so many gardens, which, besides the expense of building itself, bears with it the ceaseless expense of illustrious life, so that one can receive those who continually go and come to see such a sumptuous place.' And it was shown by his surviving tax returns, which were quoted: after building he became poorer. On the other hand he had also built, according to witnesses, in order to store his *entrate*, his goods in kind due from his tenants; they state specifically that his share of the harvests and vintages from his land in other districts was brought to Thiene, and that he had undertaken both the palace and the numerous outbuildings beside it not simply because he had inherited money, but because he had no room to store the enormous influx of produce. The house was built 'not only for magnificence but also to house his *entrate*, which were overflowing the old buildings even though those were very big'.

In the Wars the house was looted by Maximilian's troops, and when Francesco's grandson Francesco refurbished it he added, for storage space, an extra storey: the line of the original battlements of the old house can be seen beneath the eaves. He decorated both front and sides from ground to roof with frescoes (only fragments survive, or are recorded in an old photograph), and he began laying out the splendid gardens, which are frequently mentioned. He also, towards the end of his life, had the interior redecorated, with frescoes attributed to the young Veronese on the upper floor which have largely disappeared – but their reported subjects recall what must have been the atmosphere of the 1539 gathering, 'men and women who play at a table, a banquet of knights and ladies, a hunt, a dance'. Similar subjects, though painted later (perhaps in imitation), are found in the *sala* and loggia of Palladio's villa at Caldogno (Plate 5). Today, rather misleadingly, the building looks and is called 'Gothic', but there was nothing *retardataire* about it in the state it had in 1539. Any rival house would need not only 'Architecture' like Trissino's but also a scale and monumentality beyond his reach, though not beyond Marcantonio Thiene's.

Francesco died in 1554, having no sons, but six brothers, among whom and their sons he chose as his main heir his youngest brother's eldest, Giovanni. In effect he therefore passed over his eldest brother's eldest, Iseppo, perhaps because he had been suspected of heresy (which the staunchly establishment Paymaster-General would not have liked); Iseppo, furthermore, married the sister of Marcantonio Thiene, of that pro-imperial family traditionally opposed to the pro-Venetian Porto. Iseppo would already have seen that his cousin Giovanni had his uncle's favour; but if he had inherited the preponderance of Francesco's estate he might certainly have been able to build the enormous extension to his palace Palladio published in the *Quattro Libri*, and to rival his brother-in-law, Marcantonio Thiene. During the 1540s Marcantonio undertook new palaces both in the country and in the town, although he already owned a large and fine palace in the town built by his grandfather at the end of the 1480s. He and his brother Adriano, with whom jointly he undertook the villa Thiene at Quinto, were also among the richest men in Vicenza; after his death Marcantonio's son Ottavio is revealed by the census of 1563 to have been outright the richest.

The Thiene's early support of Palladio, and employment on stupendous

Plate 5
Villa Caldogno, Caldogno, Vicenza. Both hall and loggia are adorned with
frescoes representing a joyous company. The festive groups around the tables
play music, backgammon and cards. The frescoes are attributed to Giovanni
Antonio Fasolo, of the 'school' of Veronese, and date to *c.* 1570.

projects, was perhaps more important for the artist than his appointment as architect to the Basilica — at any rate it came earlier. Marcantonio may have started on his extension of his grandfather's and father's town palace before employing Palladio, in which case his substitution of Palladio for the original architect might have still greater implications. The earlier architect can only have been Giulio Romano, the pupil of Raphael who had come north to Mantua in 1523 and there built for Federigo Gonzaga among other projects the pleasure dome of the palazzo del Tè, introducing a style of 'rustication' (derived mainly from the observation of Roman amphitheatres and aqueducts) that had become highly fashionable in northern Italy, and notably in Verona in the hands of Michele Sanmicheli. The palazzo Thiene is an essay in Giulio's rustication, which indeed pervades Palladio's early designs, including his first for the Basilica, though it disappears by 1545 and from the final model for the Basilica.

Though arbitrarily remodelled in the nineteenth century, Marcantonio's grandfather's house still survives on *contrà* Porti, just down the street from the Porto palaces (Plate 6a). Through a loggia at the back it gave on a courtyard that is now the courtyard also of Marcantonio's palace by Palladio, situated opposite (Plates 6b and c). Either the grandfather or Marcantonio's father after the Wars in the 1520s had next built a second wing along the adjacent side of the courtyard, fronting an interconnecting street, and now Marcantonio was continuing along its third side, using, it is likely enough, a design by Giulio Romano but, if he did, it is all but certain that Palladio modified it. About 1550 Palladio then originated a new design, that shown in the woodcut in the *Quattro Libri* (Plate 6d), in which the palace was to be extended round the fourth side of the courtyard. The *Quattro Libri* palace incorporates into a single whole both Marcantonio's new wing and the fifteenth-century and earlier sixteenth-century structures, which were eventually to be homogenized within the courtyard by a new facing like that actually built only around two sides. The fourth side, facing the main street of the town, the Corso, was also never built.

The evolution of the palazzo Thiene is significant. It began, whether designed by Giulio Romano or not, very much as an exercise in his style, employing the kind of rustication he had introduced. It then developed, first in a tiny sketch datable about 1550, into a recreation of an ideal classical patrician's house, as reconstructed from the text of Vitruvius. The *Four Books* woodcut, reflecting the drawings made about 1550, anticipates the scale and ambience, though the individual parts are different, of the Roman house that is illustrated in Daniele Barbaro's Vitruvius of 1556. In the early 1560s Palladio would bring the ideal and the realizable still closer together in his designs for the convent of the Carità (now the Accademia) in Venice, which figures in the *Quattro Libri* as a reproduction of the type

Plate 6a
Ludovico Thiene's house in *contrà* Porti, Vicenza, designed by Lorenzo da Bologna
about 1489, but arbitrarily remodelled in the nineteenth century.

Plate 6b
Ludovico's grandson Marcantonio Thiene's house in *contrà* San Gaetano, Vicenza,
undertaken by Palladio from 1542.

Plate 6c
Palazzo Thiene, Vicenza: courtyard. The Early Renaissance loggia on the left
marks the back of Ludovico's palace; Palladio's loggia abuts it, and extends round
the third side to form the back of his own palace for Marcantonio.

of Roman house that had a 'Corinthian atrium'. Palladio's direct relationship
to antiquity was the foundation of his individual style and a guarantee
that his architecture was unsurpassable and non-obsolescent.

Finished though it never was — whether through shortage of money,
or its ample sufficiency of room for one man, or difficulty in buying up
the neighbouring plot — the palazzo Thiene created a palpable stir. The
reaction may be measured on the one hand by the eruption of real
enthusiasm in the otherwise dry and factual documents of the city census
of 1563, or on the other in the generally accurate 'Angelica' map of Vicenza
of the 1570s in which the already large bulk of the palace has become
disproportionately larger still. In the census one clerk records it as 'a house
with various and different rooms on the ground floor and above, which
house [he interjects] is the most beautiful and honourable there is in the
magnificent city of Vicenza ...'. Another clerk is still more struck: 'a house

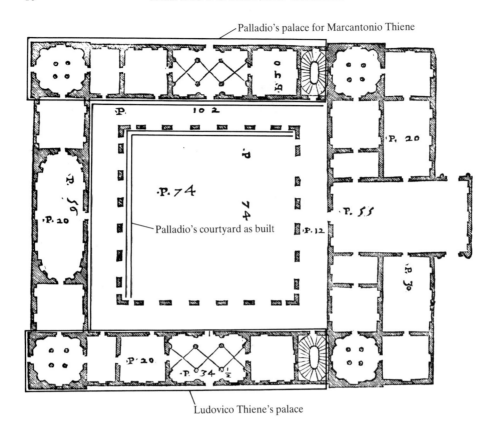

Palladio's palace for Marcantonio Thiene

Palladio's courtyard as built

Ludovico Thiene's palace

Plate 6d
Plan of palazzo Thiene as it appears in the *Four Books* (II, iii), with the positions
of Ludovico's and Marcantonio's palaces and of Palladio's courtyard as built
marked over it.

Plate 7a
Villa Thiene, Quinto, Vicenza: the northern wing of the villa, seen here from the
west, is all that survives. Originally this section abutted to its right the higher
central part of the villa, containing the *sala*. Its roof has since been altered, but
the rustication and membering of the walls on this side are original.

built in stupendous, superb and honourable style and designed and fitted
with great mastery and diligence, with many different rooms, chambers
underground, a well or cistern, and an honourable court, with two great
doors of a size to take carts, and the said rooms and chambers are with
vaults very beautiful to see and convenient for living in and staying,
[decorated with] different materials and similarly with many and various
chimneypieces and both the ground-floor rooms and those above all
vaulted, with very beautiful and large halls and corridors, with three houses
next to it ...' and in conclusion he calls it a *mácchina*, a term which was
also applied to the universe.

Although the palazzo Thiene is more prominent and better known and
preserved, Palladio's villa for Marcantonio and Adriano Thiene together
at Quinto to the east of Vicenza was originally even more ambitious (Plate
7a). At first the Thiene brothers probably pushed its construction ahead
more rapidly, and the block of the villa they built was larger than that of
the new part of the palace. The issue is rather confused because on the
one hand in the *Quattro Libri* Palladio doubled the size of the already

grandiose plan and on the other hand much of what was built has since vanished (Plate 7b). It was probably to be a double house, with separate apartments for each brother on each side of the single vast *sala* or hall. Only one apartment, the northern wing, survives, while the central block, though built (Inigo Jones saw it in 1614; 'this great lodge' he called it on his copy of the *Four Books*), has since been demolished. The building presently at Quinto therefore constitutes less than a third of the original project, and a tiny fraction of the futuristic *Quattro Libri* layout. The present entrance front was originally the short end of the building, and its pediment is spurious; similarly the garden front, which originally abutted the hall, was recomposed from salvaged pieces. The 'thermal' window (so called because Palladio derived the form from Roman baths, *thermae*) beneath its pediment corresponds to a similar window by which the great hall was

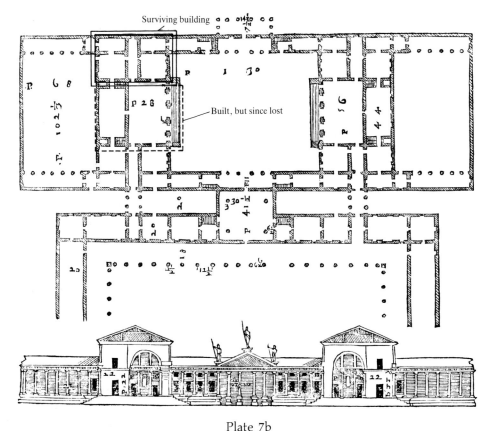

Plate 7b
Plan of the villa Thiene as it appears in the *Four Books* (II, xv), with the remaining rump and the lost central section of the villa as built marked over it.

once lit from the side. The proportions of the whole should have resembled the palazzo Chiericati in Vicenza (see Plate 11), though on a still larger scale – larger also than the villa Porto at Thiene; the main block also broke forward slightly like that of the Chiericati. Perhaps the villa was begun on Palladio's return from Rome in 1546 or 1547 and advanced rapidly at first, but the second apartment was not built perhaps because Adriano Thiene died in 1550; and when Marcantonio died in 1560 Ottavio was their sole heir.

Palladio was evidently promoted in the 1540s by a small, though powerful group within Vicentine society, until, a little more than a decade after he had been taken up by Trissino, he was put on a salary to execute the Basilica and became in effect the city's official architect. There are nevertheless signs that even then, as the creature of a particular faction, he was not immune from the consequences of Vicentine 'discords'. Clearly he came from the direction of the originally pro-imperial Trissino-Thiene grouping; he was never employed by the correspondingly pro-Venetian Porto, except, as if to prove the rule, by the Iseppo da Porto who had married Marcantonio Thiene's sister and whose position at the head of the clan had been usurped. No members of the Porto, despite their pre-eminence, appear among the donors who provided the funds with which the Basilica was begun, let alone on the rotations of the committee that steered through the execution of the Basilica until it was finally completed in 1617; no Verlato, either, whichever Verlato it may have been whom Trissino noted as Marcantonio Thiene's enemy. On the one hand a large number of those who served on the Basilica committee also employed Palladio privately, or would do; on the other it is unrepresentative of the composition of the aristocracy as a whole. There were other important noblemen and whole families in Vicenza, who had nothing to do with Palladio – and consequently have been forgotten. Marcantonio Thiene, blazoning his name on the façade and courtyard of his new palace, certainly in that sense triumphed over the Verlato.

Others, though as 'highly eminent and not unfamiliar with building' as those elected to the Basilica committee were said to be, might have had different tastes. Stefano Gualdo, who had entertained Charles V and was a friend of Giangiorgio Trissino (one whom we find at Cricoli soon after its 'opening' in 1538 and to whom Trissino had at one point entrusted his affairs during an absence) did not turn to Palladio during the 1540s, but he did lay out new gardens to the design of the Tuscan Bartolomeo Ammannati, similarly a rising artist, three years younger than Palladio, who was working in Padua at the time though he later settled in Florence. Although the choice of Ammannati shows an orientation to central Italy partly like Trissino's, it was also partly opposed to it, since Ammannati represented a strand in Mannerism that had little to do with Raphael, much more to do with Michelangelo, and it may be that even before Trissino's death in 1550 Gualdo had distanced himself from the circle in which Palladio moved. Palladio does not mention him among the lights of Vicenza at the opening of Book I of the *Quattro Libri*.

In the 1550s there occurred a more definite and visible cultural polarization when a second academy was founded in rivalry to the Accademia Olimpica. The Olimpica was founded in 1555; a year later, we find another group, prominent among them Girolamo Gualdo and Giovanni Porto, founding an alternative academy 'dei Costanti'. Its aims were similar, but its membership, by contrast, was exclusively aristocratic (while the likes of the lowly Palladio were members of the Olimpica) and its founders also took care to exclude any among the aristocracy who had heretical leanings – which was rather a large number of the Palladian party, if such it was. It must be said that Giovanni Alvise Valmarana, who had spoken in public in support of Palladio's plan for the Basilica, was also a member of the Costanti, and the issue of heresy was probably a much more forceful divider than any debate over architecture.

A still clearer glimpse of an alternative faction was an attempt during the late 1550s to deprive Palladio of his salary while work on the Basilica was halted or slowed due to lack of funds. The motion was carried in committee and then defeated on appeal to the Great Council, after support had been rallied. Among the proposers we find a Roberto Verlato and a certain Gerolamo Ferramosca; Ferramosca turns up again in 1563 attempting to transfer a minor official commission from Palladio to an alternative architect, Giovanni Domenico Scamozzi, who was building a villa for Ferramosca at Barbano, a fine building, indebted to Palladio but not frigidly imitative (Plate 8). Giovanni Domenico Scamozzi was the father of Vincenzo Scamozzi, the architect who inherited Palladio's unfinished commissions on his death but with whom it rankled bitterly to be in his predecessor's shadow; one of his first projects was a villa for a Leonardo Verlato at Villaverla (Plate 9).

By this time, however, it was largely beside the point who the architect was. The point was rather that the Vicentine aristocracy as a whole, in so far as they were a whole, had been remarkably successful, *via* architecture, in their stake for cultural prestige, considering the small size of their city, its subject status and the dearth of achievement in its earlier history. But although in those respects it was at a disadvantage, it is worth stressing that Vicenza had one considerable comparative superiority, money, during the years in which Palladio was building (Palladio does not fail to mention the fact in the *Quattro Libri*, I, proem). One of the Venetian rectors wrote in 1556 that the city was more populous – from which one may more or

Plate 8
Villa Ferramosca, Barbano, Vicenza, built by Vincenzo Scamozzi for Gerolamo
Ferramosca. Although it has no close parallel among Palladio's villas it has the
same standard elements — imposing loggias, outbuildings with a classical order —
and its colonnades are a variation on those of Palladio's palazzo Chiericati (see
Plate 11a).

less directly infer, prosperous — than it had ever been, even in the thriving
years immediately before the Wars, so populous that house prices had
shot up. Another wrote later in the century in terms revealing that
Vicentine wealth impressed even the Venetians: '. . . there being in this city
very many very affluent subjects [of Venice], but also extremely rich both
in property and in cash, which they do not leave idle, but keep employed
in various businesses . . .'. Marcantonio Thiene, for instance, is proof that
they did not keep their money idle: he is known to have dealt in silk,
through agents, on the market at Lyons. The *podestà* goes on to cite as an
economic indicator the price of dowries, reaching 12,000 to 14,000 ducats.
Although the greatest of Venetian grandees might command, say, 20,000
or an absolute maximum 25,000 ducats, those are very considerable sums
of money: they would buy 300 acres or perhaps more, and they would
build a fine palace.

The committee for the Basilica reported in 1558: 'There is no doubt at
all that this our palace, in quality of architecture and beauty, yields to no

Plate 9

Villa Verlato, Villaverla, Vicenza, built by Vincenzo Scamozzi for Leonardo
Verlato. Perhaps its closest parallel among Palladio's villas is one known only
through his woodcuts, the villa Mocenigo at Marocco (see Plate 70). The palace
of Francesco Thiene (see Plate 22) similarly has an applied order set high over
the entrance. Partly because of that, its façade seems comparatively remote and
unapproachable, frigid in the manner of many Baroque palaces.

other public building of any kind in Italy . . .'. Once Palladio was established,
and, towards the end of the 1550s, the tangible results of his designs
began at last to become conspicuous, architecture became embedded in
the civic pride of the city to a remarkable degree. An instance is the
condition laid upon the notary Pietro Cogollo in the following year that
he would be granted citizenship if and only if he spent the sum of 250
ducats on the façade of his house; although it was not stated which
architect he should use, it was probably Palladio. In 1601, uniquely in
Vicenza, it was decreed that any new aspirant to the nobility must also,
besides fulfilling the other conditions common to legislation throughout
the Terraferma, build himself a new house in the city to a value fixed by
the Council. Probably the Vicentines believed, as Palladio states (QL III,
ii), that if the 'front' streets look well visitors will suppose the back streets
to be as good.

5

Palladio's Later Career

In 1496 the medieval Palazzo della Ragione, or town hall, parliament and law court, of Vicenza partially collapsed, undoubtedly because its southern end stands on low-lying ground that drains badly; it is apparent even today how the central Piazza of Vicenza and the nearby streets slope down towards it. The Vicentines called in the Venetian *proto* or *capo*, Antonio Rizzo, who made a model by the guide of which rebuilding began. Then the Wars of the League of Cambrai supervened, and it was not until 1525 that the matter was mentioned again in Council. Opinions were solicited anew, first from the then *proto* of Venice, lo Scarpagnino, then from his successor, Sansovino, then in 1539 from Sebastiano Serlio (otherwise organizing the stage and set for the Porto family's entertainment at Thiene), then from Michele Sanmicheli of Verona, then in 1542 from Giulio Romano of Mantua; then in 1546 Palladio, returning from Rome probably for the purpose, submitted designs and was asked to make a model. In 1549 the Council decided finally between the models of Rizzo, Giulio Romano and Palladio; three weeks later Palladio was put on a salary and the work began that summer.

The core of the building remained: the hall of the Great Council and various offices and committee rooms, and the numerous shops, storerooms and offices beneath. What had collapsed were the two storeys of galleries or loggias that surrounded it; Palladio's brief was only to replace these, more permanently and more fittingly (Plate 10). The responds to the old Gothic vaults and arches remain on the inner walls, although Palladio introduced new imposts above them for the new galleries. He was constrained by the medieval fabric to narrow the corner bay in respect of the others, and for that the doubling of the angle columns compensates; their extra mass also helped to stabilize the building at its weakest point. It was rechristened the Basilica, by Palladio in the *Four Books*, on grounds of both function and form: before the building-type was adapted for large churches, the Roman basilica was a law court and town hall, like the Palazzo della Ragione; and if any Roman basilica had survived intact (for instance, the

Plate 10
The Basilica (Palazzo della Ragione or town hall), Vicenza. The copper-covered
roof marks the medieval core of the building, round which Palladio replaced
the two storeys of loggias. It is largely the use of the *serliana* motif — two
apertures flanking a central arch — that gives the building its liveliness, its
effective balance between void and solid, light and shade.

two-storeyed one at Fano described by Vitruvius) it would surely not have
looked any grander than this.

An active and influential group of noblemen not only backed Palladio
but probably put him up to submit his drawings in the first place. For
several, though by no means for all, Palladio was already building or
would later build palaces or villas. Giovanni Alvise Valmarana, for whose
widow Palladio would eventually undertake the palazzo Valmarana, and
Girolamo Chiericati, for whose palazzo Chiericati Palladio had already
made drawings, though it was not yet begun, spoke for his design in the
Council debate of 1549 determining the final decision. The first *proveditori*
selected to oversee and audit 'such a very important undertaking' included
again Giovanni Alvise Valmarana and Nicolò Chiericati, Girolamo's
brother. Other noblemen closely connected with Palladio succeeded them,
for instance Girolamo de' Godi whose villa at Lonedo Palladio had built

and was improving; Ludovico Trissino, for whom and his brother Francesco (of a different branch to Giangiorgio) Palladio planned both a palace and a villa, neither executed; Giambattista Garzadori (an unexecuted palace); and Giácomo Angarano, for whom Palladio built some of a villa and designed a palace, and whom he particularly commends in the *Quattro Libri*. The committee's satisfaction is indicated by the proud terms of their report of 1558, that the Basilica yielded to no other public building in Italy; that was even before the second storey had begun construction, in 1564. In the troubled times around 1570, it was briefly decided to suspend the building operations, but soon after the Council found the threat of the project's abandonment and decay impossible to bear, and voted again instead only to reduce expenditure on it. Building went on into the seventeenth century; its slow pace was nothing unusual: it may be compared with that of Sansovino's Library of St Mark, which was not finished until 1591.

The transformation by Palladio of the city of Vicenza, as opposed to its countryside, would hardly have become visible until the end of the 1550s, for his palaces were mostly begun after the Basilica, frequently several years or more after. In 1540 he had undertaken and rapidly completed the palazzo Civena (now largely remodelled and extended); but the palace for Marcantonio Thiene, with which Palladio was involved from 1542, reached its impressive semi-completion only in the mid to later 1550s. Iseppo da Porto's palace was complete in 1552; Girolamo Chiericati began his palace in 1551, but built only one wing and then ceased in 1554 (Plates 11a and b). Perhaps also another palace, on the other side of the Isola (the open space between the palazzo Chiericati and the river), later destroyed, was initiated during the 1540s for Anténore Pagello, a man about whom very little is known, but whom Palladio mentions in the proem to his *Four Books* beside Giangiorgio Trissino and Marcantonio and his brother Adriano Thiene as 'very well studied' in architecture. The palace fronted the Isola but at the rear gave directly on to the waterfront of the Bacchiglione, and we hear later of building stones, for instance, being shipped from here. Palladio was much more active both in this decade and in the next in building villas.

In the 1550s the comparatively small group for which Palladio worked extended and Palladio's reputation became self-propagating. In this decade, for instance, he undertook palaces in Verona (for Giambattista della Torre, an acquaintance of Giangiorgio Trissino; now largely destroyed or transformed) and in Údine (the Antonini), as well as official business in other towns, for instance Brescia. He also began to extend his practice to Venice, perhaps offering one among the many projects, coming from all over Italy, for a new bridge over the Grand Canal at Rialto in 1554. In 1555 he was

Plates 11a and b
Palazzo Chiericati, Vicenza. After the Basilica, the palazzo Chiericati is the most
striking and successful product of Palladio's work of the 1540s. The building of
the colonnaded front or portico out over public land, so Girolamo Chiericati
submitted to the Great Council, was 'for the greater "conveniency" and
"ornament" of the whole city'. The way in which the columns overlap or graft
at the joint of the central section and the wings has good Roman precedent.

apologizing for an absence from Vicenza due to business in Venice. He
competed, unsuccessfully, for a position there, and designed a palace that
was never built; he also in this decade built a number of villas up and
down the Veneto for Venetian patrons. By 1561 he was firmly established
at Venice with a commission for the convent buildings of the Augustinian
canons of the church of the Carità, part of the present Accademia (but not
very much of the uncompleted work survived a severe fire of 1630). From
the end of the 1550s, even though recommendation through friends and
relatives still counted for much, Palladio's standing and reputation were
established and national. However, one can discern in Vicenza a group
rather more like a circle of friends, interpenetrating with Palladio's earliest

attachments and with the lobby that won him the Basilica.

Among these friends figured particularly Francesco Thiene and his sons Odoardo and Teódoro, who in the latter part of Palladio's life in Vicenza, until he moved to Venice in 1570, were his landlords. Not closely related to Marcantonio Thiene, nor nearly as rich, Francesco Thiene was probably an old friend of Giangiorgio Trissino, who when he went to Rome in 1547 with Palladio and the painter Maganza had also taken Francesco's nephew Marco, while Francesco's niece Lucia married Giangiorgio's favoured second son Ciro. Francesco's own sons married outside the city, Odoardo to an Isabella Gonzaga of Mantua and Teodoro to a Diamante Pépoli of Bologna (where her brother Fabio Pepoli would be instrumental in the 1570s in obtaining for Palladio a commission to design a modern façade for the great church of San Petronio, still lacking one to this day). However, his daughters married, respectively, Dorotea Girolamo Chiericati's son Valerio and Attilia Iseppo da Porto's son Leonardo.

Other persons known to have belonged to the circle were Giacomo Angarano and Mario Repeta; it was a circle tinged, and therefore perhaps rendered more intimate, by heresy, Iseppo da Porto for instance being suspected, Mario Repeta being investigated by the Inquisition and Odoardo Thiene eventually becoming a citizen of Calvinist Geneva in 1576. It is tempting to wonder whether the heresy also tinged Palladio, and if so whether in any way it affected his architecture; but I think any idea of a conspiracy, of a closed group within society operating to obtain its own ends, is inapplicable, largely because it was not until the 1560s that the Church or the secular authorities became persecutory. Divergent beliefs about such issues as predestination, which was widely discussed, were renounced only when discussion was repressed, and were in effect respectable, or at least pardonable, certainly among laymen, until that time. As Mario Repeta declared to the Inquisition, they met regularly in their villas to discuss not heresy but poetry, and 'so as to find themselves at table together with their ladies'. Undoubtedly they discussed issues of heresy as well – but not conspiratorially. Those who decided or were forced to flee in the 1560s or 1570s were constrained to do so by retrospective persecution: if they had seen it coming, but evidently they did not, they might indeed have been secretive. As for what may have rubbed off on Palladio and his architecture, he was also a household intimate of the eminently orthodox Patriarch elect of Aquileia, Daniele Barbaro; and it is not the function of physical structures, even of churches, to preach.

It is sometimes assumed that Palladio's early Vicentine villas (even designated inappropriately *villini*) were comparatively small, but the villa Godi, his first building commission, concedes nothing in scale to the later

Plate 12
Villa Gazotti, Bertesina, Vicenza. The contrast to the plain walls and unforceful
membering of the earlier villa Godi (see Plate 62a) is remarkable; and there is
also change inside. The *sala* of the Gazotti is no longer flat-ceiled and oblong
like the rooms of the Godi and of preceding villas but groin-vaulted and in the
shape of a cross. See further chapter 19.

ones – though in style it is less monumental. The Godi, begun as early as
1537, stands rather apart (see further p. 202) from the closely interrelated
series of villas Palladio built outside Vicenza apparently after his return
from his first trip to Rome in 1541. They include the villa Gazotti at
Bertésina (Plate 12), for Taddeo Gazotti, not a nobleman, but making quick,
speculative money as a farmer of the salt tax in Treviso; however, in 1545
the authorities found his accounts unsatisfactory and he was forced to sell
his new villa, still incomplete, in 1550. From its mouldings and the nature
of its pilasters to its evident recall of the pavilions of Giulio Romano's
palazzo del Tè, it is closely linked in style to the palazzo Thiene in Vicenza;
its general design resembles, on a smaller scale, that of the Thiene villa at
Quinto. Another villa, in the original design featuring block columns
beside the windows like those of the palazzo Thiene, and for the portal a
serliana unit like the bays of the Basilica, was the one for Giuseppe

Valmarana (no close relation to Giovanni Alvise Valmarana) at Vigárdolo
(see p. 212). A third at Bagnólo for Giovanni Pisani, Venetian, but with
connections with Vicenza where he had been *podestà* in 1525, was one of
Palladio's boldest designs, though unfortunately it was altered (see p. 214).
Two more villas, the Saraceno and the Caldogno, have frontispieces similar
to the Gazotti and Pisani – a pediment over plain or rusticated arches –
and date to about the same time, perhaps slightly later. With Palladio's
villa for Biagio Saraceno (Plate 13) it is interesting to compare another
(Plate 14), built by an unidentified architect at about the same time for
Biagio's brother Giacomo or his heir on the neighbouring estate at Finale
di Agugliaro. None of this early group, which includes the villa Thiene at
Quinto, have temple fronts, though they have emphatic frontispieces; they
all, however, have large halls lit by semicircular 'thermal' windows.

Two more villas, besides the Thiene, belong to the later 1540s, after
Palladio's longer sojourn in Rome with Giangiorgio Trissino. Giacomo
Angarano, whose villa in Angarano Palladio lauds for its delicious fruits
and wines 'and much more for the courtesy of its owner' was evidently
building in 1548; Palladio was frequently at Angarano that summer. Only
the portico enclosing the courtyard or *cortivo* survives; the main house
was probably in fact never rebuilt. In 1550, at Angarano's instigation,
Palladio built a new bridge nearby at Cismon del Grappa. In 1549 Bonifazio
Pojana undertook in his ilk, Pojana, a new villa which has survived well
preserved and unaltered (Plate 15); its frontispiece is another variation on
the *serliana* (taken from Bramante) but otherwise it has the shape of a
mature villa. Its contemporary interior decoration recalls antique models
(Plates 16a–c).

It was first in the 1550s that Palladio introduced the temple front that
soon became the hallmark of his villas. At the villa Pisani at Montagnana

Plates 13 and 14
Villa Biagio Saraceno, architect Palladio, and villa Giacomo Saraceno, architect
unknown, both in Finale di Agugliaro, Vicenza. The brothers Giacomo and
Biagio Saraceno divided their father's estate equally between them, and probably
during the 1530s and 1540s undertook their respective neighbouring villas.
Giacomo's villa (Plate 14, below) is attributed to Sanmicheli but for no good
reason; it is more likely to have been undertaken during the 1530s by the
Pedemuro workshop while Palladio still belonged to it. Biagio's villa (Plate 13,
above) is by Palladio in the 1540s. Both villas are set in similar 'courts' defined
by the main house, outbuildings and walls; both rise from clearly marked
basements. However, the effect of the earlier villa is both busier and more
compact; it lacks both the dominant central element or 'frontispiece' (though it
had a coat of arms blazoned over the main door) and the amplitude of Palladio's
design.

Plate 15
Villa Pojana, Pojana, Vicenza. Dating from the end of the 1540s, the villa shows
Palladio's mature coordination of large, medium and small rooms of different
vaulting patterns, providing a 'sculptural' effect.

Plate 16a
In a larger room beside the *sala* Roman military heroes parade, in a fashion
directly paralleling Palladio's own reconstructions of the atrium of a Roman
house (Plate 16b).

Plate 16b

From the *Four Books* (II, viii), discussing Roman houses according to Vitruvius:
'The following design is of the *sale* which were called 'tetrastyle', because they
had four columns.' The disposition of statues and of the compartments of the
ceiling find precise parallels in the decorations of the villa Pojana and several
other villas. Palladio continues: 'These [*sale*] were made square, and they put in
the columns to make the height proportionate to the breadth, and the room
above more secure.' This remark suggests that his sense of proportion was
primarily visual rather than based on an intellectual appreciation of theoretical
measurements (see further p. 209).

Plate 16c
Villa Pojana. Two rooms are finely decorated with paintings by Bernardino
India and others: outstanding is the *studiolo* or 'study' off the main hall, a small
room that could more easily be kept warm, decorated with *grottesche* and
landscapes precisely according to Pliny's description (see p. 123).

Plate 17
Villa Chiericati, Vancimuglio, Vicenza. Unusually, this villa's 'frontispiece' is a full
temple front, with columns on the flanks as well as in front; Palladio more
commonly provided an arch at the side (as on the palazzo Chiericati or on the
villa Rotonda). That may be a reason for supposing it to be his first temple-
fronted villa.

(see Plate 32 on p. 107) the temple front is over two storeys, and applied
on one side, inset on the other; the villa should be compared with the
rather similar town house, also with a hall of four columns, of the palazzo
Antonini at Udine. The Montagnana villa was one of several commissions
coming in the early 1550s from outside Vicenza; in this case the link was
presumably the Barbaro, to whom this branch of the Pisani was related.
Palladio was also probably discussing at this time the villa for Giovanni
Chiericati at Vancimuglio (Plate 17), and if so that, though not built till
later, has claim to be the first with a single temple front, rising the whole

height; but Palladio had already designed a giant order, though applied, for the main block of the villa Angarano, if the *Quattro Libri* woodcut may be taken as evidence. Equally the palazzo Chiericati, designed in 1549, begun in 1551, has a front of orders, though it is not crowned with a pediment.

Shortly afterwards Palladio developed beyond the mere coordination of villa and outbuildings in a pleasant symmetry to the hierarchical stacking of the outer buildings round the main block. His new ideas are apparent both in the further commissions from his immediate circle in Vicenza and in those for new, important Venetian clients, who usually were better able

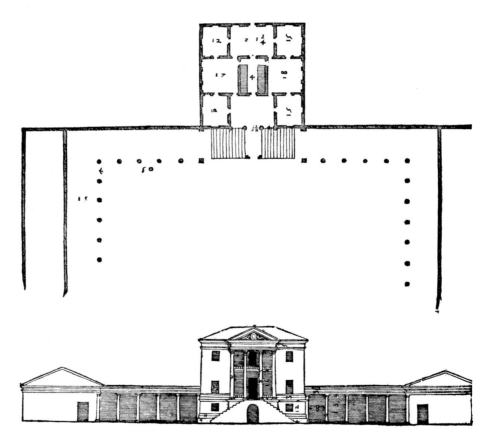

Plate 18

Villa Ragona, Ghizzole, Vicenza, from the *Four Books* (II, xv). The building, or rather rebuilding of an existing house, seems never to have taken place. The design can be dated on style to the early 1550s. Palladio remarks specifically that the portico has 'that "conveniency" mentioned above, that is, of being able to go everywhere under cover'.

Plate 19
Villa Badoer, Fratta Polesine, Rovigo. This view shows the villa with its two 'arms' opening to encircle the courtyard; it is the only surviving example of this quintessentially Palladian idea. (See also Plates 48a and b illustrating this villa.)

to put them into operation. Although Giovanni Chiericati's villa was eventually built, only one *barchessa* of the complex Palladio designed for Francesco and his sons Odoardo and Teodoro Thiene at Cicogna in Paduan territory went up, and a design for one Girolamo Ragona of Vicenza at Ghizzole that features in the *Four Books* seems never to have been started (Plate 18). The same may be said of the villa at Meledo for Francesco and Ludovico Trissino. On the other hand the large house, in two orders, with service quarters that Palladio built for the Venetian Cornaro at Piombino Dese was wholly completed and survives intact (though it was decorated only much later), and the same is true for the Badoer at Fiatta Polesine (Plate 19). The design for Girolamo Ragona looks to be transitional: it shows the surrounding porticoes that embrace the courtyard and extend from the residential block like arms, but they are square on; in the Badoer and the Thiene at Cicogna they have become quadrants. The simile of embracing arms is suggested in the *Four Books* by Palladio himself; what gave real majesty to the idea was the grafted inspiration from Roman hilltop temple complexes such as Palestrina. Later of course Inigo Jones and after him the English Palladians were much taken by these 'circular logges', and Bernini adapted the idea for his colonnade round the piazza of St Peter's, Rome.

In 1554 came Palladio's first publication, a little book on the antiquities of Rome. In the same year he had another look at them in the company of Daniele Barbaro and in 1556 Barbaro's edition of Vitruvius with Palladio's woodcuts was published. Palladio was probably already working then on the Barbaro villa at Maser, a rebuilding and refurbishment of house and outbuildings already there, which Palladio linked together into a single form. Next came the villa at Malcontenta on the Brenta canal for the brothers Foscari, who had links with the Barbaro, and in the 1560s the villa Emo at Fanzólo, recalling on a rather larger scale the Barbaro at nearby Maser. Other villas Palladio designed in the late 1550s or early 1560s never came to fruition, though they appear in the *Quattro Libri*, or have since been destroyed: two for the Venetian Leonardo Mocenigo, one at Lisiera for Giovanni Francesco Valmarana, Giovanni Alvise's brother (which survives in such horribly bodged condition it would better have been altogether destroyed), and one for Mario Repeta which was burnt down in 1672. The villa Zen at Cessalto, Treviso, on the lowlands to the east near the sea, also survives, but has now deteriorated beyond the likelihood of repair.

There is no obvious difference in nature between Palladio's villas for Vicentines and his villas for Venetians, with the exception of the villa Barbaro at Maser (see p. 99). Not unnaturally, landowning Venetians complied or competed with the trends and standards set by the Terraferma nobility: there was a sense in which they were colonizing foreign territory (jokes were made that they took an anchor with them when mounting a horse, and threw it out to bring the animal to a stop; that they sat on it facing backwards, and so on). It was reported, too (by an English ambassador) that while looking 'to landward buieing house and lands', they were at the same time 'furnishing themselfs with coch and horses, and giving themselfs the goode time with more shew and gallantrie than was wont', in sum learning 'more of the gentleman'. In one sense perhaps they aped and conformed; in another they certainly felt they should make the kind of show an embassy required, and therefore out of self-respect and pride they emulated, or out of a sense of superiority they outdid. It is notable, too, that several of Palladio's villas for Venetians were planted on routes to and from the city, most conspicuously the Foscari at Malcontenta (Plate 20), on the main thoroughfare between Venice and Padua and the rest of the mainland; its temple front clearly makes a grand statement towards the waterway (or would do if those masking weeping willows, which compound the silly legend of an eponymous discontented woman, were cut away altogether). The villa Pisani at Bagnolo and the Badoer further south in the Polesine were also on waterways, and the villa Pisani at Montagnana dominated a crossroads.

Plate 20
Villa Foscari, Malcontenta, Venezia. The villa is large because it was built for two
brothers, Alvise and Nicolò Foscari (commemorated, as usual, on the frieze).
Engravings show the villa the opposite of secluded, instead dominating a kind
of piazza. Its imposing temple front gives on to the largest of all Palladio's
surviving *sale* behind.

During the 1560s several signs emerge of Palladio's spreading fame:
one, close to the grass roots, is a notice in the Vicenza census of 1563 of
a farm building *'alla palladiana'*, which may mean no more than it had a
Tuscan or Doric order, of the kind Palladio had introduced, but it reveals
the stamp he had set on the villa, or more particularly on the farm building.
The following ditty captures nicely the proselytizing fervour of his classicism:

> Palladio does not visit prostitutes;
> Of if he does like to visit them sometimes
> He goes to exhort them to undertake
> An antique atrium in mid brothel.

In 1566 he was invited to join the Florentine Academy, and in 1568 he
received lavish praise in Vasari's revised edition of *The Lives of the Most
Excellent Painters, Sculptors and Architects*. In 1570 he became in effect (he
was not in fact appointed) city architect in succession to Sansovino, whose

Plate 21a

Villa Almerico (Rotonda), Vicenza. An earlier villa with a comparable hillside position, and in which the architecture provides ample opportunity for taking the view, is the villa dei Vescovi at Luvigliano, which has two loggias and a terrace circulating all the way round (see Plate 46).

consultancy to the church of San Francesco della Vigna he had already usurped in 1562, and moved to live in Venice. In 1572 there comes a complaint that he is always dining out and is not an easy man to find on a matter of business.

As he took on new ecclesiastical projects in Venice – the Carità commission, the façade of San Francesco della Vigna, then in 1565 the church, refectory and cloisters of the monastery of San Giorgio Maggiore – Palladio was building fewer villas, and none for Venetians, although he had several projects under way for Marcantonio, Anníbale and Federigo Sarego (or Serego) of Verona. There is a design for a house for Federigo Sarego in the *Quattro Libri*; for Marcantonio Palladio was working at three or four properties besides that of Pedemonte where his villa still stands. Its double loggia between massive rusticated columns should, according to the very extensive *Quattro Libri* design, have given on to three additional wings round a whole additional courtyard. Palladio was employed by Sarego not only as an architect but also as an engineeer, installing new conduits and drainage systems to irrigate his newly planted rice-fields; he is more than once called 'engineer' in documents and he was credited in a book on the subject for a design of a machine to raise water.

As it were a late child, Palladio's last villa, the famous villa Rotonda, was commissioned in 1566 (Plate 21a). Its builder, Paolo Almerico, had just returned from Rome where he had followed a career in the Vatican. Since he is reported to have been a cultured man, and had a natural son, he may have been either disgusted or ousted by the new Pope elected early in 1566, Pius V Ghislieri, who was rabidly religious. At any rate, Almerico returned to his native city, which he had left after inculpation in a murder (acts of violence not being uncommon among the nobility), in order to retire. Palladio calls the villa 'suburban' and includes it among his town houses; Almerico had to sell his family house proper in the town in order to build it, but it was a villa since there had been a farm on the spot before and since it was for his retirement (see p. 142). He was fortunate to live to enjoy it several years. Almerico himself (and not Palladio) called it the Rotonda, patently after Santa Maria Rotonda, as the Pantheon was then known; and it may even have been Almerico, rather than Palladio, who suggested the idea of recreating the Pantheon in a villa. It should be appreciated that the recreation was for the owner, within, standing under the dome that, within, sharply slopes and soars with an effect like the Pantheon; without, the villa resembles Hadrian's monument hardly at all, nor ever can have been intended to. Although Palladio changed the camber of the dome in the woodcut in the *Quattro Libri* (Plate 21b), that need not mean that he originally designed the dome to rise higher; he may have wished merely to express more forcefully its inner resemblance to the Rotonda. Although their exterior aspect was appreciated as well, the four temple fronts were also primarily for the benefit of the owner, who from them would enjoy the views stretching in all four directions.

The year 1570 was one of crisis: there was an enormous drain on resources to arm for the Turkish war, which caused further widespread trading and capital losses. In Vicenza in 1570 Palladio was directing the work on the palace of Montano Barbarano (for that reason, Barbarano wrote to Federigo Sarego in Verona, Palladio could not go to him), but, what with the war, Barbarano seems to have incurred such debts that on his death the palace had to be sold. Palladio was also replacing, opposite the Basilica still under construction, the offices of the military governor, the Loggia del Capitaniato, on which the victory of Lepanto was soon celebrated in stucco. In the same year Palladio celebrated his own career with the publication of the *Quattro Libri*, which took its place as a standard work throughout Europe beside Alberti's fifteenth-century textbook *De Re Aedificatoria*. Palladio's last years, however, were severely shaken by the deaths within a few months in 1572 of two of his sons. Although he had moved his household to Venice in 1570, he maintained his links with

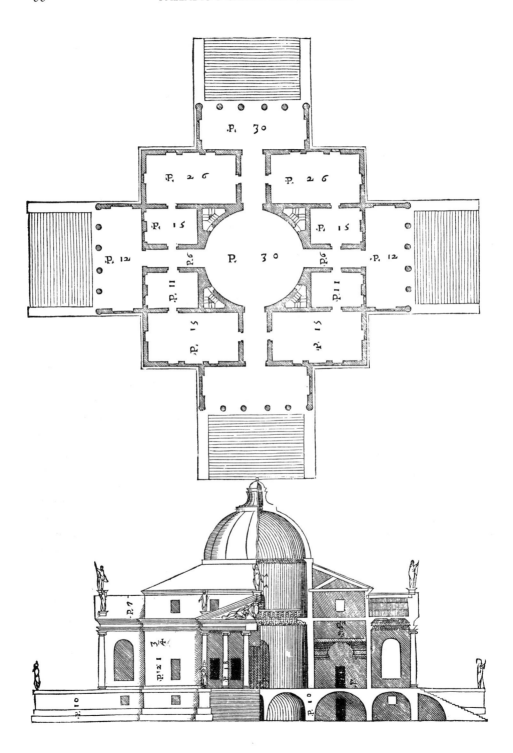

Plate 21b

Villa Almerico, Vicenza, from the *Four Books* (II, iii). In the *Four Books* Palladio
frequently altered the woodcuts away from the reality in order to emphasize
certain features, and that, rather than any change of mind, may explain why he
represented the dome so much higher and more dominant than he built it. Even
so, the woodcut makes it clear how closely the block or shape of the building
resembles the norm of Palladio's mature villas: the dome is merely a modification
or variation of the usual *sala*. Palladio reserved a programmatic reconstruction
of the Pantheon for his church of the Redentore in Venice.

Vicenza, where he made arrangements to be buried, and where he seems
to have designed before his death in 1580 two new palaces, one for a
Francesco Thiene (of yet another branch) and one for Alessandro Porto
(also of yet another branch), who, however, were related to each other,
since Francesco had married Alessandro's sister. Both palaces were taken
over after Palladio's death by Vincenzo Scamozzi: one, Francesco Thiene's
(Plate 22), is both large and complete, dominating the entry into the Corso
from the piazza, one of Palladio's most harmonious and serene works, if
it was by him; of the other, Alessandro's (Plate 23), only two bays were
built, but they are some of the most 'masculine' in all Palladio's architecture.
Palace building (or more often rebuilding), though sporadic, continued
after his death in the mould he had set, sometimes magnificently.

When in 1570, on the death of Jacopo Sansovino, Palladio became
architect to the city of Venice, the rôle in practice and status was not
equivalent to his position (which he did not relinquish) in Vicenza as
salaried architect to one building, the Basilica. As it happened, during the
last ten years of Palladio's life Venice had the opportunity to undertake
its own Basilica, when the Ducal Palace was badly damaged by fires in
1574 and 1577. But Palladio's designs were rejected, and no grand gesture
was made. The Venetian aristocracy either individually or as a class did
not see in Sansovino or in Palladio or in architecture a means by which to
improve the city's standing: it was only after complaints about its squalor
that the Piazza was tidied up by Sansovino, not reorganized. Great palaces
were built, although Sansovino's mighty Corner Ca' Grande, for example,
was undertaken only because a much prized Gothic predecessor had burnt
down. The concept of the Grand Canal as an architectural showpiece did
not emerge in the sixteenth century.

In 1576 there was again crisis: the Senate proferred a votive temple if
Providence should remove the particularly terrible plague then raging.
Palladio was requested to submit alternative designs for a round and a
'quadrangular' church. The latter was chosen, and the Redentore rose
rapidly, though it was not completed before Palladio's death. The troubles

Plate 22
Palazzo Thiene al Castello, Vicenza. Though the palace was certainly not built
by Palladio but by Scamozzi, it follows through the line of development
achieved in his latest palace, the Barbarano in Vicenza, and in others unbuilt.

Plate 23
Palazzo Porto (Porto-Breganze) al Castello, Vicenza. This palace was built by
Scamozzi but is not likely to have been designed by him – its grandeur, its
forceful motifs, demand an attribution to Palladio. The rich, heavy swags of the
frieze have parallel in the 'tempietto Barbaro' (see over).

of the 1570s undoubtably prejudiced other projects: still Palladio built no palaces in Venice. He built no villas, either, although Vincenzo Scamozzi, reworking the Rotonda, built the Rocca Pisani for Palladio's former clients the Pisani of Bagnolo in 1576, and others were building them. In the last year of his life Palladio obliged the Accademia Olimpica with the design for a theatre — a long-standing interest, traceable through his study of the Roman theatre at Verona, through his work with Barbaro on the reconstruction of the theatre described by Vitruvius, and a theatre he had erected in 1565 for a society in Venice (though that, he reported in a surviving letter, had been a wearisome, purgatorial project). According to tradition, he died at Maser, presumably supervising the erection of a new small chapel, a round building just as Marcantonio Barbaro had argued the Redentore should be (Plate 24).

Plate 24
'Tempietto Barbaro', Maser. Small chapels were frequently added to villas from the second half of the sixteenth century onwards: they seem to have been not so much for the convenience of the patron as for the staff and labourers of the estate.

PART 2
Palladio's Mentors

Plate 25
Giangiorgio Trissino as an intellectual, by Vincenzo Catena (Louvre, Paris),
painted probably when the sitter was in his early forties.

6

Giangiorgio Trissino

Giangiorgio Tríssino (Plate 25) not only was extremely well travelled and knew a large number of the leading figures of the time, but he was also, at the end of the 1530s, when Palladio seems first to have met him, and when he was approaching 60, widely respected both as a scholar, poet and critic and, in the more conventional rôle of a nobleman, as a courtier and ambassador. His family was as old and as Vicentine as anyone's in the town, deriving its name from the ancient fief of Trissino in the Valdagno in the foothills of Vicenza — the region from which comes today the mineral water Recoaro; in addition to what his own land brought in, Giangiorgio was entitled to the tithes of this village among others. When in the early 1530s he came back to reside in Vicenza, reducing his attendances at Italy's courts if not exactly retiring, he could write contentedly to a friend that he was respected more than anyone else in the town; he had, after all, carried the Pope's train at the coronation of Charles V at Bologna in 1530, a signal honour and one that counted in his society — it was precisely the kind of thing genealogists liked to record. In the preface to the first of his *Four Books*, when Palladio, forty years later, wished to congratulate the city of Vicenza for its 'many gentlemen ... who for nobility and learning are not unworthy to be numbered among the most illustrious', the first name to be called was that of Giangiorgio Trissino, 'splendour of our times'; and however one assesses his literary achievement there was no one else in Vicenza in the sixteenth century who begins to rival his prominence.

Trissino had not studied at a university; instead he had married young, aged sixteen (twice that age would not have been unusual), and he embarked on his intellectual and diplomatic career only eleven years later, after his wife had died, in 1505. Before that, one presumes, he had been happy to enjoy life and youth, with the pair of hounds, the hawk and the good horse he had had even as a child, orphaned at seven; it is evident from his later career that he always liked women. His first wife, Giovanna, was also a Trissino; she left him two sons, one of whom, Giulio, survived to become the bane of his father's life. In 1505, leaving his children and affairs to the care of his mother, he began his circulation of Italy's courts, first at Milan, then at Ferrara, where he remained most firmly connected, and also at Mantua, where he played the gallant to Isabella d'Este. He cultivated the acquaintanceship particularly of intellectuals, and assiduously studied the classics, particularly Greek.

He established his reputation, however, in Florence and Rome. He had moved to Tuscany in 1513 to visit the baths probably at Bagni di Lucca, having suffered a nondescript illness or fever for some three years; dietary regulation and cupping or even more drastic bleeding had not been effective, but he seems then to have thrown the malaise off. Florence at the time was a leading centre of Greek studies; and in that year the Florentine (Medici) Leo X had been elected Pope — he was the most humanist of all the Renaissance popes, and particularly keen on Greek scholarship. Trissino found favour with Leo — naturally, considering that the Pope had appointed as his secretaries Jacopo Sadoleto from Modena and Pietro Bembo from Venice, chiefly on the merit of their reputation in *belles lettres*; Trissino had to his credit by this time several well-turned *opuscula* and an important tragedy, *Sophonisba*. By 1515, he too had been pressed into Leo's diplomatic service, being sent to Germany to try to find terms for agreement between the Pope and Maximilian: Trissino was a natural choice for the task because his family, in Vicentine politics, had usually been pro-imperial, and his relative Leonardo da Trissino had led Maximilian's forces into Vicenza during the first campaign of the Wars of the League of Cambrai. Leo X also obtained for Giangiorgio a pardon from the Venetians, who had exiled and condemned all noblemen who had not appeared before them when they retook Vicenza, and in 1516 he sent him to Venice as papal *nuncio*. However, a note sent back to the government from a Venetian stationed in the south survives, informing the Council of Ten before his arrival that Trissino was coming more to settle his own affairs than on any matter of importance. That must have deflated a little the ceremony of his reception, and in fact nothing more substantial came of this mission than had come from the trip to Germany. Recalled in 1517, Trissino for the moment received no more such duties, and spent time once again in Vicenza, but he maintained close links with Leo X's court, where he had made lifelong friends such as the Pope's relative Bishop Niccolò Ridolfi. After the death of Leo X, he was able to re-establish those links upon the election of the next Medici Pope, Clement VII, in 1523. He also served Clement VII as an envoy to Venice more than once, although in the same year, 1523, he married again.

His second marriage was rather rash. His new wife, Bianca, was a famous beauty of his youth whom he had perhaps long loved (a letter he had written to her in 1507, sixteen years before, accompanying an alabaster vase of unguents, has survived); anyway, he married her quite quickly after she became free at the death of her husband Alvise, to whom Giangiorgio was executor, in 1522. Dispensation was required, Bianca not only having been married to another Trissino, but being also herself, like Giangiorgio's first wife, *née* Trissino. They did not wait for it to come through to live together, but by 1535 Bianca had reclaimed her dowry and was living independently; but then again Giangiorgio was at her deathbed in Venice in 1540. They had a son, Ciro, to whom Giangiorgio was closely attached, and whom he would have made his heir, had he not had a son by his first marriage, Giulio. Giangiorgio had already decided Giulio was a runt (perhaps not unreasonably, because he was congenitally thin, frail and chesty) and had entered him into the Church. Newly, incestually married father and celibate son, nineteen years old, soon quarrelled, Giulio refusing to have his movements dictated and Giangiorgio refusing to provide him with money. At last Giangiorgio boxed his son's ears (so Giulio claimed), and then, while Giangiorgio, as so often, was abroad, Giulio and his maternal relatives claimed his rights in a gang, besieging his stepmother in the house while he emptied his father's barns of their goods. Such behaviour was not unusual: state justice had not yet supplanted personal vendetta.

During the 1520s Trissino migrated between Rome, Vicenza and Venice; he went to Venice on diplomatic service for Rome or Vicenza. He began publication of his various compositions and treatises on composition in Rome, where the *questione della lingua*, the debate over the form of Italian to be used in literature, was mostly hotly debated; later, after the Sack of Rome in 1527, he republished them in Venice. In the debate he was with Baldassare Castiglione in the camp that supported 'courtier's' Italian, essentially the current vernacular common to Italy's regional courts; the camp that prevailed, however, was Pietro Bembo's, supporting a much more artificial language modelled on the often outmoded expression of Petrarch and Boccaccio. Had Trissino's theories won, he would have been a more important figure; today his achievement is often reduced to his translation and publication of Dante's *De Vulgari Eloquentia* (On good writing in the vernacular), and his attempt to introduce Greek ε and ω into the Italian alphabet (to distinguish short 'e' and long 'o'). (Later, Palladio adopted the ε for a time, and its appearance on a drawing is now a useful indication of his authorship and the drawing's date early in his career.) While it was not yet apparent that Bembo's ideas would carry, Trissino enjoyed considerable prominence.

Even after the Sack of Rome Trissino remained in attendance on Clement VII: hence his rôle at the coronation of Charles V at Bologna in 1530.

Shortly afterwards, however, approaching fifty, he confessed himself 'tired of working and sated of courts'. A successful action against a collateral branch of the family had won him the tithes of the Valdagno, and he was 'less poor than ever before'. He seems to have decided to settle down, both to enjoy his dignities in his native city and to serve it in a statesman-like fashion. In a memorandum from the early 1530s, he set out the means by which he thought he could resolve the city's quarrels and factions. He failed not only to do that, but even to rub shoulders himself with his peers without friction, or to resolve his own quarrel with Giulio, or to stay with his wife, or eventually to remain in Vicenza at all.

During the 1530s he was often called upon to represent his city at Venice, particularly in 'a case of the very gravest importance', in fact a dispute over the administration of two small towns in Vicentine territory, Marostica and Lonigo (to these Venice appointed its own governor; Vicenza claimed she should administer them). Trissino's patience was tried to its uttermost by his fellow ambassador, of the Porto family, on whom 'having been an ambassador of two Popes and an Emperor, I do not expect to have to fawn'. Although disgust and exhaustion with service at court are a *leitmotif* of private letters of sixteenth-century Italy, Trissino's complaints as an elderly man reduced to pettifogging are poignant, particularly in the midst of the other troubles that were shortly to descend on his head.

After his wife had left him, Trissino decided to rebuild for himself, in addition to his town house and to his family home at Cornedo in the Valdagno, a third house about two miles outside Vicenza at Crícoli (Plate 26). Its façade after Raphael was in fact derived from Sebastiano Serlio, and only just before Alvise Cornaro had added an upper storey to the loggia in the court of his house at Padua almost to the same design, but Trissino's conviction that Leo X's Rome was the proper model must have been his own. He called the house a castle, and one of its 'towers' still has painted fictive diamond pointing copied from Roman military architecture; Raphael's villa Madama had also had 'a little defence' (see p. 115).

A document proves Palladio to have been with Trissino at Cricoli in February 1538. Come the summer, Trissino rented a house in Padua, and was most likely the means by which Palladio met there Alvise Cornaro, even if Cornaro, though highly influential in matters architectural, was in no sense a scholar or humanist, like the general run of Trissino's acquaintance. Through Trissino or Cornaro Palladio doubtless met the architect Sebastiano Serlio, and at Cornaro's house would have examined not only Serlio's drawings but also an extensive series of drawings of antique buildings by Giovanni Maria Falconetto. Some of these he would not have known; others he would not have seen reproduced so accurately; others

Plate 26
Villa Trissino, Cricoli, Vicenza. In 1538 friends reported having been
'sumptuously' entertained there; and that 'everyone liked the place marvellously,
and were equally pleased by the building, especially since they were given to
understand that, as far as was known, the greater part of the design was
Trissino's own'.

again were of local monuments, notably the considerable Roman remains at Verona. They would have whetted his appetite and fed his knowledge of Rome, the *fons et origo* of classical architecture, which shortly afterwards, in 1541, in Trissino's company, he was enabled to see for the first time with his own eyes. In these years Trissino must also have introduced Palladio to learned and influential circles in Venice, where he had another house, and where, in 1540, he was with his wife at her death. He surely introduced him, for instance, to Daniele Barbaro, with whom Palladio later, in the 1550s, collaborated to produce a celebrated edition of Vitruvius. It is likely enough that Trissino had in mind a similar collaboration, since he projected, though he did not take very far, a treatise on architecture of his own.

In 1543 the Bishop of Vicenza, Niccolò Ridolfi, found it opportune to visit and for a time to reside in his diocese. It was the first time he had set foot there, although he had been appointed in 1524. His appointment, incidentally, illustrates the loss of power and face the Venetians had suffered during the Wars, for ever since they had annexed the region the bishoprics had been their plum: this Ridolfi was a Medici cousin, a supplantee of the papacy. Surely because he came from elsewhere, and not from Venice, the Vicentines decided to welcome him magnificently, with a ceremony and apparatus imitating royal and papal entrances, all along a processional route leading from the city gate to the Bishop's Palace. This event was clearly Trissino's show: Ridolfi was an old friend of his, for whom he had previously seen to the bishopric's business, and in the few days before his formal entry Ridolfi stayed with Trissino at Cricoli. Trissino devised the 'programme' of allegorical figures in paint and stucco which greeted the procession from the arches and so on erected along the route; these were designed by Palladio. Trissino also exerted himself to bring to the ceremony, and so honour it still further, important and distinguished persons; he succeeded in inducing Ranuccio Farnese, the Pope's grandson, to come, *'per veder meglio la civiltà di questa nostra patria'* ('to see better the nobility of this our city'), as he wrote to him. The inspiration from Rome and Florence under Leo X is very clear: before entering the city, Ridolfi was entertained at Cricoli much as eminent guests on their way in to Rome would have lodged at the never completed villa Madama which Cricoli miniaturized, and the programme Trissino devised recalled that of Leo X's entrance into Florence in 1515. But nostalgia was not the motivation; it was recognized instead that these forms and ideals, being shaped to an unprecedented degree by the informed study of classical architecture, offered the way forward for the present and the future – represented at the ceremony by Ranuccio Farnese, scion of the then Pope.

Ridolfi entered the city in a ceremony that involved and depended on the fine arts to a greater extent than any before: it marks the point at which, we may assume, the Vicentine nobility in general began to divine that public architecture might be a good means to promote themselves and their city abroad, to give it a better name. If so, then Ridolfi's entry amounts, historically, to the turning of a page, opening the glorious chapter of Palladio's career, which means also the most glorious of Vicenza's, as his contemporaries almost knew. Quite how much of this general orientation was to the personal credit of Giangiorgio Trissino is difficult to estimate. Clearly he could not sustain the rôle of its political arbiter, but he continued to serve frequently as his city's representative, and in the orientation to the Roman High Renaissance and in the preparation of Palladio he determined the style in which his city would enhance its prestige through the arts. When he went to Rome in 1541, taking Palladio with him, his intention may have been to secure a benefice for his son Giulio, with whom he was newly reconciled. However, in 1545 he undertook a much more extended sojourn in Rome and took with him a small tutelage, consisting of Palladio, the painter and poet Giambattista Maganza or Magagnò (whom Trissino had christened, less adhesively, 'Terpander') and Marco Thiene, whose sister Ciro would marry. Marco actually calls their group in a letter an 'academy'. Terpander worked hard at his painting; Palladio assiduously set about taking measured drawings of the antiquities in and around Rome, breaking off only to return briefly to Vicenza to present his drawings for the Basilica, the spectacular central monument now required by the city.

The last years of Giangiorgio's life were disastrous. Giulio had heretic tendencies, word of which probably hindered his advancement in the Church, and thus prevented an alleviation of his chronic shortage of funds, and increased his demands on his patrimony. When he went to Rome Giangiorgio handed over the administration of his possessions to Giulio, but he took them back on his return complaining that Giulio was ill-treating the tenants and running up debts; and in 1547 he made them over or fixed their 'sale' to Ciro. A running battle developed; eventually Giangiorgio and Ciro entered Giulio's house and ransacked it for keys and papers, whereupon Giulio, with a band of militia provided by the Vicentine justices, burst in on his father at his villa at Cricoli, and would have dragged the old man from the gouty bed in which he lay. When the case came before the magistrates, they dispossessed Ciro and Giangiorgio.

Suddenly impoverished, Giangiorgio mobilized the resources he had acquired in his career, adding one further weapon, his newly completed *Italia Liberata da' Gotthi*. He attempted to borrow horses from one of his best connections, Cardinal Madruzzo (with whom we later find Palladio), but in the preparations then under way for the Council at Trent the Cardinal felt he needed as many as he had for his own train. Trissino had to be content with mules, but set off to Augsburg anyway, determined to await the arrival of the Emperor, to present his poem (in which Justinian is the hero; the preface points the parallel between Charles V and Justinian) and to ask in return some Italian benefice for his old age. But the Emperor never came; he delayed in Brussels. Meanwhile it was pointed out to Trissino that the Emperor no longer retained in Italy any possession of any worth, having granted away all he had had long ago. Trissino therefore turned round and went to Rome, not passing Vicenza on the way: he had not viewed his peers rosily before, but now he saw the city as a nest of vipers, and Venice, whence the news came that his appeal against the Vicentine magistrates had been rejected, was equally vicious. In Rome he died, excruciated by gout and one may imagine by frustration, in the lodgings of Marco Thiene.

Trissino's literary œuvre, which was a greater achievement than his preparation of Palladio, is often criticized as pedantic and lifeless, but these

terms are not relative to his time. When one considers that his tragic play
Sophonisba was the first to have been founded on the theory of tragedy
laid down by Aristotle in his *Poetics*, and thus the first to demonstrate the
'three unities' by which classic French drama, from Corneille to Racine,
was ruled, pedantry or classicism can hardly be regarded as a defect.
Trissino in this play and in *Italia Liberata* also established the use of blank
verse — in this at least he anticipated Shakespeare and Milton. Posterity's
criticism condemns more his lack of other qualities than his classicism,
which had real virtue in its ability both to state the rules and to create
satisfactory works of art bound by them or illustrating them. That is an
achievement closely analogous to Palladio's in architecture, and one may
well assume that Palladio learnt to harness theory and practice partly by
the example of Trissino's charioteership. It should also be appreciated,
again with an eye on Palladio, that Trissino was inventive in his choice of
antique models, partly because he was such a very good Greek. For
instance, the *Sophonisba* contains elegant and seamless translations from
Sophocles and Euripides, and the *Italia Liberata*, written 'with Aristotle's
precepts' but 'with my mind on Homer', produces a unique sensation: in
a scenario of chivalric romance recalling Ariosto's *Orlando Furioso* one
recognizes Homeric similes, all expressed in a refined and rotund vocabulary stemming from Petrarch. The bold, scholarly and appropriate use of
antique models is characteristic of Palladio's architecture, which was carried
out according to the precepts of Vitruvius but was inspired by a personal
exploration of the archaeological evidence — Palladio's fascination with
Roman baths, for instance, was novel.

7

Alvise Cornaro

Palladio met Alvise Cornaro (Plate 27) probably in 1538 through Giangiorgio Trissino, who took lodgings in Padua in that year. In Padua Cornaro seems to have achieved considerable influence by force of personality, though he was not (to his regret) an aristocrat either of Venice or in his native city. For Palladio he was a means to new ideas and people – his acquaintanceship included Sebastiano Serlio, one of whose books, of 1544, contains a preface with a remarkable tribute to Cornaro as an architect. From Cornaro Palladio obtained and copied many of the drawings of classical buildings made by the architect and architectural painter Giovanni Maria Falconetto, who had lived in Cornaro's household until his death in 1535. But also Cornaro had ideas and views of his own both about architecture and about agriculture, which almost certainly influenced Palladio and in any case are a valuable sample of the ideas circulating at the time about country matters. Though they could be opinionated and eccentric, Cornaro's writings make him something of a spokesman for the attitudes of Terraferma landowners.

Cornaro is called 'a great figure' in Paduan life of his time, a 'generous patron', of the playwright Ruzante and of the architect Falconetto. However, most of what is known about him is based on his own estimation, and the man was also a charlatan, a boaster and a liar, perhaps particularly in old age. He was a self-confessed plain-speaker, stressing the practical and empirical in support of his parade of ideas – a refreshingly novel voice, in many ways. His series of pamphlets on architecture, agriculture and on the proper conduct of life, 'the sober life', are not without absurdities, but they seem to offer a glimpse of reality when compared with the usual elegant abstractions of Renaissance humanism such as Trissino's surviving fragment of a treatise on architecture. Cornaro was a sharp businessman, behind whose passionately argued schemes for the improvement of the general lot there also lay personal profit. As factor for the Bishop of Padua he kept within the bounds of honesty only by fudging the accounts. He was eventually sacked, but it is typical of Cornaro that on the eve of

Plate 27
Alvise Cornaro, engraving after a portrait by Tintoretto.

dismissal he put forward another great project from which all would benefit
if the other party first put up the money. Cornaro was not even his real
name, and though he liked to let it seem he was a nobleman, he failed to
persuade the Venetian courts when he applied, with an ingenuous sincerity,
to be recognized as one.

The Cornaro (or Cornér) were an important, large, ancient and wealthy
Venetian family; but Alvise's real name was Rigo or Righi. His story (which
he seems to have imbibed from his father) was that his Cornaro ancestors
had gone out to the Peloponnese in the fourteenth century, and while
enjoying their estates there had neglected to update their registry in the
Great Council in Venice, as they realized too late when they were forced
to return to Italy after the Turks conquered the Morea in the later fifteenth
century. Alvise's grandfather was an innkeeper, the owner of a tavern well
situated at Portello, or the quay where the ferry from Venice docked when
it reached Padua; this passed to Alvise's elder brother, and Alvise inherited
the basis of his wealth from his mother's side. From his maternal uncle, a

cleric noted for his business acumen, he inherited his house near the church of the Santo, on the via Cesarotti, and his starting capital. He astutely increased it considerably. In the end he even achieved for his only daughter, to his great joy and satisfaction, the rank he desired for himself, by marrying her to a genuine scion of the Cornaro family; all the same he postponed indefinitely paying over the large dowry on which the match was negotiated.

There still survive, though not in a good state, Cornaro's Loggia and Odeon (Plates 28a and b), architectural embellishments he added to the house his uncle left him, which no longer exists; also his gardens in the shadow of the Santo, to which one crossed via a tunnel, have gone. The Loggia, which was designed by Falconetto, was at first a one-storey structure, to which a second storey was added perhaps at the same time as the Odeon was undertaken, in the early 1530s. It was remarkable that in the economic doldrums of the early 1520s anyone should undertake such a frivolous thing as a loggia, but when first completed, in 1524, it was merely an open arcade five bays long and one deep. Thanks to Falconetto's archaeological interests, it introduced for the first time into the Veneto architecture founded more closely on classical example than the prevailing Early Renaissance style – in details such as the *Victories* in the spandrels of the central arch, or the keystone heads, which Falconetto derived from Roman examples he knew in his native Verona, or the half columns and the triglyphs and metopes of the entablature. Even Falconetto's signature on one of the piers deliberately imitated the signature of the architect on the Roman Arco di Gavi in Verona. In the house itself, though he never managed to refurbish it architecturally, Cornaro had painted copies from designs by Raphael.

The Loggia was a gallery in which to stroll and converse (*passeggiare*), converting to an open-air dining room. It is often said to have served, or even have been built, as a backdrop for the performance of plays by Ruzante, which at least on one occasion were staged 'in Cornaro's house'; however, this does not seem possible, for several reasons. When all was made ready for a performance, the stage can only have been in front of the Loggia, and so would have masked its bottom half. Ruzante's plays are about peasants (Ruzante was the stage-name of Angelo Beolco; it means 'frolicking'), and in one of his manuscripts there is an illustration of the set, consisting of three huts opening in doors at the bottom and windows at the top: these huts would have fitted with the arches of the Loggia at best unhappily, and would have negated unavoidably the Loggia's own architecture. Above all Ruzante's gross, dialect-speaking characters were hardly suited to a stage the like of the elegant Loggia, by all the terms in which it is subsequently praised. Only the last of Ruzante's

Plates 28a and b

Alvise Cornaro's Loggia and Odeon, Padua, in the courtyard beside Cornaro's house, in a print from the map of Padua published in 1784. The Loggia at the rear and the Odeon on the right were adjuncts to the house on the left; the Odeon is shown here before current restorations.

plays, the *Vacharia*, dating from 1533, had classical reference, being a modernization of Plautus's *Asinaria*. When staged 'in Cornaro's house' it was also reported to have 'a very good set', which cannot have been the Loggia itself (references to the set in the play preclude it), but which would have made the Loggia redundant. If the Loggia had been a theatre, it would be the only permanent, stone backdrop of the sixteenth century known. As it is, by all the unequivocable references recorded, sets and stages were invariably built of wood, and were usually dismantled immediately; Palladio's Teatro Olimpico in Vicenza is an exception, but even that is also built wholly of wood. Cornaro's Loggia was an ornament, like the arch that Falconetto built for him at his estate at Este, a pavilion, like the many dining pavilions that adorned villa gardens. It belonged with Cornaro's garden across the road. As such it was highly praised: Vasari called it 'bellissima e ornatissima'; Palladio called it 'bellissima' in his *Four Books*.

The second storey of the Loggia derives, like Giangiorgio Trissino's front to his villa at Cricoli, from Raphael's villa Madama in Rome – this time more strictly, rather than reflecting Serlio's variation of the design for inclusion in one of his books, as Trissino's does. For Palladio it remained a fundamental model, or rather a theme on which to work his own further variations; some of his early façades even reveal exact replication, for instance in the provision of plinths for the window-sills as well as for the pilasters. In the *Four Books* Palladio singles out for praise still another aspect, the Loggia's staircase, which is disposed around a square stairwell in a manner that he claims was invented by Alvise Cornaro; he may also have been impressed by Cornaro's two staircases, placed symmetrically about the centre, which is something Palladio adopted for the first time in the early 1540s, and which thereafter became a standard feature of his architecture.

Like Trissino, although he employed Falconetto for the Loggia, Cornaro made his own designs, perhaps including that of the Odeon, although its basis is a plan which Falconetto had used earlier in one of his gates for Padua. This plan must have had particular interest for Cornaro, since it derived from a Roman building in San Germano in central Italy then identified – wrongly, as it happens – as the country house of Marcus Terentius Varro, author of *De Re Rustica*. It made the Odeon a kind of recreation of what was called the 'studio' or study of his agriculturalist forebear. It had, however, little relation to agriculture, but was probably designed for music-making. Consisting of a central square surmounted by a dome, it was an excellent space for a small gathering, though perhaps not ideal acoustically. Its round, central dome may even be seen as a precedent for Palladio's villa Rotonda. It was a strange plan for a Roman villa, and in fact the building identified as Varro's villa was actually a small Roman bath-house in the same town, Varro's villa having long since disappeared.

Cornaro could not, like Trissino, have given Palladio the chance to increase his classical culture. One may doubt whether he had much to teach the younger professional in architecture, beyond a little vocabulary or formwork — whatever his talents as an amateur designer and for all the good sense of his drafts towards a treatise on architecture, which was intended explicitly for owners, not architects, and anyway dates from the 1550s. Possibly some of Palladio's associates may have come to him, or his clients, from Cornaro's circle, for instance Falconetto's son-in-law the stuccadore Bartolomeo Ridolfi, or the painter Gualtiero Padovano. The preface to the 1544 Venice edition of Serlio's book on private houses strongly recommends Cornaro as the man a prospective builder should go to see: 'If a gentleman ... wishes to know how one builds a house in town, let him go to casa Cornaro in Padua ... If he wishes to make a beautiful garden, let him take his model from Cornaro's ... If he wishes to build in the country, let him go to Codevigo [Cornaro's main estate] ... If he wants to build a palace fit for a prince, let him go to Luvigliano, where he will contemplate a lodging worthy of a Pope, or an Emperor.' Cornaro was influential in setting and articulating a taste, and for that reason alone would have been a man to know and to be known by.

Cornaro is most important as a practitioner and proponent of what he called *la santa agricoltura*. 'Holy agriculture' was partly a philosophy of life, and at the same time the means by which he made his money, by a process more like modern property development than innovative agronomy. Cornaro did two things: he reclaimed land, that is, he bought it cheap, put in dykes and drains to render it arable, then either sold it or leased it; and he negotiated profit-sharing contracts with his tenants, by this incentive increasing output. Neither the one nor the other was new, or practised only by Cornaro (Leonardo da Vinci had, for instance, put his mind to such drainage schemes, among other things), but Cornaro seems to have started early — as soon as the return of peace permitted — and he contracted his factorship of the Bishop of Padua's lands probably in the joint expectation that he would increase their yield. That was in 1529; and in 1530 Cornaro formed his own land reclamation company. Yet things had gone very wrong by 1541. The Bishop had been reduced to holding Cornaro prisoner for the money he owed him, and Venetian magistrates had ordered Cornaro to cut the dykes he had made, which they were told were endangering the state of the lagoon.

However, Cornaro's dykes seem not in the end to have been demolished, and he came to a settlement with the Bishop of Padua. For he had continued to claim that the Bishop owed him money, rather than he the Bishop — essentially on the grounds that when he had rented the factorship, the Bishop had promised to advance him 2,000 ducats with which to terminate the tenants' old leases (which meant paying them for any improvements made during their occupancy); but the Bishop's money had not been forthcoming, so Cornaro charged against the Bishop's account the money he believed he would have made on the higher yields that the redistributed and renegotiated leases would have brought. There were also, however, certain petty dishonesties in the accounts: a figure of 5,587 lire was found to be more exactly 2,587 lire, for instance, or in a note the Bishop asked Cornaro to buy bricks on his behalf at the same rate as his own kilns sold them (not a higher one). It is evident that the Bishop's staff came to loathe Cornaro, accusing him of 'lies' and of being 'full of artifice'; for his part he claimed that they were spreading stories that he had no money of his own and that his brother was making his grandchildren his direct beneficiaries, since he did not trust any money to pass through Cornaro and come out the other side.

Ruzante's peasant plays provide another sidelight on Cornaro's 'holy agriculture'. They are remarkable for the unadulterated earthiness of their characters and the grit of their dialogue, but even for the peasant whom he himself acted Ruzante had not exactly sympathy, nor any for the peasant's lot in general, however clearly he saw it. He saw it the more clearly and had the less sympathy for it by working as Cornaro's own factor, that is, as his instrument in making the peasants more productive. In fact Ruzante's plays belong in an established tradition of 'anti-villein' literature, satire or simply just spite against the peasants — hated for their recalcitrance and ignorance and evasiveness and refusal, ultimately, to behave urbanely. Ruzante, the character played by Angelo Beolco, is a lazy incompetent: at the opening of one play he comes on to see he has failed to set his nets properly to trap any birds, after which he decides to go to sleep. It seems that Cornaro, managing the Bishop of Padua's lands, tried to remove such peasants, the inefficient 'poverissimi', too poor even to possess animals, and whose lots were unproductively small, in order to introduce more industrious sharecroppers on more workable units of land.

Cornaro was not therefore Fabian. The division between the landlord, the man who enjoyed the *entrate*, or what came in, and the tenant, the

man who worked out on the land, was not questioned or crossed. Writing
some years later, in 1558, in his treatise on 'the sober life', Cornaro presents
a vision of an idyllic country community, such as he claimed to have
created on his (main) estate at Codevigo by land reclamation. It is entirely
a world of enlightened self-interest, in which the better conditions for
human breeding Cornaro has obtained are recorded as a service to God,
who gains the souls. The village at Codevigo is 'very beautiful, both
because it is full of beautiful streets, which meet in a beautiful square in
the middle of which is its church, and because it is divided by a broad and
swift passage of the river Brenta, on both sides of which there is open
ground, all of fertile and well cultivated fields, and is now, God be thanked,
very well inhabited, which it was not before, instead quite the contrary,
because it was marshy and full of bad air, and the residence more of snakes
than men. But when I had drained it, the air changed to good, and people
came to live, and the souls began to multiply greatly, and the place was
brought to the perfection you see today: such that I can say truly that in
this place I have given God altar and temple, and souls to adore him — all
of which gives me the greatest pleasure, solace and contentment, every
time I return to see and enjoy it ...'. He had banked the river, built the
bridge over it and drained the marsh prevailing on the lagoon side.
Appositely, in his argument with the Venetian authorities about his dykes
in this area, he had pointed to Torcello, which was once a flourishing city
but was devastated by malaria — in which devastation it remains — or, as
Cornaro says, by the 'bad air' that drains and irrigation can ameliorate.
Statistics are not available to prove or disprove the growth of Cornaro's
'model' village. The population, however, was increasing everywhere.
Cornaro is an articulate representative of a general trend in which those
in the cities increased their power over those in the countryside, whom
they wished increasingly to exploit and direct, creating at the same time,
as they might see it, a Sabine georgia.

Cornaro propagated a theory of 'the sober life', which may also, though
less directly, be relevant to Palladio's villas. In itself the theory was nothing
remarkable, simply a regime avoiding excess, and therefore imbalance of
the humours, by which disease or death were believed to be caused (indeed
broadly speaking they are); more obsessively Cornaro attributed Ruzante's
early death to insobriety, and would claim that the regime had kept him
alive till the age of ninety-five, while he confidently expected to reach a
hundred — which he might have done the more easily, since when he said
he was ninety-five he was actually eighty-two. For a variety of loosely
connected reasons the way of agriculture, according to Cornaro, was the
only 'sober life': it was preferable to a career in arms, which meant living
off others' loss, or to 'crossing the sea with infinite mortal risks' (this seems

to be an echo of a sentiment in Horace, whose 'golden mediocrity' also meant staying at home) or to other careers which were 'full of contraries' — this of course implies both difficulties and medical 'contrary humours'. From the 'sober life' Cornaro in effect excluded politics, from which he was debarred. It was a prescription he would surely not have made had he been brought up a Venetian aristocrat; but it is a line that might appeal to certain members of the landed classes of the Terraferma — those who wished to forget that their fathers had welcomed the ejection of the Venetians, for instance. By means of 'agriculture', furthermore, Cornaro claimed he had made enough money to live like a gentleman: he could spend freely — according to the old, ultimately chivalric ideal that *noblesse* was proved by largesse — and he could support writers, musicians, architects, painters and sculptors. These, together with his 'honoured' buildings, 'convenient rooms' and 'beautiful' gardens, which he had created, were his gentlemanly recreation and his fulfilling pleasure. And, unlike others, thanks to his 'sober life', he would live long enough to enjoy them.

Cornaro's writings were almost all published in the 1550s, although some remained as drafts he never finalized. They are repetitive enough to justify the assumption that he had already formed his views when Palladio met him, and that they were quite widely disseminated by word of his own mouth by the time of that eulogy in Serlio's book of 1544. It is also clear that other landowners — Veronese proprietors for instance, and Venetians on land in the Padovano, including Venetian neighbours of Cornaro's at Codevigo — were already exploiting their land along the lines that Cornaro would keenly propagandize. Around Vicenza both the local nobility, such as the Thiene, and the Venetians who had bought their way in more or less recently, such as the Pisani at Bagnolo, were undertaking similar agricultural redevelopment.

8

Daniele and Marcantonio Barbaro

The brothers Daniele and Marcantonio Barbaro, owners of the villa Barbaro at Maser, which, with architecture by Palladio and frescoes by Veronese, is a supremely beautiful building, one of the most attractive banners of Italian Renaissance culture — the brothers Barbaro were both highly esteemed by their contemporaries, the one an influential prelate and a distinguished scholar, the other a prominent figure in the Venetian government, serving notably as the Venetian representative in Istanbul in the difficult circumstances before and after the Battle of Lepanto; one a complete Renaissance humanist, the other an exemplary Venetian patrician. But they remain impenetrably shadowy personalities, Daniele in particular, because he wrote and published, and there exist a great many words from his pen; yet, however much one delves into his writings, their author remains remote. Occasionally a glint suggests that the Barbaro were human: Daniele is reported on one occasion, by way of an expression of his joy at the news of a friend, to have kissed Pietro Aretino, the poet, with whom he corresponded; however, their remarkably uninformative letters are conspicuously lacking the kind of vivid detail that individualizes people or makes them scrutable.

Take, for example, the turning-point in Daniele Barbaro's career, when he received a letter while on embassy in 1549 in England, where Somerset was Lord Protector, telling him that he was to be appointed Patriarch elect of Aquileia. In his reply to the Venetian government he protested that the civil career he had been pursuing, working his way up through the various offices and in England for no other reason, was all now being taken from him; that the appointment would gain him nothing or rather would cost him; and that anyway he was not at all suitable. He nonetheless did not refuse the election, and the Council of Ten in Venice, who were arranging the matter, which was rather delicate, ignored his protestations. How sincerely did he feel them? It is almost impossible to tell. It is not known whether the nomination, which had been made by the actual Patriarch of Aquileia, Giovanni Grimani, came out of the blue or had been mentioned

Plate 29
Daniele Barbaro, Patriarch Elect of Aquileia, by Paolo Veronese
(Rijksmuseum, Amsterdam).

beforehand. Although Barbaro had been pursuing a civil career, he had also from England written letters addressed to his aunt in a convent in Murano (but for wider circulation), which were reflections or reworkings of a tract by St Bonaventure. He was not married, although his younger brother Marcantonio had taken a wife six years earlier. Still more to the point, his great-uncle Ermolao Barbaro before him had been appointed by the Pope Patriarch of Aquileia (although the then Venetian government had refused to accept the appointment, which in their view trespassed on their own prerogative), and his uncle on his mother's side, Francesco Pisani, had been Bishop of Padua and a member, with the Grimani, of the so-called *papalisti* group of families to whom fell the most lucrative ecclesiastical benefices in Venetian territory. Also Marcantonio Barbaro's mother-in-law was Giovanni Grimani's aunt. The choice of Daniele Barbaro to be Patriarch elect cannot have been surprising or have appeared to anyone inappropriate.

The doubling of the Patriarchs of Aquileia, it should be explained, was a device whereby the actual Patriarch could appoint his successor or vicar, the 'elect' Patriarch, before his own promotion or death. It was also in the Venetian government's interests to control the succession, not only for the same reasons that motivated any secular power to control ecclesiastical investiture, but also because Aquileia, in effect a prince-bishopric on the German model, constituted an important legal title and practical instrument of Venetian control over the northernmost coastal region of the Adriatic, the Friuli. The area was a march between Italy and Austria for which Venice had fought repeatedly with the Hapsburgs and to which the Emperor still nourished claims – and made an attempt to put forward his own candidate even after Daniele Barbaro's death in 1570, pointing out with truth that much of his flock spoke German, not Italian. The Venetian government rather than Giovanni Grimani was the moving force in Barbaro's election, pressing on him if not whom he should choose at least that he chose, so that the succession be assured.

Giovanni Grimani's reluctance to choose, and his eventual choice of Barbaro, have their own explanation. In the first place Grimani seems to have disliked his nephew, Pietro Querini, who obviously had expected the election, since he held the same bishoprics that Grimani had held before he became Patriarch elect. Snubbed, Querini and his allies immediately created trouble for Grimani at Rome, trouble which exacerbated or possibly initiated the sordid wrangle over Grimani's supposed heresy that began now and continued until there was a final ruling in 1566. (The issue was the thorny one of the predestination of souls to Heaven or Hell; the Patriarch had given a dubious ruling when a friar in Udine was accused of preaching against 'free will'.) The wrangle denied the Patriarch the cardinalate he and also his government expected, since his predecessors had invariably received one, and dogged not only Grimani but also Barbaro, although Barbaro, thanks to his obvious uprightness, was untainted by it. In the second place, the system of 'electing' the next Patriarch was precisely the kind of rigging that was coming under attack from the current movement of reform in the Church, or counter-reform as it became when reform became heretical. The possession or virtual pocketing of the Patriarchate by the Grimani, who had passed it to nephew to brother to brother since the beginning of the century, now seemed particularly blatant, and the Venetian government was beginning to find it objectionable as well. There had already been some difficulty when Giovanni became Patriarch elect to his brother Marino in 1546. Now there was further difficulty in inducing the Pope to ratify even Barbaro's election, since the right to designate a successor had in the meantime been restricted to cardinals, such as Grimani should have become but had not of course, because of the charge of heresy. Immediately he was appointed Barbaro stepped into an endless and ever more complicated round of litigation and intrigue, which probably his own appointment had partly precipitated, and which in the event justified Grimani's reluctance to elect at all.

Both Daniele and Marcantonio were diplomats, dignified patricians, expert in the dispensation of order, in the mastery of feeling, in the expression of their better, second nature. With a characteristically rationalized appreciation of the wider, political issues, just as he had accepted the Patriarchate elect, so Daniele consistently refused the cardinalate which Grimani, who outlived him, never received: his acceptance would have been a humiliation for the Venetian government, which had committed itself behind Grimani's good name and his prior entitlement to the cardinalate. Did Barbaro not want the cardinalate which, when he became Patriarch elect, Aretino had predicted for him? His merits undoubtedly deserved it. His great-uncle, on whose scholarship his own was founded, had accepted one, in despite of his government. If he did, Daniele repressed his want, like a second Scipio, conqueror of his enemies but still greater conqueror of himself. Daniele seems also to have remained in untroubled relations with Giovanni Grimani, although when the Grimani affair was finally concluded — with Grimani purged and certified orthodox, but still denied the cardinalate — Barbaro admitted to the Pope that the man was haughty. He must have been well aware that Grimani was the reason for the stasis of his own career and that ultimately Grimani's troubles were largely Grimani's fault. But if Barbaro admitted a defect in Grimani to the Pope, that was when diplomatically there was no longer anything to lose; in fact it showed a studious and conciliatory grace in defeat. Again, in what seems an exquisitely calculated gesture, Barbaro included in his will a bequest to the incumbent Patriarch of the cup which Edward VI had given him on his departure both from England and from a civic career — though one cannot say that the chalice bore any poison.

Daniele Barbaro was born in 1514, his brother three years later. Both were schooled in Verona, where their father was governor, and then went to study at the University of Padua. Marcantonio passed out rather more quickly, leaving in 1535, and travelling with his father-in-law's embassy to France; Daniele studied philosophy in Padua for ten years, to become an ornament around 1540 of the humanist salons in Padua and of the garden parties in Murano that Giangiorgio Trissino also attended — and in one or the other place Trissino is presumed to have introduced Palladio to him. Marcantonio was the first to receive a government post, to place his foot on the first rung of the ladder of Venetian offices, in 1541; it was not until 1545 that Daniele received office, and it was specially created for him — to administer the founding of the botanic garden at Padua. Like Padua's anatomy theatre, the University's botanic garden was one of the earliest anywhere and still survives; Barbaro was a moving spirit behind it. In 1548, however, Daniele was elected *proveditór di comun*, a city magistracy of a standard kind, combining policing, licensing and adjudication with, in his case, jurisdiction particularly over the lives and livelihood of boatmen and ferrymen operating in the lagoon and the canals and rivers of the immediate mainland.

Daniele was, then, late in starting his political career; he had made his mark as a humanist first. He had pursued studies not only into Aristotle (the great speciality of Padua) but also, notably, into Hero's *Mechanics*: that connected back to his interest in gardens, since Hero describes numerous automata and his jokes and tricks were an inspiration for the soaking devices (*giochi d'acqua*) that were an inevitable element of sixteenth-century gardens, but it also reveals his practical bent. Particularly Daniele threw back to his great-uncle Ermolao, whose *Castigationes Plinianae* or cleansings of the text of Pliny's *Natural History* were an outstanding work of scholarship, founded not simply on philology but also on the workbench. In the 1540s Daniele devoted much time to the editing (and probably revision) of Ermolao's unpublished work. He also wrote poetry and a tragedy — in obvious correspondence to the interests both of Trissino and of the circle of Alvise Cornaro in Padua. Both brothers were practical: by all accounts Marcantonio himself made the stucco figures and ornament for the grotto behind the villa at Maser. Daniele not only used, but also 'made at home' sundials and astrolabes. There is an important account of the *camera obscura* in his treatise on perspective of 1569.

The interruption of Daniele's magistracy by his dispatch on embassy to England was usual enough, and an embassy was an unavoidable, if expensive, step in a political career; although he received a grant towards his travel and the state he would have to maintain, it was invariably inadequate and usually slow in forthcoming, and Daniele was one among many who complained on their return of unrecovered costs. Daniele complained particularly because, having spent so many thousands of ducats, he had not one jot furthered his career. Marcantonio also wrote, twice, to point out how it would or could cost their family: but again, the brothers' real aim may have been to pass Daniele's career credits, so to speak, on to Marcantonio. Once Daniele had become Patriarch elect, his life did not greatly change: he still had much diplomacy to do, between Grimani, the Pope and Venice; he had petty administration to do, the pastoral work of the diocese. At first he was, genuinely, much troubled with money, for although the Pope had been induced to grant this 'poor' but worthy man Barbaro (so he was described to him) 1,000 ducats a year from other sources, the other sources were recalcitrant. Among these matters Daniele's ordination was one of the most trivial, as the Venetian ambassador to the Pope added explicitly – mere routine, and easily backdated. Quite possibly he never was formally ordained, and one wonders whether he dressed usually as a layman, and as a priest only on ceremonial occasions (for instance in his portrait by Veronese (Plate 29); none is known of Marcantonio).

The course of Marcantonio's career remained uninterrupted, though he was perhaps rather slow to rise. In 1555 he was appointed to the new office of *proveditor dei beni incolti* (superintendent of uncultivated land), with which for the first time the State undertook the supervision and coordination of the projects of deforestation, irrigation and drainage that were transforming the countryside; it also attempted to control 'fencing', the appropriation of common land. Marcantonio now owned the property at Maser; once Daniele had transferred his patrimony to his brother, it was probably Marcantonio who tended and ran it, practising the new 'agriculture' – following his father, who had bought and sold to make the property more compact and therefore economic. It is recorded by contrast that his grandfather had 'never seen' the property. It was quite small, a little over 40 acres, that is just the size the agricultural manuals recommend a gentleman should run personally. Possibly his expertise in matters agricultural earned him the office of *proveditor dei beni incolti*. Marcantonio was next made governor of the town of Brescia, and in 1560 became one of the *savi di Terraferma*, a court of appeal hearing cases against all the mainland governorships. In 1561 he was appointed ambassador to France, then in a state of turmoil and rising civil war: Guise the year before had defeated Condé, and in 1563 the Huguenot Wars began in earnest. Venice was deeply involved, since the city had lent Caterina de' Medici, regent for Charles IX, a large sum towards the cost of fighting the Huguenots; Marcantonio's dispatches, which survive, show him close to the workings of power.

Meanwhile in 1560 Daniele Barbaro had been designated official historian of the Venetian Republic. He had earned the honour partly by the quality of his epistolary style – his dispatches and his concluding 'relation' of the state of affairs in England had impressed the Council of Ten, and even the Pope was induced to voice admiration for the elegance of his letters during the continuing Grimani dispute (many of Daniele's letters were published in collections in his lifetime; but they are moral essays, concerned not to convey information but to varnish a truism). Partly also he had crowned his reputation as a scholar by the publication in 1556 of his authoritative commentary to Vitruvius, on which he had been working for nearly ten years, aided by Palladio who drew the woodcuts (he had perhaps prepared them during the trip he had made with Daniele when he had gone on Grimani business to Rome in 1554). Barbaro's appointment was the more significant since the previous incumbent had been Pietro Bembo, the most eminent man of letters of his day, who had also followed an ecclesiastical career, finally to become a cardinal – the comparison was implicit. Unfortunately Barbaro managed before his death ten years later to take the history no further than a preamble and summary of events before the point at which he intended to begin, where Bembo had broken off, at the death of Julius II in 1513. The preamble reflects a sense of the way that events can overtake human intention, typifying the resignation inculcated into the sixteenth-century Italian outlook.

While Marcantonio was ambassador in France, Daniele took the place Grimani might otherwise have taken at the Council of Trent, which had reopened in 1562. His rôle was not insignificant: he contributed influentially to several debates, for instance that on utraquism (communion by the faithful in both bread and wine); he chaired several committees (one of them on the calendar); his diplomatic influence is evident in the instruction the Venetian ambassadors received in Venice in 1563 to take advice from Barbaro when they got there. To some extent the brothers Barbaro may have been working together in the diplomacy involving the French delegation to the conference; the rise of French Huguenism naturally lent a certain urgency to their proceedings. Certainly Daniele's approach at the Council was political rather than theological, spiritual or concerned with conscience: he argued for instance on the issue of utraquism not that communion in both kinds was or was not sanctioned by Christ, but simply that if this point were conceded to those Germans who wanted it then other demands and concessions would inevitably follow. That is, incidentally, an attitude typical of Venetian polity – always preferring inflexibility to fairness, in the untrammelled knowledge that all humanity is malicious. During these years, since Trento is so close, Daniele was also able to spend much time at Maser: in mid-June 1562, for instance, it was reported that 'many prelates are taking leave to quit the town, some for reasons of business and others for pleasure; many have already done so, and also yesterday Monsignor Barbaro went to his villa in the Trevigiano'; he returned in early July.

The villa (Plate 30) he was then visiting was perhaps complete as it is now (before certain later depletions), and the building work (it was in fact a rebuilding of the brothers' grandfather's house) is thought to have been concentrated in the second half of the 1550s. It seems to incorporate some ideas Daniele and Palladio would have derived newly from Rome. In 1559 it already had its 'beautiful gardens', which may or may not imply the presence also of its waterworks and therefore the grotto behind the house. The decoration, however, may well have continued into the 1560s.

Plate 30
Villa Barbaro, Maser, Treviso: exterior from the front. The unusually rich stuccowork of the pediment (and also of the grotto behind the villa) reflects Marcantonio Barbaro's pastime of composing in stucco. The sundials on the outer wings reflect Daniele's mathematical bent. For views of the interior and of the grotto see Plates 39a–c and 43a–c.

Veronese was probably in Rome in 1560 and Marcantonio can hardly have undertaken the stuccowork until his return from France probably in 1564. At any rate, in 1566, in Marcantonio's tax declaration, the possession is declared as '48 *campi* (just over 40 acres) surrounded by a wall, all, both cultivated and uncultivated, joined to the building with its courts, orchards, streams, woods, vales and hills'. It sounds complete as well as idyllic.

After the resolution, or cessation, of the Grimani dispute in 1563, and the conclusion of the Council in the same year, Daniele Barbaro's public rôle and career became less eventful. In 1567 he issued a revised version of his commentary on Vitruvius and in 1569 published his work on perspective. According to its frontispiece the second work was intended for painters, sculptors and architects, but like the Vitruvius commentary, which systematizes and schematizes as much as it elucidates and demonstrates, so the work on perspective inclines more to the theoretical than to the practical — although it was consistently Barbaro's contention that the practical should derive from the theoretical, or at least not stand independently. In that sense Palladio was his perfect instrument. Probably the Pope would have sought again to make him a cardinal, and perhaps found a way to achieve it, if he had not died, aged fifty-four, in 1570.

Marcantonio was then in Istanbul, with little immediate prospect of return. He had been sent out there in 1568, when Turkish ambitions in the eastern Mediterranean and the Sultan's desire to pick a quarrel with the Venetians had become manifest. When the coming war broke out he was imprisoned, though not *incommunicado*; he then had the task, after the Battle of Lepanto, which was meant to be a famous victory but left both land and sea to the enemy, of negotiating a peace from a position of unadmitted weakness. He himself compared dealings with the Sultan to keeping aloft and intact a glass ball, which would smash both if grasped too forcefully and if not seized forcefully enough — by which he said he meant neither irritating nor encouraging Turkish 'ignorance' and 'arrogance'. His success and skill in concluding a tolerable peace was acknowledged when he was elected, while still abroad, a Procurator of St Mark, the most prestigious of the offices of state after the dogate, though in the same way more ceremonial than powerful.

Likewise, soon after he had returned from Istanbul, Marcantonio's rôle at the reception in Venice in 1574 of Henri III of France, who was making his way from Poland, from the rule of which he had fled, via Vienna and Venice back to claim his deceased brother's crown, was in terms of protocol extremely important: he held the King's parasol. Otherwise he was appointed to govern the Friuli, having to resolve a new dispute between the Patriarch of Aquileia, still Giovanni Grimani, and the new Pope Sixtus V; in the same capacity he argued for the foundation of the fortress of

Palmanova to meet the growing threat of Turkish encroachment over land, and oversaw its construction – that star-shaped barracks surviving intact but bleak and desolate today is also a Barbaro monument. During the rest of his career Marcantonio was frequently involved in official matters artistic, arguing at length in the Senate on the form of the church that had been voted in thanksgiving for the cessation of the plague of 1576–7, that is, on Palladio's Redentore. He was also responsible after Palladio's death for the construction of the tomb for Doge Nicolò da Ponte in 1585, and he was on the committee for the new Rialto bridge in stone of 1587 (until then there had been a succession of wooden bridges). In 1580 he had added the chapel to the villa at Maser, having Palladio adapt the round-church Redentore design for which he had argued unsuccessfully. His son Francesco succeeded Giovanni Grimani as Patriarch of Aquileia in 1593; Marcantonio died in 1595.

In several senses Palladio was still more closely involved with the Barbaro than with any of the Vicentine aristocracy. In his will Daniele mentioned him as 'Palladio our architect', among the household servants, and Palladio is said to have died at Maser, still a member of the Barbaro household – once that kind of 'service' had been undertaken it was for life, and only in exceptional circumstances and extreme provocation broken off. (The idea, extrapolated from Palladio's failure to mention Veronese's decoration in the commentary to his woodcut of the villa Barbaro in the *Four Books*, that there was a quarrel or coolness between Palladio and his patrons, is unlikely; he did not mention Veronese perhaps simply because, on the tightly designed page, there was not room.) For Daniele and for Marcantonio individually and together architecture was not merely an interest but had wider importance. Marcantonio argued architecture in the public arena, and Daniele in his commentaries to Vitruvius urged his peers with heartfelt earnestness to appreciate that architecture was more than the building trade: it was a science that needed and repaid study. And yet it is clear, also, that in Venice architecture was not all it was in Vicenza: it became a matter of prestige for the Vicentine nobility as a whole (more or less) in a way that it never did for the city of Venice as a whole. In Vicenza Palladio was a kind of political instrument, and the Basilica and its palaces in the town or country were a kind of cultural stalking-horse by which to advance the city in the eyes of Italy. In Venice Palladio and architecture were not a means to any kind of end or advancement, and not a substitute statecraft, though architecture was employed on occasions for reasons of prestige, in order to keep appropriate state.

There is the same contrast, I think, between Palladio's other villas and the villa Barbaro. The villa at Maser does not compete; it does not colonize or impose; it was not, like the villa Foscari at Malcontenta or the Badoer at Fratta Polesine, on a trunk route, but lay on an unfrequented bifurcation of the road down from the Brenner Pass — Daniele Barbaro was merely fortunate it was close to Trento. Even in its site (though that was pre-determined) the Barbaro is unassuming: it is not set on top of its hill, but only so far up its slope as to render it invisible except from due south (its road runs east-west). It has of course not a temple front but an applied order. Though it has rich ornament, its decoration is frivolous — no statues of emperors, no exemplary histories, but the dalliance of the gods, among whom Venus and Bacchus are the soul of the party. For various reasons the Barbaro is often regarded as untypical of Palladio, whose sole authorship is sometimes doubted — but it would have been absurd to retain 'our architect' and to let him design for others but not for ourselves. The anomaly may rather be explained by the villa's lack of pretension. It was uncomplicatedly a retreat, recalling on the one hand the pleasant gardens on the Zudeca or Murano that Venetian aristocrats owned, and on the other hand, perhaps still more, the kind of villa typical during the same period round Rome, where the ornament is frequently elaborate but the architecture is seldom imposing; instead it is almost subservient to the garden. As such, the villa Barbaro was not called upon to manifest the status of its owners, in which they were anyway secure.

The Barbaro were in many ways the very model of the higher Venetian patriciate, and were directly involved in the events and developments by which their commonwealth was shaped during the sixteenth century. With all that, it seems to be the case that although their family was old and well connected, they were not exceedingly rich: Maser's forty or so acres were rather modest, and both brothers needed a career in order to maintain their fortune. It is not clear where their money came from otherwise, whether it was in trade or not. Theirs seems a classic example of the Venetian aristocracy's movement to the land, since they so cherished the house at Maser their grandfather had never seen — it shows also that the movement was a gradual process, since their grandfather, for all that he may not have seen it, nonetheless owned it, and since Marcantonio went out to Constantinople, if only to sign away Venice's loss of her last piece of the Greek Mediterranean.

PART 3
'In Villa'

9

'Matters of Villa'

'Villa' is an impossibly corrupt term. To English ears today it sounds too much like 'chalet', or villa as in 'holiday villa', implying a contemporary building (otherwise it might be called a farmhouse). In some ways, however, the 'holiday villa' is a resurgence from the dead letter to which 'villa' had been reduced earlier in this century, when it was merely a type of small house with a garden propagating urban sprawl, as in the street-name 'Park Villas'. 'Holiday villa' has at least brought back the idea of recreation, which is an association vital to the villa in Renaissance Italy, as a pleasant place to stay, and as somewhere away from the pressure and business of normal life, not home but a second home. On the other hand the word has lost the formal association it still had in the nineteenth century, as something vaguely Italianate, or even Palladian, a compact, squarish, small block of a building probably with a low-pitched pyramidal roof and perhaps a terrace or balcony. But in English, even before it became definitively suburbanized, the word has always meant nothing grand or glamorous, but a modest or middle-class building. It is therefore not the right term to use for Palladio's country houses, for example the monumental villa Cornaro (Plates 31a–c).

However, there is no other term and the usage is established. But how did it come to be used? Though known to the English Palladian movement, it was rarely employed: it occurs but once in the Palladian textbook *Vitruvius Britannicus*. Neither its proprietor Lord Burlington nor its architect

Plates 31a and b
Villa Cornaro, Piombino Dese, Treviso. View from the front and interior of the great four-columned *sala*. Zorzi Cornaro, who commissioned the house after he had inherited from his father in 1551, was a prominent member of the extremely wealthy Venetian Corner or Cornaro family, who for some time had owned extensive lands in the region.

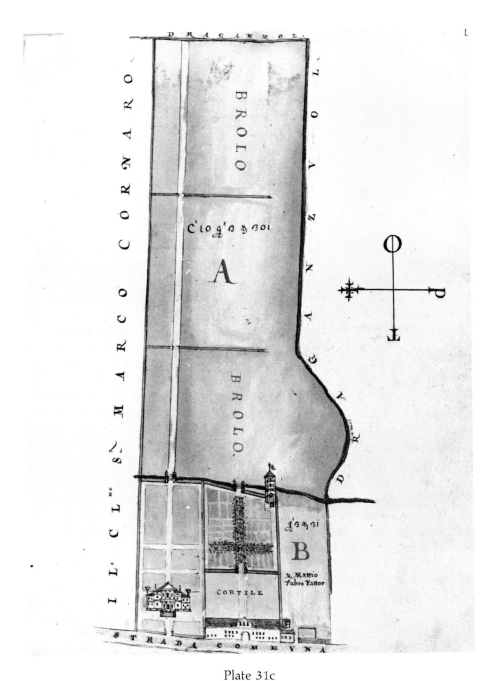

Plate 31c

Villa Cornaro, Piombino Dese. This map of 1613 (in the Museo Correr, Venice) shows the house as a stately home or palace, and the factor's house and farm buildings to have been altogether separate, though adjacent – the usual arrangement of Palladio's villas (see again p. 188). Note also the dovecot tower by the garden bowers (see further p. 115).

William Kent seem ever to have applied the word to what might be regarded as the classic English Palladian 'villa', Chiswick House. Isaac Ware, in his translation of Palladio's *Four Books of Architecture* dedicated to Lord Burlington in 1738, frequently used the word (and that is why we use it for Palladio's country houses), but he did so for convenience (otherwise he would have had to find a series of awkward periphrases). He distorted the sense, or range of sense, that Italian *villa* had for Palladio. Ware does not seem to have made the term more common. The English villa may fairly be said to have been invented not by the Palladians but by the Picturesque movement. In 1793 Charles Middleton gave a comprehensive definition of the villa, already moving towards the current usage: 'Villas may be considered under three different descriptions – First, as the occasional and temporary retreats of the nobility and persons of fortune from what may be called their town residence, and must, of course, be in the vicinity of the metropolis; secondly, as the country houses of wealthy citizens and persons in official stations, which also cannot be far removed from the capital; and thirdly, the smaller kind of provincial edifices, considered either as hunting seats, or the habitations of country gentlemen of moderate fortune. Elegance, compactness and convenience are the characteristics of such buildings ... in contradistinction to the magnificence and extensive range of the country seats of the nobility and opulent gentry.' Although the English visitor to Palladio's villas today may well feel the force of that 'contradistinction' to the 'opulent' and so much larger country houses of English Palladianism, that is an accident of history. In Palladio's own time his villas were not small or 'compact', they were conspicuously magnificent. Subsequently everything became more palatial, and there is the same difference between Palladio's villas and English Palladian country seats as between Palladio's villas and later villas in the same part of the world, such as the enormous villa Pisani at Strà on the Brenta, dating from 1736–56.

However, Middleton's words, despite the shift that has taken place, relate closely to Palladio's own. The qualities of 'elegance, compactness and convenience' directly reflect Palladio's own terms of reference, though they are coloured by the shade of that 'contradistinction'. While 'convenience' may be an equivalent to the *commodità* to which Palladio's Book II was principally directed, it bears false overtones of a retreat from publicity and pomposity: in reality there was nothing Biedermeier about Palladio's villas. Middleton's 'compactness' is more transparently anachronistic, though it relates perhaps to the 'perpetuity' or solidity that was one of Palladio's cardinal principles. And 'elegance', in 1793, might almost be a pretty pink thing, delicate like Rococo and neoclassical Robert Adam, at any rate lacking grandeur and virility, such as Palladio actually sought.

Quite the contrary, Palladio was concerned not with villas in these terms but precisely with 'the magnificence and extensive range of the country seats of the nobility and opulent gentry'.

Possibly few would quarrel with the idea that villas, or rather a certain type of villa, should be 'in the vicinity of the metropolis' or 'not far removed from the capital'. But even this qualification is misleading. Palladio's villas were not alternatively either suburban in this sense or 'provincial'. There was abroad a notion of a type of house called a *villa suburbana*, which Alberti had discussed in *De Re Aedificatoria*, but it was a classical type, one which Palladio did not and could not revive. A *villa suburbana*, for Cicero or Pliny, was a house near Rome, near *the* city, not merely outside any city. Later, the term could be applied to other cities by analogy, but only if they were metropolises. It could be applied in England or France, which have and had both a metropolis and its corollary provinces, but not so well to Venice, its immediate mainland and its further dominions, and it collapses when applied to Vicenza and its territory. Burlington's Chiswick House or Mereworth in Kent might qualify as *villae suburbanae*, for later generations if not for their builders, but their model, the villa Rotonda, though it is a short ride or half an hour's walk from the centre of Vicenza, did not and cannot. Vicenza was not a metropolis. When Palladio himself calls the villa Rotonda 'suburban', that is his justification for placing it among his town houses and not among his country houses: for there was no intermediate category. Since the owner had sold his house in the centre of the town in order to build it, it was not an 'occasional' residence but his sole main one. It is again inappropriate to describe Palladio's villa Pisani at Montagnana (Plates 32a and b) as a *villa suburbana*, just because it is sited immediately outside the admittedly splendid walls of that small town: the market square is 200 yards away. It is equally difficult to claim that, the Pisani being Venetian, the house was suburban to Venice, for Venice was more than a day's journey away and reached after first passing through Padua. Except in the conspicuous case of real Renaissance *suburbanae* outside Renaissance Rome, the term is incorrect and misleading,

Plates 32a and b
Villa Pisani, Montagnana, Padua. Similar in date and design to the villa Cornaro (see Plates 31a–c), and again a Venetian commission, but rather smaller. Even so, the four-columned *sala*, with contemporary statues of the Four Seasons by Alessandro Vittoria, makes an impressive waiting-room. Palladio's woodcut in the *Four Books* shows beside the main house two outbuildings reached by bridges; though these were never built and would have interrupted the fine Doric frieze that girds the villa the idea can be found borrowed or developed in several later Palladianizing villas of the region.

because it suggests a ghost category of pleasure villa, not properly a residence, which might even have no bedrooms and was visited only within the day – Middleton's 'occasional and temporary retreats'; but there was no intermediate type or function of house distinguished by Palladio from a town house or from a residential villa with a farm (which could be visited within the day if you liked). All villas, wherever they were, were second houses chiefly for pleasure.

In Renaissance Italian, *villa* meant primarily not a house at all. The villa was the estate rather than the house: *andare in villa* meant 'to go to the country'. In his own words Palladio designed not villas but 'houses of villa', with their appurtenances for the 'use of villa' or 'of the villa', where 'villa' means not even the place but the farm, although occasionally he falls into the way of calling the house itself a villa, as it may be called in Latin. Ware in his English version of Palladio's *Four Books* distorted this sense, for instance by translating Palladio's habitual phrase *'cose di villa'* (matters of the farm) as 'things belonging to a villa', referring to the house. Although Palladio once says *la villa* in the Latin sense meaning the house, he did not set out to build villas or country houses reproducing classical villas or country houses, or he would have said so in the *Four Books*. He says instead, when it comes to 'structures of villa' (QL II, xiii), that of these there are two sorts, one for the owner and his household, the other for the produce and the animals. The former, the house, should suit the condition or status of the owner, 'and is done as is done in cities, and we have treated of it above', for a house 'in villa' is not intrinsically different from a house in town. Then, after describing and illustrating his own *'case di villa'* (houses in the country) Palladio has a brief chapter on those of the ancients (QL II, xvi) – their *'case di villa'*, not their 'villas'. He mentions Pliny, meaning to allude to his famous description of his villa at Laurentinum, but he refuses to discuss him, limiting himself instead to the few words Vitruvius gives the subject. He describes and illustrates 'only the part of the villa' (meaning farm), explaining, once again, that for the house the reader should refer above, where he has already discussed Vitruvius's domestic architecture. Palladio made no fundamental distinction between houses in the country and houses in the town; he had no separate category he called 'villa'.

The opposition between town and country, though operative during the Italian Renaissance, had nothing like the force or tension it has since acquired, during and after industrialization. The real differences, in the Renaissance, between a town house and a country house were few; the only important difference was between townspeople and country people. There was no separate term for town and country houses: *villa* was not generally used, and the word *palazzo*, contrary to modern expectation, was used indifferently during the Renaissance for gentlemen's houses either in the town or in the country. It is true, or becomes true during the Renaissance, that the design of town and country houses may differ; but before Palladio's time, certainly in northern Italy, the external and internal disposition of houses in the country and the town was more often than not identical.

English and Italian 'villa' derives after all from the same Latin as French *ville*. As for the etymology of the Latin word *villa*, it is probably a corruption of *vicula*, which is a diminutive of *vicus*, meaning both a street and a hamlet, either in the country or in a town. A 'villa' is at root a group of buildings, a habitation. In classical usage it had come to mean an estate in the country in particular, but it described the estate more than its being in the country, and Nero's Golden House, which he built, to his subjects' grievance, in the very centre of Rome, was also a villa. Other related words have oscillated in similar ways. Italian *terra* means 'earth' but also 'town' in several phrases, not 'country' as one might expect: *in questa terra* means 'in this city'. In fact *terra* applied equally to the town and its province, between which, in Renaissance Italy, there was a relationship more binding than, for instance, that between an English market town and its shire. The countryside was the territory of the town, or, to use the kind of analogy then popular, the town was the head and the country was the trunk, and they were symbiotic. Almost all that divided city and country was the physical wall of the town, and even this division was blurred by urban sprawl in many cases, including that of Vicenza.

In the Renaissance, the city depended absolutely on the local countryside – both for its food and for its raw materials, not only wood, brick and stone but also the basis for textiles and oils of all kinds. It obtained by trade for the most part only luxuries. On the other hand, as a farmer runs his farm, so the city ran the countryside, and Palladio's villas, invariably built by citizens, are a sign of growing interference by the management. Most, probably almost all citizens, including artisans, owned or rented property not only in the city but also in the countryside. This is still the case so often in Italy today, and the Italian prejudice, still strong today, that the food and drink from your own patch is best can be traced back at least to Alberti's early fifteenth-century treatise *Della Famiglia* (*On the Household*). There was little or no urban proletariat in the Renaissance; the only proletariat were the peasants, to whom the city was often alien, while every citizen would be at home in the countryside. It was only for the peasants, who were sometimes hated with a virulence that was in effect racist, that a fundamental division between town and country existed; and in this matter of villas their needs hardly enter. They were usually regarded as evasive and recalcitrant, dishonest and vile by nature: they were the equivalent of the animals in the farmyard, literally because they ate revoltingly and smelt, and spiritually because their failings were innate. They were born of the dung, and their sufferings were all their own fault. And in Renaissance Italy there was no such thing as a landed gentry who visited 'town' — the metropolis — rarely if at all, whose life was a country life. Landowners and their agents, smallholders and even a tenant class above the peasant labourers belonged both to the city and to the country.

Unlike the French or English aristocracy, who might have one life on their estates and another at court or in government, with a long journey between, Italian landowners could come and go between town and country in a matter of hours. Although smaller cities like Vicenza had become politically dependent on larger ones, or on national powers, even so fiscal management, first-recourse justice and civic government remained local; and since, conversely, Terraferma citizens had absolutely no part in the Venetian administration, Venice never became 'town' to them. Thus city and country remained a single organism. Even for Venetians this was largely true, since they, too, owned land for the most part within close range of Venice, in the Padovano or Trevigiano (territories of Padua and Treviso) immediately bordering the city's historic countryside. Venice was partly a special case, in being a port and in having expanded beyond the support capabilities of its hinterland. But while the Paduans frequently complained in the sixteenth century of Venetians buying up their land, the Vicentines and Veronese were given no cause to do so. Those Venetians who wished to farm or to enjoy country pursuits generally did so not far from home.

The relationship between city and country was not polar but hierarchical. The houses built by Palladio in the country always belonged to *cittadini*, citizens. When there is report of noblemen who live predominantly or exclusively in the country, who have 'rusticated', that is because they have fallen on hard times, and would be in no position to employ Palladio. Palladio's villas were more truly *palazzi* in the country, built with unprecedented magnificence and firmly eschewing any tinge of the rusticity by which they were surrounded. The town house that Palladio planned for Marcantonio Thiene was ambitious enough; the 'villa' he would have built for him was still more palatial.

10

Site, Sight and Height

The essential difference between a house built in the country and a house built in the town is situation, or is due to situation. Therefore, examining the architectural tradition that Palladio and his patrons inherited, it is well to start where Vitruvius started, where also most Renaissance writers on architecture – Palladio among them – started, that is, with the site. Choose a good position, said Vitruvius. One could do that in the country; in the city there was constraint. In Italy, a good position in the country meant somewhere open, visited by a cool breeze; it meant in particular, following current medical theory, somewhere where the air was good (it was bad, for instance, on low, marshy ground), or was changed (enclosed in a valley it would grow fetid). The matter of air became particularly important after the Black Death had struck in the middle of the fourteenth century: plague continued to strike every generation until the middle of the seventeenth century, and was most commonly believed to be carried by infectious air; the surest way to escape it was to take refuge in the country, because, as it was believed, there the air was generally much better. It was therefore prescribed that a villa should be set on an eminence. For this there were also several other practical determinants. Few of Palladio's patrons were building on a virgin site; sometimes the earlier building had been a castle (for example, the villa Badoer, Fratta Polesine), and even if not it had perhaps included at least a fortified tower. Height made it possible to see the enemy coming, and made it difficult for the enemy to get at you, if it were a small marauding band with no motive to stay for long.

However, in times of peace and order the good view provided by height was enjoyed for its own sake. Not only the Romans had enjoyed views, but also medieval kings: for instance La Zisa, the twelfth-century pleasure palace built by the Norman King Roger II in the midst of his extensive gardens and hunting grounds behind Palermo, still has steps up to its flat roof. So has the castle or hunting lodge built by his thirteenth-century successor Frederick II at Castel del Monte in Puglia, set on a hillock commanding a view in every direction. The site was obviously

Plate 33

Castel del Monte, Puglia. Though Emperor Frederick II Hohenstaufen built several strikingly geometric buildings, Castel del Monte, which he never saw completed before his death in 1250, is the most perfect of them, an octagon orbited by eight octagonal towers (and these are centred on the points of the star created by extending the sides of the octagon that makes the interior courtyard). It has been seriously proposed (but cannot seriously be believed) that Castel del Monte inspired Palladio's villa Rotonda.

chosen for the sake of the view, and the castle has seats by all the windows. Castel del Monte (Plate 33) was built in the form of a perfect octagon, for which symbolic explanations have been sought; but the site itself required a building that should face all points of the compass, especially if it had been chosen for its eminence in the first place. Few other princes built on so grand a scale as Frederick, but there are numerous signs of a common tradition throughout Europe: for example, the towering keep of the great castle of Vincennes outside Paris built by the French kings in the fourteenth century, which was a defensive and military installation, but set in the midst of the royal hunting forests over which the king's personal apartments had a splendid view. The distractions of kings had soon been taken up by the nobility and the very rich: dating from the later fourteenth century, Boccaccio's descriptions in the *Decameron* of the villa to which his protagonists retire to escape the Black Death repeat the fact that the house, and its various pavilions, are set on a gentle eminence. In the fifteenth century the indications multiply: a famous one is Aeneas Piccolomini's description of the view from the palace he built in Pienza after he had become Pope Pius II — in which he also discourses on the sweetness of the air. The retreat built by his successor Pope Innocent VIII atop the Vatican hill in the 1480s was naturally called the Good View (Belvedere).

That medieval tradition, which itself had derived from antiquity, was reinforced and eventually overcovered during the Renaissance by a wealth of classical references. The requirement of height became more specifically one of a gentle rise, following the remark of Pliny the Younger about his villa at Laurentinum (outside Rome towards the coast) that 'while you are not aware you are climbing, you realize you have ascended to it'. Of course, having reached the top without perspiration, one expected a view; the view was the visitor's notification that he had in fact ascended. One finds Pliny's ideal widely echoed, especially after Raphael and his patrons had made a thoroughgoing attempt to reconstruct the facilities of Pliny's villa in the villa Madama outside Rome; Raphael had deliberately echoed Pliny's phrase in a letter describing his plans for the villa, explaining that the road up to the main entrance 'climbs so sweetly that it does not seem to climb, but until one has arrived at the villa one would not have realized that it is up high and dominates the whole countryside'. Before the end of the sixteenth century the notion had spread even to England: Sir Philip Sydney in the *Arcadia* described a pavilion as 'Truly a place for pleasantness, not unfit to flatter solitariness, for, it being set upon such an insensible rising of the ground as you are come to a pretty height before almost you perceive that you ascend, it gives the eye lordship over a good large circuit, which according to the nature of the country, being diversified between hills and dales, woods and plains, one place more clear, another more darksome, it seems a pleasant picture of nature, with lovely light-someness and artificial shadows'. Palladio frequently gives notice of the good situation and light climb to his villas: that of the villa Rotonda, or of the closely related villa Trissino at Meledo, or of the villa Sarego at Pedemonte near Verona, 'placed on a very beautiful site, that is, above a hill of very easy ascent, which "discovers" part of the city, and is between two valleys; all the hills about are very pleasant, and copious in good water' (QL II, xv).

Italian Renaissance connoisseurs without doubt had some appreciation of 'the horrid', despite Ruskin's claim that before the English 'Picturesque' revolution the appeal of landscape had resided in what it might reveal, the 'available and useful', not in its dynamic, the drama of its form, light and shade. However, in the Renaissance people preferred to enjoy nature more as one would a garden or a park, ordered and fruitful and full of game; they liked 'movement' in the landscape, too, but movement literally, that of travellers on their way, shepherds singing and piping, any evidence of human settlement. They were as happy to look out on a city as on to fields and hills. Another well-known citation was taken from an epigram by Pliny's contemporary Martial on a cousin's villa, from which, he said, 'you can put a price on all Rome (*totam licet aestimare Romam*)'. Notably the humanist scholar Angelo Poliziano (Politian) alluded to Martial in a letter written from Cosimo de' Medici's villa at Fiesole, which overlooks Florence, that from there '*totam licet estimare Florentiam*'. In order to attract his correspondent, the Neoplatonist philosopher Marsilio Ficino, to visit him at the villa in high summer he also stressed that, although it was hidden away and solitary among the shady woods, 'we are never deprived of a breeze'. Despite his words Politian, as a guest, probably valued the prospect rather than evaluated the prospectus, but the owner Cosimo de' Medici's expression of dislike at the idea of looking out on any fields he did not own is recorded. And Palladio in his *Four Books* suggests that the best place for a villa was in the middle of an estate, 'so that the owner without much trouble can "discover", and improve, his properties round about, and the fruits deriving from them can expediently be carried by the labourer to the manor' (QL II, xii).

The idea, 'I am monarch of all I survey/ My right there is none to dispute;/ From the centre all round to the sea /I am lord of the fowl and the brute', generally informed the Renaissance delight in landscape. Also in other ways the aesthetic of the castle continued to influence the conception of the so-called villa. 'Lordship', if only of the eye, remained a desideratum. Castles that look more castellar than real − the turretted fantasies of numerous French châteaux, or English castles such as the late Tudor Richmond Palace − were built not only in northern Europe during the fifteenth and sixteenth centuries: one finds turrets and the teeth of battlements without bite on numerous buildings in Italy, too. The battlements of the villa Porto at Thiene have been mentioned; the early sixteenth-century villa Giustinian at Roncade, Treviso, is surrounded by a battlemented wall and four large towers and has a turretted gate, which might possibly have served for defence; but it also has battlements coronetting its inaccessible chimneys. Similarly, genuinely military installations were made not only to be but to look 'robust': Palladio's contemporary Sanmicheli built fortresses and city gates for the Venetians that advertise their mightiness with unmistakable self-consciousness. There was no contradiction felt between the expression of power and the classical idea of a villa, as Raphael's letter on the villa Madama illustrates. Having described its 'insensible' approach, he goes on directly to say of the main entrance:

'And in the first sight (or impression) you have of it [*nella prima apparentia*] there are two round towers either side of this entrance; these, apart from the beauty and grandeur [*superbia*] which they give the entrance, also provide some defence for those who have retired within; between them a very beautiful Doric portal gives entrance to a courtyard ...'. The towers were never built, because the villa was never finished, but they are clearly visible on the plans.

Such twin towers could be traced back to Roman and Byzantine fortifications and gateways, and in the medieval West to the great gate that Frederick II built guarding the Roman bridge at Capua, facing the road north to Rome at the border of his southern dominions. On the equivalent of a balcony between two towers, the effigy of the Emperor, accompanied by allegorical figures, symbolized the 'august' rule of Justice within imperial territory. The gate was admired in the Renaissance, and influenced directly, first, the twin-towered arch that Alfonso of Aragon built in Naples in the 1450s, and indirectly soon afterwards the twin towers of the Ducal Palace of Urbino that look out majestically over the road up to the town from the west. The nexus of associations involved, some of which had once had a practical basis, while others were biblical, included the idea of a balcony from which the ruler was presented to the people, and from which he metaphorically and almost literally oversaw them. Although some of these notions would ill apply to the villa Madama, they underpin or explain to some degree the *superbia* the towers flanking its entrance were felt to impart. Significantly Raphael added that 'you could truly say that the Ponte Molle [the Roman bridge over the Tiber] was made specially for this villa so that the road [from the villa] should arrive precisely at the bridge'. The villa, as a *rondpoint* on which lines of approach were trained, needed an emphatic vertical accent.

Towers occur quite frequently in Palladian villas, usually in pairs: in the villa Pisani at Bagnolo, for instance, or the Thiene at Cicogna (Plate 34) or the Valmarana at Lisiera. Some may have been taken over from a previous building – though Palladio invariably introduced the second one, to make the symmetry – in which they might once have served as watchtowers and refuge towers, or later as dovecots. Palladio's towers are usually described as dovecots, but doves, a valuable supply of meat in winter, were extremely noisy: the towers at the end of the range in the villa Emo at Fanzolo (Plate 35) were certainly dovecots, but those forming part of the house, as at Bagnolo or once at Lisiera, are less likely to have been. At the villa Barbaro at Maser the outlying tower-like forms bearing sundials were certainly never dovecots, and their upper floor was closed and inaccessible. Even as dovecots, anyway, these towers could still serve as lookout points and often might have contained a habitable room.

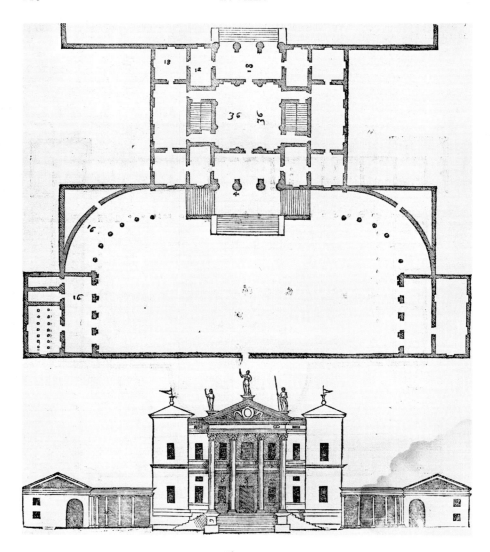

Plate 34
Villa Thiene, Cicogna, Padua, from the *Four Books* (II, xv). Of this ambitious
design for Palladio's one-time landlords Odoardo and Teodoro, sons of Francesco
Thiene (see p. 52), only the *barchessa* down on the right of the woodcut seems
ever to have been built. The towers at the front appear from the plan to have
been matched by two at the back, making the villa look all the more like a castle.

Stressing, in his agricultural manual *La Nuova, vaga et dilettevole Villa* (The
new, pretty and delightful farm), that the villa should be designed for
superintendance, Giuseppe Falcone remarks: 'So standing downstairs at

Plate 35
Villa Emo, Fanzolo, Treviso. The nucleus of the estate in which the Emo stands
is preserved: the left-hand dovecot gives a good view of the farmyard on that
side, and both survey widely the flat territory around. The Emo seems originally
to have had a park, and some of the land immediately beside the villa may
always have been wooded. Its interior is richly decorated with frescoes by Zelotti
('school' of Veronese).

the door under the porch, or upstairs at the windows, the owner will look
out on the whole courtyard, or rather he should see to it that the dovecot
has four windows, so he can better "discover" the whole farm – who
comes, who goes, and what is going on around the place'. Anton Francesco
Doni, whose *smanio* for villas has been mentioned, was more concerned
with the aesthetic, requiring, besides everything else, 'a little room in a
corner, with mirrors from top to bottom and on all four sides, as large as
they can be found, and lit by two great windows, in which you can see
far and near in every direction'.

Otherwise Palladio transmuted the 'castellar' tradition, in particular the
quality Raphael called *superbia*, into new forms. He did so above all by
the provision of a pedimented and columnar frontispiece or 'temple front',

which, though not his own invention, is one of the hallmarks of his architecture. He explains himself in a paragraph concluding his note in the *Four Books* on the *'case di villa'* of the ancients: 'In all the buildings "of villa", and also in some of the city, I have placed the frontispiece on the front façade, where the main doors are, because such frontispieces emphasize the entrance of the house, and contribute much to the grandeur and magnificence of the work. In this way the front part is rendered more eminent than the other parts, and also frontispieces of this kind [in particular the pediments] turn out very suitable for the display of the devices, or arms, of the builders, it being usual to place these in the middle of the façade. The ancients employed them in their buildings, as can be seen from the remains of their temples and other public buildings; and, as I explained in the proem of the First Book, it is very probable that they derived the form and the principle from their private buildings, that is, their houses.' The temple front indeed derived, as archaeology has revealed, from the Mycenaean *megaron*, though that was not so much a private house as the royal palace: Palladio divined the majesty latent in the form. At the same time, by his notice of the coat of arms 'in the middle', he recalls northern European gatehouses, which by the time of the late Middle Ages were invariably central, rose above the height of the surrounding walls, and prominently featured above the portal the castellan's coat of arms. Not least, the protruding frontispiece, as one can deduce from other remarks by Palladio and others, not only marked the transition from outside to inside, but also served the owner as a loggia, from which he would enjoy the view over his countryside.

The Veneto, it will be recalled, is sometimes completely flat. However, from well before Palladio the system of a *piano nobile* had evolved: the ground floor provided the base on which the living quarters of the villa were placed, and not infrequently there was a loggia on the second floor as well as the first. Palladio early on established the system of a clearly articulated basement, upon which the villa visibly stood as if on a mound. Even before he had adopted the temple front characteristic of his later villas, he habitually placed a strong string-course marking the limit of the ground floor, and he slightly narrowed in the profile of the floor above it (the effect is made still more obvious in the woodcuts of the *Quattro Libri*). He may have noted a passing reference to a *'basis villae'* in one of Cicero's letters, but more probably he was accommodating usage. The wider basement might have appealed to his clients as the equivalent of the sloping batter at the root of an imposing castle or tower. It should be appreciated that even into the seventeenth century Palladio's villas were often called 'castles' — his early building for Giuseppe Valmarana at Vigardolo (see p. 212) is an example; and a castellar sloping batter is sometimes found in other architects' work. Palladio himself, with his usual rationalism, claimed that walls thicker at the bottom than the top made the building stronger and more durable – qualities at once natural to good architecture, in conformity with Vitruvius, but ultimately also castellar. He justified the provision of a basement on the grounds that the *piano nobile* 'shall be safe, clean and healthy for habitation, since the floor will be removed from the damp of the ground – besides the fact that, being raised up, it achieves greater beauty, both in the being looked upon and in the looking out' (QL II, i).

The strength of the rule may be proved by an exception, the (lost) villa Palladio built for Mario Repeta, in which the owner's house was no higher than the outbuildings: Palladio apologized for the deficiency in the *Four Books*. In his latest, most fully developed villas, the manor house presides over an elaborate hierarchy of subordinate buildings, linked by porticoes which architecturally were essential to the orchestration of the whole crescendo, though Palladio himself says only that they protected the owner, while he inspected his barns, from the weather. The finest example is the villa Trissino at Meledo, an amplified version of the villa Rotonda, never built (Plate 36). The house would have presided over the estate from up on its eminence on the analogy of Roman temple complexes such as that at Palestrina, which Palladio had studied, and on which there remained in his day the medieval fortress built in the ruins of the temple at the summit.

Palladio's invention, however, was not shackled by the temple front,

Plate 36
Villa Trissino, Meledo, Vicenza, in a model based on Palladio's woodcut (QL II, xv). Palladio stated specifically that the *sala rotonda* was to be at the top of the hill.

and he did not invariably employ it even in his later villas. For instance, the villa Sarego at Pedemonte, Verona (Plates 37a and b), has no temple front, but instead an internal courtyard preceded by a similar entrance courtyard (all that was built) ranged by Ionic columns 'made of unfinished stones, as seems to be required by a villa, to which things plain and simple, rather than delicate, are appropriate'. One might best suppose that Palladio was referring to the farmer's life, but plainness and simplicity were also characteristic of military men and architecture. For example, it was stated in 1564 in a work on fortifications that 'This sort of massive and military architecture requires little ornament, the architect needing to have an eye only for the robustness and the brave impression of the work ... some ornamentation may be added so long as it appears impressive rather than simply pleasant to the eye, such as footings, cordons with carved strips below them, and ashlar finishing, rusticated, though not deeply, at the corners of the bastions.' Not that Palladio's villas were intended to comport a military air; but that many deliberately expressed a certain gravity and might easily, on the occasion for instance of a distinguished visit, take on something of the parade ground or the processional.

The symmetry and order of Palladio's mature architecture were not limited to the building but extended out from it. Paths, gates, walls and porticoes create not only geometrical patterns on paper but sight-lines converging on the major features. Gardens also were included in the overall plan. Palladio's villas were not preceded by long avenues, but the approach to the villa, and the various given of the landscape, clearly determined the site and character of the eventual structure – most clearly, of course, in the case of the villa Rotonda. Palladio explains in the *Four Books* (QL II, iii) that its four fronts were dictated by the hill-top site: it is 'atop a little mountain [*monticello*] of very easy ascent, and is washed on one side by the navigable river Bacchiglione, and on the other is surrounded by other very pleasant hills, which create the appearance of an enormous amphitheatre' – which last also picks up on what Pliny says of one of his villas. Ignoring the dome of the villa Rotonda (which is hardly apparent on the outside), consider how important to the building are its steps, or

Plates 37a and b
Villa Sarego, Pedemonte, Verona. The villa Sarego is something of an oddity among Palladio's surviving villas because it has no 'frontispiece', no central dominant element; it has no *sala*, either. However, it is not unique: the lost middle-period villa Repeta also had no central room or strong central accent, and the centrepiece of Palladio's reconstruction of a Roman country house in the *Four Books* is the courtyard.

Plate 38
Villa Almerico (Rotonda), Vicenza, seen from the main entrance. See also Plates
21a and b, and 69 (showing the interior).

the walls which flank the steps: the steps on each side are as broad as the block itself (an exact proportion: $\frac{1}{2} + 1 + \frac{1}{2}$), serving to settle the house into the hill (Plate 38). If they were not there the building would perch on its crown like a tiny hat on a clown's pate. Was it coincidental that, while most of the villa's decoration was added later, the statues that stand proud at the ends of the steps were immediately installed, so quickly (four years after the building was begun) that Palladio could credit their sculptor in the *Four Books*?

Palladio's later, more ambitious villas were never completed; the wood-cuts in the *Four Books* reproduce buildings and projects pressing at the limits of his clients' means. Few possessed even the kind of site on which to undertake the evocation of a Roman temple complex. Most, however, had the means to reproduce in paint the 'imperious' vistas they might have liked to command. The tradition that a house in the country should have a view underlies the development of landscape-painting in villas — pure landscapes (that is, landscape backgrounds without stories in the foreground) being otherwise entirely absent from sixteenth-century Italian art. Any older tradition for that kind of decoration was again overlaid by the citation of classical sources, especially after the discovery in Rome of part of Nero's Golden House. The finest such painted landscapes surviving, those by Veronese in the villa Barbaro at Maser, are a paradoxical mix of realistic illusionism and classical evocation.

An important precedent for Veronese's Maser landscapes was the salon of Alvise Cornaro's so-called Odeon in Padua. The Odeon, though modelled as Cornaro supposed on the villa of the Roman writer Terentius Varro, was actually in the town, and its octagonal central salon, which should have been an ideal belvedere, was in fact at ground level and had no view at all. Cornaro gave the salon illusionistic height and a 360° view by painting landscapes in every other corner. Each alternate corner was shaped out into a large niche, and a balcony painted to the height and form of a real balcony: apparently one could step into the niche like stepping out on to a balcony, and look over and through the balustrades down on a landscape spreading to the horizon. Since Cornaro exerted considerable influence, and there are connections between the artists he employed and the teams of decorators working in Palladio's villas, all the landscape schemes that subsequently appear in villas in northern Italy can probably be referred back to this one.

Cornaro himself had taken up the idea from the villa Farnesina, as it is now called, in Rome, built for the Sienese papal banker Agostino Chigi; the Sienese architect and painter Baldassare Peruzzi had painted an illusionistic landscape along a wall in an upper room, and his pupil and artistic heir Sebastiano Serlio had brought the design north and to Cornaro. This was the kind of landscape, so it was believed, that Vitruvius and Pliny had (rather fleetingly) referred to, although Peruzzi's landscape derived in form from earlier Florentine painting, which itself emulated vistas stretching out to the horizon featuring in early fifteenth-century Netherlandish pictures (for example, Jan van Eyck's *Madonna with Chancellor Rolin* in the Louvre). Cornaro's consciousness of classical precedent emerges in his draft for a treatise on architecture, in which he updates in contemporary terms the idea in Pliny that landscapes and *grottesche* (the kind of abstract or fantasy stucco and painted ornament rediscovered in the ruins of Nero's Golden House) were a cheap and practical form of decoration. 'As for the decoration of halls, chambers and loggias, I state that they should be painted, but not with figures unless a great painter does them, because figures if they are not well done look terrible, but instead there should be landscapes, and also *grottesche*, which make a "belvedere"; and this is decoration of less expense than tapestries or high-backed benches [*spalliere*]'. (Tapestries and the marquetry backs of *spalliere* had been decorated frequently in the fifteenth century with perspective townscapes, landscapes and still lifes, so Cornaro's idea that frescoed landscapes should substitute for them was

Plate 39a
Villa Barbaro, Maser: view from one of the windows in the façade (looking
south). Here there were once formal gardens and then orchards (see further
p. 148). Venice and the lagoon lie in the far distance.

the more appropriate. One finds *grottesche* decoration, for instance, in the
sala of the villa Badoer at Fratta Polesine, where perhaps high-backed
benches might otherwise have stood.)

Many other ideas, for instance that the green of nature was soothing,
lie behind landscape painting in general – which contains figures that give
it a subject. Only illusionistic, story-less landscape pictures may have
substituted for a defect of the site. Unusually among Palladio's villas, the
Barbaro looks out in one direction only (Plate 39a), giving at the back on
to a hill; the arrangement was not purely deliberate, since the villa was a
conversion of an existing property. Numerous windows looked out over
the gardens and fields to the front, but on the side and back walls
Veronese's landscapes (Plates 39b and c) conjure an alternative series of
views, in an adaptation of the perspectival system used in Cornaro's
Odeon. The landscapes by no means strictly reproduce the landscape that

Plate 39b

Villa Barbaro: fresco by Veronese in the room (with *Olympians* depicted on the ceiling) opening on to the fishpond and grotto. The scene of mountains and sea is not typical of northern Italy: it is surely derived from Flemish landscapes Veronese had seen (themselves largely factitious). As Doni (quoted in the text) and others bear witness, Flemish landscapes were esteemed in sixteenth-century Italy above all others, but more for qualities such as wildness than for portrait verisimilitude.

Plate 39c

Villa Barbaro: fresco by Veronese in one of the front side rooms (on the south),
one of the series of landscapes he painted on the inner walls. The villa at the
rear has twin towers and a double loggia between; before it a carriage is drawn
up, and nearby there is a platform for mounting a tethered horse.

might be seen in that part of the world through a window — rather they show in formation the repertoire of conventional motifs that will become familiar in the seventeenth and eighteenth centuries; but they include elements from actuality, for instance contemporary carriages going by on an ordinary afternoon.

There is a letter from Raphael's friend Baldassare Castiglione describing the pleasure of watching the *va e viene* from the villa Belvedere on the Vatican. Nowadays, one has to go to more remote parts of Europe — for instance, to the more isolated parts of Greece — to appreciate what a little movement in the landscape once meant. A carriage coming down the road, like that depicted by Veronese, might have been the day's event. On its arrival at the villa, the entire staff would turn out, the owner would descend, the place for a moment would be abuzz. During the rest of the time, one expected quiet in the country, 'to flatter solitariness', although Palladio's villas were usually (like castles) built beside roads and waterways, on routes — for which Palladio gives several practical reasons in the *Four Books*. Palladio describing the villa Rotonda states that the Bacchiglione is navigable — it was an additional pleasure to see the boats going up and down it. It is a human pastime, looking out of the window, and if one is not moving through it, one likes the landscape to show life around one. In the Renaissance it was an essential pleasure of the villa, though interwoven with all the others.

Take, for example, Anton Francesco Doni. He recalls enthusiastically visiting the villa of Federigo Priuli at Treville near Castelfranco — now lost, though it was an important precedent for Palladio, since Priuli had consulted Serlio and perhaps Sansovino and it was a large, imposing house, built in the late 1530s and decorated by 1542: 'The most illustrious Priuli's villa at Treville is very stupendous, such that every great lord should depart at post haste from his realm to go and see it, and contemplate the spirit of that gentleman. Foreigners of every condition are received there and well looked after, as I can attest from experience. The house is a great joy in many ways. You are there first in a stupendous large room, in which everything is a pleasure. The floors are like mirrors, the benches are carved and gilt, there is a variety to relish of painting and colours, and friezes of unusual fantasy; easel-paintings by Titian; wall-paintings of landscapes in colour by good Flemish masters, marvellously pretty. The *spalliere*, the drapes of gold and silk, the canopies, the embroidered and needlework curtains, the gold vessels, the paintings and the sculptures are better than anywhere else. I pass over the rugs of supreme excellence, the tapestries, the linen; the metalwork and other sideboard things are as fine as industrious hands can make them. Here marvellous intellects foregather, to sing, play, talk, recite; and from the windows you can see coming from far away carriages bearing gentle women, honourable men riding horses, solely to see the fine place — and so in one vista you have beautiful women, landscapes, gardens, banquets, dances, and all the pleasures united, to the sound of fountains, of birds tame and wild, and the scents of flowers, natural from the gardens, and of exquisite perfumes from in the house....'

11

'The Alchemy of Well-being'

Clean and cool air, views over landscape, the green of nature, its flora and fauna, an easier rhythm of life, these were available 'in villa' as they seldom were in town. Such benefits of the country were widely enjoyed by the ruling classes in the Renaissance, and determined the most important differences in function between a town and a country house. 'I have taken a "vineyard" at Frascati', wrote the courtier and humanist Anníbale Caro about 1560, having spent most of his life in the service of the Farnese family, 'where I enjoy and restore myself on this air greatly, and what is important is that I seem to have found the alchemy of staying well'. The country, as Palladio immediately makes clear when introducing his designs for country houses in the *Four Books* (QL II, xii), was valuable above all for the 'recreation' it offered, recreation in the widest sense including refreshment, relaxation, play, exercise and the restitution of mind and body. All the activities Palladio mentions in his introduction ('Of the site to be chosen for structures of villa') derive from the country situation: there is a view, so his proprietors can look; there is space, so they can walk or ride; and there is isolation, so they can read or think quietly, and be private.

Palladio has treated of city houses and also the houses of the Greeks and Romans after Vitruvius, Book VI; he turns secondly to houses in the country. His introduction makes a standard antithesis of country and city, although it also has a topical thrust. He begins: 'City houses are truly very splendid and convenient for gentlemen who have to live in them for all that time they will need for public administration, and the running of their own affairs; but they will gain just as much utility, and perhaps consolation, from houses in the country, where they will pass the rest of the time in looking upon and improving their possessions, and increasing their estate with diligence and skill in agriculture. There also by exercise, which one can take in the country on foot or on horseback, they will preserve their health and strength, and there finally their spirits, tired of the agitation of the city, will take great refreshment and consolation, and they can attend quietly to the study of letters, and contemplation — as for that purpose the wise men of old times used often to follow the practice of retiring to similar places, where they were visited by good-hearted friends, and their kin....'

Palladio takes it for granted that gentlemen would possess at least two houses, one in the city, the other in the country, and that they would commute from one to the other whenever they wanted but also seasonally. The 'seasons' were those of long tradition and were held in common throughout Europe; they have still not quite disappeared from twentieth-century life, since the 'seasons' of opera, or 'the season' in which one 'came out', were originally the seasons of *rentrée* to the town from the country for the winter. There was a complementary exodus during the spring, since it was cooler and more salutary out of town during the heat of mid summer, and it was especially important that the owner should be in the country for the late summer and autumn, coinciding with the harvesting and hunting seasons. The European nobility would not usually return to town until November, the English monarch still does not open Parliament until November, and once it would have been difficult to hold any parliament any earlier, while the nobility were on their estates — even among the small towns of Italy, where the estates were hardly very distant. For instance, there is a report from Padua of 1445 that on 7 September it had been impossible to make up a quorum in the Great Council, for the reason that 'because the vintage is now on almost all the citizens of Padua belonging to the Great Council are to be found "in villis" in order to see to their vintages'. Numerous other such remarks recur in official papers. Even four hundred years later, we hear that the Venetian nobility bitterly resented being required by their Austrian rulers to return to their administrative posts out of 'season'. It is an obvious consequence that Palladio's villas were built against the heat rather than against the cold, although one finds fireplaces invariably provided, because the spring is usually cold in Italy; anyway, the weather might be vagarious, and the owner would probably also visit the villa, comparatively unattended, at other times of the year, not only when he transferred his household for the season.

Having referred explicitly to the governmental duties which traditionally become noblemen, keeping them in town, Palladio seems to allude again implicitly to current conditions of political life when he says that 'they will gain just as much utility, and perhaps consolation, from houses in the country'. The word he uses, *utilità*, meant generally profit, but here seems specifically to pun on *utilia*, legal and administrative duties or in particular the fees earned (or less directly accrued) from them. If so, Palladio is suggesting that agricultural pursuits might be as lucrative as government posts. The choice of the word *consolazione* seems an even more patent allusion to legal wrangles, the frustrations of the political hothouse, that 'rancour and odium' between the factions of the nobility which are well enough recorded in Vicenza. As well as simple contentment Palladio must mean the amelioration of some pain or ill, the pain, for instance, of party feuding and petty politicking in the civic government. When Palladio goes on to mention the 'agitation' of the city from which his patrons may escape, he has at his elbow Horace, Juvenal and a host of authors who had lamented the noise and turmoil of city life; but *agitazione* also means actual civic unrest, of the kind the Venetian rectors found to arise particularly in the winter, when 'the nobles have come in from outside in the country to live in the town'.

Palladio merely hints, but elsewhere there was a much more forthright and sometimes bitter expression of the disadvantages or evil of the city, which often stood, in fact, for the politics of the day in general and the backbiting of courtly life in particular. Complaints of the kind had already appeared in the early fifteenth century in Leon Battista Alberti's *Della Famiglia.* In the sixteenth century they were almost universal, though their targets were usually generalized and their point blurred by justification in classical precedent. An example is Bartolomeo Taégio's *La Villa,* published in Milan in 1559, which is dominated by a dialogue for and against the city or the country. Its debate is shallow, but the writer's very inability to find good arguments to support his prejudices is indicative of the depth of his feeling. It is typical that while Taegio digs out a rich collection of classical and more recent authorities he fails to mention that Milan was at that time a divided and conquered city, having been ruled earlier by the French and then by the Spanish. Surely that situation lent the real gloom to his long list of the ills of the city: robbery, murder, iniquity, conspiracy, lawyers' falsifications and prevarications, the corruption of judges, the condemnation of the innocent, and the oppression of widows, orphans and the poor. The horrors to the sense of sight he stresses might in other contexts be taken as signs of good government – prisons, gallows, public executions, stocks, chains; hospitals full of disease. He adds stinking streets, crying beggars, funerals, and attacks art for the falseness of its apparent beauties. By contrast he lauds not only nature but the natural, exaggerated into the unnaturally natural, such as ploughmen adorning their shares with flowers, the rough songs of peasant girls, and one thousand happy, fruitful and festive recesses where quietness and felicity have their habitation. Certainly Palladio's mention of 'diligence and skill in agriculture' is not too far from the sentiment current in all Italy that 'agriculture' was something genuine, honest and natural, while 'city' politics were corrupt and degenerate.

Frustration or fatigue in the city seems to have come first, and then came the interest in the country. To put it rather crudely, town life was real life and country life was escapist. Villas were places of recreation, even though Terraferma noblemen might now spend more time on their estates because in the city they had little to do or little they could do, and might justify or rationalize their retirement to the country by the invocation and exercise of *agricoltura*. Cincinnatus the farmer statesman returning to his plough, the emperor Diocletian retiring to his 'villa' at Spoleto — so many citations of classical precedent (Diocletian was probably the outright favourite example) only take on meaning in a political context.

Appropriately Palladio's progression is from 'looking' to 'improving' (literally 'adorning') the estate and then to its increase with the aid of *agricoltura*. 'Agriculture' was a gentlemanly pursuit or pastime, regarded as a pleasure in the way that gardening is today; it was not distinguished from gardening proper. It was an art or science in so far as it was a nobleman's occupation — not because so much time invested in it improved yields per unit of land as modern agronomy might. Its only science in the modern sense was that of empirical observation: to ascertain that the labourers laboured, to avoid being cheated by the factor or by tenants, to maintain buildings and to direct irrigation and deforestation and enclosure. That required 'diligence' as Palladio says, and specifically such personal attention to the details of the estate occasioned his employment to build villas. As Giuseppe Falcone recommended in his agricultural manual: 'Inside the owner's apartments I would require every conveniency that one could desire, so that the owner will live there with better will, and will not so much miss the advantages of the city'. In his *Idea dell'Architettura* of 1609 Vincenzo Scamozzi says the same: 'The building of a villa is much recommended, since there is no doubt that persons who have a good house at their estates and farms, where they can put up conveniently, go to visit them more often, from which there results a very great increase and benefit to their yields.' The ideal of all the manuals is that the owner take a personal interest in his estate: the extreme and infeasible precedent of Mago of Carthage, who gave up his house in the city altogether in order to practise *agricoltura,* is more than once cited.

Despite its 'diligence' and 'art', the 'agriculture' the nobleman might practise *in villa* was a sideline or recreation, like gardening, though that, too, requires diligence. However seriously he might take it, agriculture was not serious business, which was public; the villa was rather 'principally', as Palladio goes on to say, 'for private and household business' (on which perhaps many were prepared or were driven to spend more time than before). Life *in villa* was a holiday, simply because it did not involve politics and affairs. In town one had affairs, *negotia*, the kind of business proper to a prince or gentleman, that is, for the State; in the country one had play or relaxation, *otia*, privately — this was a fundamental antithesis, although it might be qualified, depending partly on the state of current affairs, by claims that the otiose had greater value. It had, for instance, many times been claimed that otiose 'contemplation' was preferable to the 'active' life of ruling or gaining glory, a debate to which Palladio's mention of 'contemplation' deliberately alludes.

The debate was a hoary one, rooted in the old Christian dilemma, whether it was preferable to serve God by withdrawing from society or by remaining within it. Quite apart from those who felt the monastic urge directly, the spiritual values of 'contemplation' were still, by various humanists, preferred to social and political demands. The debate was, of course, carried on chiefly by intellectuals, who favoured their own leanings, but also, given the dissatisfactions and frustrations of political service and ordinary justice, men of every ability were the more inclined to be persuaded or to deceive themselves that culture counted for more. Typically, Palladio goes on to endower 'the study of letters, and con-templation' with golden tinges of classical reminiscence: 'For the same reason [quietness] the antic sages [*savi*] used often to make a habit of retiring to such places [in the country], where, visited by great-hearted [*vertuosi*] friends, and kin, possessing houses, gardens, fountains and similar pleasure-giving places, and above all their culture [*vertù*], they could easily achieve what happiness one can achieve here below.' Those are strong words, equivocating the priority of 'active', public service, in town. For Palladio employs the word *vertù* in different senses at once, so as to transfer its original, 'active' value to the 'contemplative' realm. Visitors to his patrons' villa will, Palladio suggests, resemble those antic *savi* (meaning in Venice office-holders as well as wise men in general), who were *vertuosi*, meaning ambiguously good, 'great-hearted' or accomplished. He strongly implies that the *vertù* that the ancients, in a striking zeugma, 'enjoyed' with their fountains and gardens consisted not only in culture but also in moral virtue, for it was moral virtue alone, as Christian belief had it, that led to happiness ('such as one can achieve here below'). Not cynically nor naïvely, but in compliance, I reckon, with the general *Weltanschauung*, Palladio suggests with an adroit reshuffling of clichés that the best possible mode of conduct, almost one's duty, was to enjoy the life of ease and pleasure the villa represented.

That is not an isolated instance. One finds similar conclusions in a letter of 1544 from Annibale Caro to his friend Bernardo Spina, who was in the service of the Marchese del Vasto, governor of Milan for Charles V. Spina had told Caro when they had withdrawn together privately to his study that he had had the idea, or whim as Caro calls it, of becoming a friar. Caro is against the idea, asserting, though his own employer was the

Pope's son, that laymen are just as close to God as friars. Instead, Spina's aspirations could better be satisfied by retiring to his villa: '[Do not be] either a hermit or a friar, but a man, a decent man, a friend to God. As such, retire first into yourself, which is the finest hermitage you will find, and then in order to shun company retreat to a villa with your books, with your "honest pastimes", exercise, hunting, fishing, agriculture, in an "ease with dignity", in a religion without hypocrisy, removed from the crowd but not from your friends, away from ceremony but not from conveniency, from trouble, not from virtuous action. In this way I think you can be "consoled", and good and holy, without being a friar.' If despite my arguments, Caro concludes, you still want to be a friar, you must have a melancholic sickness . . . 'You a friar? At least take on a humour befitting a gentleman.'

Caro's 'honest pastimes' are a phrase taken from Pliny, describing himself in his villa; his 'ease [ozio] with dignity' is taken from Cicero, revealing, if one pursues the reference, the same kind of shift as in Palladio's play on vertù. For Cicero the phrase had been almost a slogan of his republican, establishment party, the Optimates, and he had written in a well-known passage in the Pro Sestio, 'What therefore is before the minds of the helmsmen of the state, what should they aim at, and whither should they direct their course? Towards the very best thing, that which all sane, good and happy men most desire, ease [otium] with dignity. Those who want that, are all optimates; those who achieve it should be held to be statesmen and conservators of the public weal.' In Italy in the sixteenth century, it seems, the nobleman's inbred inclination to political responsibility was introverted, or was diverted away from the macrocosm of international politics towards an attempt to achieve his 'optimate' goals in the limited, enclosed microcosm of a piece of the Italian countryside. Similarly desire for what Caro calls 'religion without hypocrisy' can be equated with the heresy rife particularly in Vicenza. Everywhere, any aspiration, whether religious or political, was liable to turn away from the proper institutions towards a substitute expression in private life, in the more responsive environment of the countryside villa. There one could enjoy in the mind the 'virtue' choked in the waste of action. The villa remained what it had always been, a late summer residence where one took time off; but it took on a new importance in a time of political impotence as a miniature state in which one could assert the missing control, improve, execute, and achieve 'such happiness as one can achieve here below'.

12

Health and Fitness

Relaxation *in villa*, though taken during 'the rest of the time', was as much a part of the rhythm of life as its duties. Those on whom duties greatly weighed, such as monarchs, or those who wore themselves out in prayer or study, such as intellectuals, especially needed relief or 'recreation'. According to a simile frequent in medieval discussions of the matter, the mind can no more be perennially sharp and active than a bow-string can remain taut: it needs to be unstrung if it is to string well. Relaxation was necessary to good health; conversely health, among those who wished to make their peace with God, was the main justification for pleasure or relaxation.

Regarding the preservation of health, the approach of medieval and Renaissance medicine was generally psychosomatic, since the four elements, the basis of its theory, were the determinants of both mental and physical order or disorder: melancholy, for instance, was a condition both of the body and of the mind. Accordingly to defend oneself against disease one needed not only a fit and clean-blooded body but also a cheerful and sanguine temperament. When Palladio speaks first of exercise, then (indirectly, by citing the example of ancient sages) of conversation, he was giving the usual Renaissance prescription by which to keep one's spirits up (the 'spirits' in question being the various vapours believed by contemporary medicine to operate both the emotions and the constitution). As Isabella d'Este once put it in a letter to a pining friend: 'Above all, I hope you will force yourself to take regular exercise, and to join in pleasant conversation, in order to drive away melancholy and grief, whether they arise from mental or bodily causes.' The use of the villa as a means to the preservation and restoration of health emerges nowhere more obviously than in Boccaccio's *Decameron*, which opens in plague-stricken Florence, and with a group of young nobles meeting together to decide that the situation is hopeless, and that they must flee. Not only do they flee, but once in their villa they tell each other stories, specifically designed to keep their spirits up: they forbid each other sad stories, and encourage dirty stories, because dirty stories are the most likely to make their hearers laugh. This did not mean, however, that the manners of Boccaccio's young aristocrats were not refined: the dirty stories are about people of a lower class or a different country, and their tellers and audience themselves observe a formal and punctilious decorum.

Closer in time to Palladio, Pietro Bembo's *Gli Asolani*, published in 1505, represents, like the *Decameron*, the talk of young nobles in the country, and was placed in the same category of 'recreational' literature. Bembo's protagonists have met for the wedding, held in or near Ásolo, of one of Queen Caterina Cornaro's ladies-in-waiting; to pass the time, they discuss love in turn and according to rules like those imposed upon Boccaccio's young nobles, and at the same time of day, during the midday heat (as an alternative to siesta, which one of Boccaccio's people says is not so healthy). 'Queen' Caterina, having married the King of Cyprus and inherited the island on his death, was compelled by the Venetian government and her brothers to yield it to the Venetian state, receiving in return a 'court' and the funding for it at Asolo. She owned at Altívole, on the plain below the little town, a villa corresponding in many ways to that described in the *Decameron*: it had a central building and several separate outhouses or 'pavilions'; it was surrounded by a series of three walls, creating an inner court and garden, an outer court, and a park or *barco*; the park was stocked with animals; a river ran through the estate and fed at least one fountain. Whether Bembo's *Asolani* is sited here, or up in the little town, is not clear – perhaps more likely in the town, since one of the protagonists goes wandering in the hills, where he meets a hermit. But there survives, in the one wing (of the outer courtyard) now remaining of the villa (Plate 40), a loggia perfect for a group to sit in, directly recalling the loggias in which woodcuts show the *brigata* of the *Decameron* sitting; its walls are enlivened by festive *grottesche* decoration, and it is open on both sides to any slight afternoon summer breeze. It could well have served also as an open-air dining room (Plate 41). Reports of other decoration include a prominent fresco representing Aristotle bridled and ridden by the courtesan Phyllis – a medieval tale with the obvious moral that the urge to pleasure overcomes even philosophers, and a manifesto of the 'recreational' nature of the villa. Although plague is not mentioned in Bembo's *Asolani*, it is recorded a year before it was published that Caterina's nephew, Cardinal Marco Cornaro, was coming to stay at Altivole with only a few of his people 'to escape some suspicion of the plague'.

The importance of the villa as a refuge against plague or as a quarantine should not be underestimated. A typical occurrence is recorded in the summer of 1522, when the young Leonardo Giustinian, having landed from a ship returning from Africa on which plague had been discovered,

Plate 40
Villa Cornaro (known as the '*Barco* of Queen Caterina Cornaro'), Altivole,
Treviso. The room open on both sides (on this side to the court of the villa, on
the other to the park) might well have served as an open-air dining room
(compare those in Plates 41 and 71).

fled once within reach of Venice to his father's villa at Roncade near
Treviso, together with several companions; there might have been no
notice of his normal behaviour if he had not been in trouble for returning
to Venice before his quarantine had expired. According to a declaration
they made to the authorities in 1537, certain brothers of the Venetian
patrician Barbarigo family kept a house in the enchanting countryside
round Montebelluna specifically 'for the times of plague'. And, although
infectious air was not the right explanation for the spread of plague, flight
to the country was an efficacious remedy, as statistics prove: in 1578, for
instance, it was estimated that 767 had died of the recent great plague in
the countryside round Vicenza, while 2,357 had died in the city, although
the city had only about one sixth of the population of the countryside.

However, the walls around the park at Altivole or round the villa in
the *Decameron* or originally round many of Palladio's villas were not so
much for the exclusion of outsiders as for the inclusion of the animals: the

Plate 41

Vision of an open-air dining room by a waterway by a garden, attributed to
Benedetto Caliari (son of Paolo Veronese). The picture (now in the Accademia
Carrara, Bergamo) came from a Bergamo villa where it had probably formed
part of a series. A noblewoman is about to be taken for a row; another fishes.
Notice the drapes laid on the seats before they sit.

park was kept for hunting, or at the least to provide game for the proprietor's table. At Altivole there was an isolated tower out in the park, presumably a dovecot, but it may also have provided a view of the hunting. When Palladio in the passage quoted above mentions exercise, he includes hunting, though it is true he is not very explicit. Hunting was one of those typically chivalric occupations about which not much (but not nothing) was said or written in the Renaissance in Italy — as opposed to the Middle Ages and to northern Europe, from which there is a considerable hunting literature — but which went on nonetheless. As the sport of kings, it was intimately bound in with the tradition from which the villa emerged. La Zisa, Roger II's lodge at Palermo, had been set in the middle of a spacious park well stocked with game. Since there can have been no strategic justification for the placing of Frederick II's castle at Castel del Monte deep in the hinterland of Puglia, it must have been intended as a hunting lodge; Frederick's extraordinarily naturalist work on falconry was a signal contribution to medieval hunting literature.

In the *Decameron* Boccaccio stresses the abundance of animals in the gardens surrounding his protagonists' country retreat, and though he never has them hunt they eat meat. From the later fourteenth century, behind the Visconti palace still standing in Pavia there was once an enormous hunting park stretching all the way to the Certosa di Pavia. From the fifteenth century reports of hunting expeditions undertaken by the large and small courts of northern Italy are frequent, and Lorenzo de' Medici even wrote a comic poem about a hunting expedition, in which, however, some of the participants were neither competent nor keen. Although it was a pleasure for many, and for some no doubt a passion, it was not, in Italy, fashionable, or a means of display. Among the great, Pope Leo X Medici may be mentioned as a keen huntsman (though clerics were ordinarily debarred from the sport), and his master huntsman was, as it happens, a Vicentine. But the large hunting lodge Leo X kept in the Roman Campagna was exceptional, and the hunting of large game — deer, boar, even bear — of the kind that remained popular throughout this period in northern Europe certainly declined earlier in Italy. It was believed that the introduction of the gun had caused a scarcity of larger game. When in 1532 Stefano Gualdo organized a hunt during the visit of Charles V to his villa near Vicenza, the Emperor's bag was only a couple of hares. That would have been a contemptible catch in the eyes of his father Maximilian, a renowned huntsman. Charles V caught his hares with dogs, though falcons were also used — with the aid of professional falconers.

If Palladio's patrons had practised hunting very widely or keenly he would surely have mentioned it; he was nowhere required to make architectural provision for it, such as kennels. Writers of agricultural

manuals also have little to say about it, though Giuseppe Falcone remarks
that the hunting of hares 'is an art that truly brings a thousand pleasures,
and restores the spirit flagging in the study of letters or the exercise of
arms, or in the hopeless wrangles of the city, or in some other melancholy'.
He commends it as 'a true preparation for matters of war', rather hollowly,
since he goes on to say it is not dangerous. However, close by or in the
hall of every villa there would have been an arquebus and other weapons,
with which every nobleman could, when he wished, murder animals or
other noblemen, or at least, if he followed Falcone's advice, fire twice a
week in order to deter robbers.

Every villa would have had a spit. The doves kept in dovecots were
there for the eating, and birds, which, if not hunted, would be limed or
snared by the villa's household, were an important source of meat. Both
dovecots and fish ponds (Palladio mentions fish ponds at the villa Pojana
and in front of the grotto at the villa Barbaro) were, though expensive
investments, valuable larders. Fishing would seem to have been just as
popular as hunting small game. Hunting and fishing conveniently provided
the kind of little gift with which it was usual to keep the channels of
courtesy flushed and one's obligations in good credit: if dispatched from
a prince or great noble to a dependant such gifts would be a favour, but
they were also a common accompaniment to a letter, for instance, between
friends and peers. Not only game and fish but any products of the villa,
as well as all kinds of artefacts, would circulate in this way – quails, hares
or fish, or flowers, cheeses, fruit, wine, artichokes, olives, even young trees.
It is still a usual hospitality in Italy to offer some choice local item of food
or drink, which the recipient will savour not simply for its quality but also
for its particularity. These numerous gifts must have helped immensely to
enliven staple diets. There were no 'corner shops': as Falcone again points
out, it was easy to run out of things – one might have oil but no vinegar,
bread but no wine, while the city, even if close by, might easily be debarred
by a river in flood or by the appalling roads. He recommends hunting to
relieve 'bucolic boredom' in more ways than one.

Although the riding and walking Palladio mentions could easily, and
commonly did, embrace hunting, on the other hand it was also a pastime
in the Renaissance simply to go for a walk or to go for a ride. Stables
Palladio certainly provided, and marks them on his plans. Or one could
go for a row, when, on a hot summer evening, it was 'more pleasant to
be on water than on land'.

Whether riding, or going out for a drive in a carriage, one might easily
by chance or design arrive at a neighbouring estate, and visits were
probably the most essential pastime of all 'in villa'. The average landowner
spent much time travelling, whether on business or on pleasure. Although

there was a trend, in order to facilitate *agricoltura*, to build up holdings into one estate, that could be a slow process, and most, perhaps virtually all landlords had *possessioni* scattered in several different districts. But anyway any great man would expect to be entertaining almost constantly, and if someone were not calling on him he would be calling on someone. One would call either for dinner (in the middle of the day) or after dinner or to stay the night. For instance, Palladio's patrons Francesco and his son Mario Repeta held dinner parties on alternate Saturdays at their villa at Campigli, and often put their friends up; Palladio reports (QL II, xii) that the rooms of the guest wing (extending down one side of the courtyard of the villa, which was destroyed in the seventeenth century) were each decorated with allegories and examples of a different Virtue; it was Mario Repeta's rather serious-minded joke to lodge his guest in the room he thought most appropriate to his character.

We have the authority on these matters of Alvise Cornaro, whose *agricoltura* and *villeggiatura* were an integral part of his vaunted 'sober life', by virtue of which he claimed to have reached a robust old age. 'I have also', he says, 'another means of taking recreation, because I go in April and May, and again in September and October, for some days to enjoy my hill, which is in the Monti Eügánei [south of Padua; his estate was at Este], and in the most beautiful site among them; it has its own fountains and gardens, and above all a convenient and beautiful apartment, and in this place I sometimes indulge in a little hunting, appropriate to my [old] age, convenient and pleasant. Then I enjoy for as many days my estate at Piano [Codevigo, his main estate and farm] ... At these same times of year I also go every year to revisit one of the cities around, and take my pleasure in the enjoyment of the company of my friends who live in them, by being with them, and talking to them, and through them with others who are there, men of good intellect: with architects, painters, sculptors, musicians and "agricultors", since with such men this our age is well endowed. I see what they have done recently, I see again what they have done before, and I always learn things I am glad to know. I see their houses, gardens, antiquities, and not least the squares, churches and fortresses, leaving out nothing from which a man can take pleasure and learn something. But above all I enjoy the going and coming on these trips, on which I contemplate the beauty of the situations and of the landscape I pass through. Some are on the plain, others in the hills, near a river or with fountains, with many fine buildings and a garden around....'

Partly because he was an old man, partly because he regarded debauchery as one of the great evils of the age along with Lutheranism, Cornaro does not mention sex, though most people in the Renaissance would have regarded that, too, as essential to health — for men, anyway. Failure to indulge and obtain release might damage the complexion. Palladio does not mention sex, either. However, one of the stories of the *Decameron* takes place in a *possessione* or villa outside town, and begins with the situation that the unmarried son of the owner 'used from time to time to bring a woman for his pleasure and to keep her there a day or two, and then send her away'. It seems rather unlikely that similar practices should not have continued into Palladio's time. Reports from rather later suggest that there was more liberty for dalliance *in villa*, since there was no one of importance about to look on.

Cornaro's recipe is also indeed a programme for retirement, and that was one more important traditional function of the villa. In his book on merchandizing and the perfect merchant Benedetto Cotrugli in 1458 had recommended that the businessman should retire in his old age to the country, and there read the Scriptures. The richest and most powerful of a city of merchants, Cosimo de' Medici, had capped that, not only reading the Church Fathers but also hiring his own philosopher, Marsilio Ficino, to expound to him. Two years before his death he wrote to Ficino, 'Yesterday I came to the villa of Careggi not to cultivate my fields but my soul. Come to us, Marsilio, as soon as possible. Bring with you our Plato's book *De Summo Bono* . . . I desire nothing so much as to know the best road to happiness'. He died at Careggi, his principal villa, as did his younger brother Lorenzo, and his grandson Lorenzo the Magnificent. When Annibale Caro wrote of the 'alchemy' of Frascati he, too, had only a few years to live. A significant number in the Renaissance managed to retire, including the prince of princes himself, Charles V, ruler of most of Italy, who retired, in 1556, to a villa — not, as is usually credited, to a monastery, though the monastery available beside it was one of its facilities.

13

Gardeners' Delights

The walls enclosing the garden behind the villa Badoer now defend nothing but weeds; dull grass has replaced the variegated species once perfuming the gardens of the villa Barbaro at Maser, and the fountain once by the gate to the orchard stands in a coach park shielded by railings against vandalism. Palladio's villas today are all bereft of their tubs and trellises, their paths, hedges and bowers, their fountains, their topiary, and all the botanical varieties in which Renaissance owners took a keen interest, judging by the long lists writers like to give of them. The pity is the greater, since Palladio declares when introducing his villas (QL II, xii) that 'gardens and orchards are the soul and pastime of the villa'.

For many, probably even most, in the sixteenth century, the layout of gardens was a more important matter than the architecture of the villa's house, and no owner interested in the latter would neglect the former. When Pliny wrote of his villa he described its gardens, which were integral to the architecture and decoration. Enriched by the Arabs, the association of pleasure, privacy and greenery had persisted through to the Renaissance intact. In the Middle Ages the garden became, if anything, too potent a symbol of sensuality: in the *Lives* of the Saints gardens are one of the worst tortures to which evil pagans could submit aspiring martyrs. Implacable tyrants would go so far as to lock the Christian in a walled garden, in which the scents, balms and colours of the flowers were a cue, inevitably, for the appearance of a seducing siren. Otherwise, in poetry, the details of desire and of the sexual act were blurred in a spray of petals or verdure – 'She took me beneath a cool bower, where I saw flowers of every colour, and there I felt such joy and sweetness, that I thought to see the god of love', wrote Guido Cavalcanti in the thirteenth century. In the *Trionfi* Petrarch evoked a garden land in distant Cyprus, the island sacred to Venus, where Cupid held sway, and this image fed the fantasy of a host of following poets, including Sannazaro, the first Renaissance author to visit Arcadia. Written at the end of the fifteenth century, Francesco Colonna's 'Dream of a Battle of Love by Polia's Lover'

(*Hypnerotomachia Polifili*) is a long meander through a garden landscape, in which tantalizing female figures bamboozle the narrator among classical ruins, botanical recitations and exquisite pavilions. In the sixteenth century such poetry of desire became concrete as statuary came regularly to be installed in gardens, often in close association with fountains. The fashion was led by Rome, but it was assimilated in northern Italy by the middle of the century. The ditty of the 'nymph of the spring', apparently composed to accompany a statue of a female nude beside a fountain in a Roman garden, was time and again repeated or reworked:

> I am the nymph of this place, the guardian of the sacred fountain,
>   sleeping to the soft sound of its murmuring water.
> You who touch my hollow marble, respect my sleep. Drink or wash,
>   but keep silent.

Gardens might be conducive to a state of trance, a heightened sensibility.

Gardens were sensual paradises: even if they had no houris, plants, water and statuary were highly associative, especially in the heat. Real gardens were indistinguishable from the so-called Gardens of Love — implicitly or explicitly moralizing images of partnered youngsters eating, drinking, music-making, dancing, embracing. Gardens stood under the sign of Idleness, next door to Sin. However, there were limits to the behaviour of young aristocrats together 'in society', though they might well indulge in horseplay. Several more or less institutional games involved much physical contact: variations on blind man's buff, for instance. Particularly people would use syringes to squirt water on one another, or from the second half of the sixteenth century *giochi d'acqua*, devices secret or otherwise to fire water at the apprehensive or unprepared, were installed. In gardens in summer people would sing songs together, more or less lustily; virtually all secular songs in the Renaissance were songs of courtship or love. In art and literature music-making carries a long heritage of sexual innuendo, presumably earned. So also do chess and cards. Cards had been introduced into Europe in the early fifteenth century, although the games that had been devised were still few, and card-tables were not ubiquitous as they would be in the seventeenth and eighteenth centuries. Backgammon was widely played. Gaming, though perhaps regarded as an uncultured pastime, may have become more widespread in sixteenth-century society (Cornaro seems to imply it had spread like Lutheranism). It was also sport to watch sport, including football of a kind, or notably wrestling, which it was left to the lower classes to perform — Oliver, who wrestles with Charles before the Duke in *As You Like It*, proving the rule.

However, though sensuality was so much in the air, from the scent of the plants to the calls of the birds to the expectation of shouts and laughter coming from the bower or raised by fleeing nymphs, that need not have perturbed the decorum of those who sat or strolled through it. Especially in the heat, it was usual to entertain or gather in gardens, to talk or hold discussions – recalling, depending on the disposition of those participating, Plato's Academy or Boccaccio's *Decameron*. The dialogue, that favourite Renaissance literary form, is commonly set in a garden. Commonly one would stroll through the garden and then at some suitable spot stop and summon chairs. Learned humanists recall reclining on rugs strewn beneath bowers, though they were probably spread over benches rather than on the ground. There is a great emphasis on shade, achieved by the careful nurture of vines and jasmine and so on in trellises. It was also common to picnic. Renaissance furniture, though in many ways so little developed towards comfort, included such refinements as folding picnic tables. The *Hypnerotomachia* even featured basins and fountains on wheels that the nymphs of his imagination brought before the enraptured banqueter. Open-air dining seems to have been for Anton Francesco Doni, describing all the possible delights of the villas of which he dreams, the summit of those pleasures. He says in final praise of Federigo Priuli's villa at Treville that if you stayed there a month you could find a different place to dine outside every day, but he particularly enjoyed his little colonnaded *montagnetta*. (The little mound, though everything else has gone, apparently survives.)

Water was essential to the Italian garden, by long tradition: Pliny had found his villa at Laurentinum perfect, except in one thing, that there was no spring – water came from a well. Palladio recommends (QL II, xii) that his patrons build beside a river, if they can, for other reasons but also because 'with the greatest utility, and ornament, they will be able to irrigate their lands, gardens and orchards' – those that are the soul of the villa. And in the Renaissance, where there were waters, there were nymphs – an association reflecting the sensuality implicit in the garden. Soon little temples, or 'grottoes', were provided for the nymphs (Plate 42), or alternatively for the male river-god, on the example of classical grottoes – one of which, believed in the Renaissance to have been a famous one occupied by the nymph Egeria, still survives outside Rome. Similar dank little caves that were formerly Renaissance grottoes exist today, having lost all their charm; but when in use they were sanctuaries of coolness, and abounded with water, often not merely in the basin into which the tutelary deity discharged his or her vase (or occasionally breast) but in all sorts of secret places. The grotto was the pumproom of the garden's waterworks, and the centre of the *giochi d'acqua* with which it was the guests' delight to be soaked. One that Bartolomeo Ammannati built in the 1540s for Stefano Gualdo at his villa has gone, but survives

Plate 42
Villa Porto, Thiene: grotto, built 1579–81 by the engineer Cristoforo Sorte.
Though no longer in use, it stands to this day beside a stream and was
undoubtedly the pumproom for the irrigation of the gardens.

in a description: 'One enters this fountain by three passages, each in rustic form with fine incrustation: one climbs by two stone stairs with a suitable meeting in the middle, and, in chambers beneath, there are bird-houses ... Above, there is a loggia, standing above the oval cavity of the grot below, where the water-tricks are; the loggia has three large arched windows and six other square apertures, including the door in from the stair, which are divided one from another by stucco terms. These hold up the cornice and the ceiling, on top of which there is a large lead basin ... As you go in to the fountain [the oval grotto] there are two half-length statues in stone, which squirt water, and in a niche a satyr who also squirts water, and the paving stones of the floor, the ceiling and the walls are all full of tricks. ...'

Probably people in the loggia worked the tricks on those approaching below; it seems one would enter by one door at the back, go up to the loggia, and open water on those entering the grotto by the other doors at the front. Besides the grotto at the villa Barbaro, which had water play, but not tricks, this seems to have been the finest example in the Veneto in Palladio's time, although many and still more elaborate installations were devised in this and the following century in gardens in Tuscany and around Rome.

The grotto at the villa Barbaro (Plate 43a) is closed to public access but was originally in effect like another room of the house, being on a level and on a line with the main room; it, too, like the main room, was frescoed inside by Veronese. The continuity of garden and house would be more obvious if the paintings apparently once in the barrel vaults of the central room had survived, for originally (though it is odd that not a single trace could be found during the modern restorations) above the smiling musicians in their niches and the illusionistic paintings of the household coming and going were painted garlands and trelliswork, presumably much like those still to be seen at the ends of the vaults of the front rooms (Plate 43b). In this way the grotto, though not so large or elaborate as the grotto which Daniele Barbaro had surely seen in the villa Giulia in Rome, made virtually for the habitation of Pope Julius III — since the waters alleviated the gout by which Julius was plagued — was in a real sense the 'soul and pastime' of the villa Barbaro. Closed off at the rear by a wooded hill and at the sides by outbuildings, by the main house at the front, the Barbaro grotto was always a *giardino segreto* invisible and unsuspected by the outside world. But the identity stamped by the coat of arms above the entrance to the cave of the grotto proves it was a sociable place as well as a private one. The exuberantly rich and festive decoration of the grotto still conveys something of the spirit of holiday that was meant to prevail (Plate 43c). The liveliness was above all in the water, led from a spring in the hill behind to flow not only through the urn held by the reclining god in the cave and down into the fishpond, but also through diverse parts of the statues lined in the niches outside — from the wineskin held by the

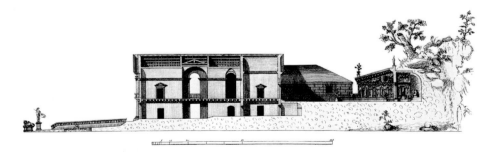

Plate 43a
Villa Barbaro, Maser: cross-section of the house and grotto, engraving from
Ottavio Bertotti Scamozzi's *Fabbriche e Disegni di Palladio* (1796).

Plate 43b
Fresco by Veronese on the ceiling of one of the front side rooms. If the barrel
vaults of the main *sala* were also originally painted, their fictive trelliswork must
have been similar.

Plate 43c
The grotto as it is today. The stuccowork is attributed to Marcantonio Barbaro
himself, since he is reported to have practised in stucco as a pastime and it
cannot be attributed to Alessandro Vittoria, the sculptor of the fountain by the
road below the villa.

satyress on the extreme right, from the mouth of Bacchus's panther, from
Diana's mouth, from the mouths of the horses Neptune rides, and from
the eyes of Venus's dolphin – and even from the breasts of the nymph
who stands above the great pediment. Splashing and trickling from these
various sources it was gathered in the fishpond before the grotto, and then
led into the house, providing – a particular luxury Palladio notes in the
Four Books – running water for the kitchen before serving the six fountains
of the garden in front of the house. The fountain surviving on the other
side of the public road was always the last and greatest of these; as now
there were two more immediately beside the protruding main block of the
house and in front of the porticoes (which Palladio himself calls loggias,
and which were therefore places not of passage but of sojourn, prospecting
and giving on to the garden). There was another fountain directly in front
of the main block, and two more of which the basins remain in the centre
of the lawns sloping down to the road. Surely these last two fountains
formed the centres of two 'mazes' or complicatedly geometric gardens;
they must have been particularly fine, given that Daniele Barbaro had been
the driving force behind the creation of the botanic garden at Padua

University. Once arrived at the bottom of the slope, the waters were led away to irrigate the *brolo* or orchard on the other side of the public road, now open fields. (The avenue of trees on an axis with the house, however, has a falsifying effect, since it extends the domain of the villa too far, too Versailles-like, out into the open country). Palladio reported that 'the orchard is very large, and full of the most excellent fruits and different trees'.

A villa, then, would usually have a garden, generally perhaps smaller than that of the villa Barbaro, made up of beds, paths and tubs laid out symmetrically, often set off by hedges which could be developed into topiary; if water was available, that was an opportunity to develop the garden further with fountains and so on. The garden would give on to the adjacent *bruolo or brolo,* which I have translated as 'orchard' but which could serve as a vegetable garden or for any crop grown for the villa; alternatively the immediate 'domain' of the villa would open on to a *barco* or park in which the owner could hunt. Before the sixteenth century it had not, however, been usual to find the finest gardens beside a villa. Even from the first half of the sixteenth century there are more reminiscences of gardens on the nearby islands of the Zudeca or Murano in Venice than attached to villas on the mainland. In Florence, the Medici gardens in which Michelangelo trained were either those of the Medici palace itself or were beside the convent of San Marco, still in the city. In Rome, the earlier Renaissance gardens were established well within the city, for instance beside the palazzo Venezia on what is now the open square beneath the Vittorio Emmanuele monument. Even the villa Giulia, undertaken in the 1540s, was close to the old walls, and the famous villa 'resorts' such as Tivoli and Frascati were not 'developed' until the 1560s. The provision of gardens in villas was an aspect of the new trend towards a longer sojourn and the architectural aggrandizement of country houses.

Even much of the pleasure in creating a garden was architectural, in so far as it involved surveying, trellising and topiary. It was the failure of his box hedges that led Giangiorgio Trissino to borrow Isabella d'Este's gardener to do their 'good setting-out and re-ordering'. Pietro Bembo wrote to a friend he had left in Rome: 'Tomorrow I shall return home, to plant new trees in the little grove which has lost several oaks and chestnuts owing to the intense heat of last summer. Your ivy [a gift] has already covered a fine large pavilion at the other end of the garden, and I have made another little pergola with ivy and larch-poles firmly fixed in the ground at regular intervals, which in two or three years' time ought to be very beautiful.' Laying out his garden in his villa at Frascati, 'among the peasants ... coming to grips with agriculture', Annibale Caro found 'to have come into my hands dividers, a compass and a spade'. He had also to stake out the vines (which in trellises would provide a particularly dense shade), and he was otherwise 'greatly occupied with the paths'. In fact, 'I am doing a few verses of my translation of Virgil, and the rest of the time I attend to the paths, and I draw the strings to mark out their lines, and this is my life'. It was probably not the paths simply that kept him so busy, but the hedges which formed them. The hedges were also frequently shaped into topiary. The present restored garden at the villa Lante at Bagnaia north of Rome (with a grotto like that at Maser) or the seventeenth-century Giardini Giusti in Verona (Plate 44) give the best available savour of what it must have been like at Palladio's villas as well — though garden design changed very little over the years and the gardens of Lord Burlington's villa at Chiswick or Westbury Court gardens in Gloucestershire, for instance, will serve not too badly.

Although the distinction between the garden proper and the *brolo* beside

Plate 44
Giardini Giusti, Verona. Though the gardens are probably seventeenth-century, the formal principles have not changed from the sixteenth. Across the river from the centre of Verona, these are city gardens, which were perhaps even more prized than country ones, though inevitably less extensive. In Vicenza the comparable Orti Valmarana immediately outside the Castello gate also survive, but have lost their formal layout.

it was felt, the same geometry pervaded both garden and orchard, and whether it involved cultivating hedges and vines or planting and pruning lines of trees it was all *agricoltura*. One more pleasure common both to the garden and to the *brolo* was that of making things sprout, or 'the pullulation of the grafted sprigs which, as our creatures, we watch grow with the most singular pleasure', as Bartolomeo Taegio put it. That was a recreation with a tradition stretching at least to the mid fourteenth century and to Pope Benedict XII, who liked to tend his vines beneath the Palace he had built at Avignon, and to his younger contemporary Petrarch. In his letters Petrarch described his little house and orchard outside Avignon at Vaucluse, and later retired to a similar *possessione*, at Arquà in the Euganean hills, that still survives (among vineyards in an unchanged, still delightful if well-known setting). In his handbook for kings, *On the remedies of both Good and Bad Fortune*, he characterized gentlemanly *agricoltura* as a pastime and in this way differentiated it, for the coming Renaissance, from working the soil like a peasant: '[Agriculture] was once held in esteem and practised by great men and discussed by great intellects. In this as in much else Cato the Censor holds a high place, of whom it was written very truly: he was the greatest senator, the greatest orator, the greatest general, but the final praise is added that he was a farmer without precedent or compare in his time. Who therefore would be ashamed to till the soil with Cato? ... Who would blush to goad and cry on oxen that Cato's voice might urge along the furrow, that voice by which many great armies had been fired to do battle, that had discoursed so eloquently on difficult cases? ... He indeed first drew up the precepts of agriculture into the form of a science, and edited them in writing, and following him came many others, who raised up that lowly and sunken work of the hand with their high and noble poetry [above all Virgil's *Georgics*]. Bearing these men in mind, and the necessity of supporting life, I do not condemn agriculture. However, neither the lustre of authorities nor the fear of famine will compel me to judge it preferable to liberal and honest arts, or even equal to them: for although in that first time of Roman rule the same men could be both leaders and farmers, things have changed in the interval, and since nature is now less robust your talents are not sufficient for such different employments. Therefore in this age I would permit men of the first rank to turn to agriculture not as a trade or a business but for leisure and relief from their cares, and occasionally to graft pliant springs on growing buds, to trim luxuriant foliage with a curved scythe, to insert wanton shoots in hollow trenches in the hope of offspring, to divert murmuring brooks down sloping channels to thirsty meadows. But for them to dig steadily or plough, to devote their whole spirit to the land, unless under necessity, that I think improper and unbecoming for a brave or a learned man, who can hardly be short of something better to do. ....' His purple description of permissible agricultural pursuits seems exactly to set the dilettante tone of sixteenth-century gardeners and *agricoltori*.

In the fifteenth century the agricultural pursuits of Cosimo de' Medici, whose country houses are often regarded as the earliest Renaissance villas, were in the same mould. 'He loved to do grafting and cropping with his own hand', according to the biographer Vespasiano de' Bisticci, who paints him first devoting two hours to pruning his vines, and then turning to the *Moralia* of St Gregory. The gardens at San Marco in Florence are the first example Vespasiano cites of Cosimo's *agricoltura*; he goes on to wonder at his ready memory, despite his greater affairs, of every tree and graft on his extensive estates. Much the same was said in the funeral oration of Francesco da Porto, the builder of the villa Porto at Thiene: he took 'an immense interest in agriculture, in which he so delighted that with justification he could take pride, like Cyrus in Xenophon, in the trees he had grafted with his own hand.' (The garden of Cyrus of Persia as described by Xenophon became one of the icons of Renaissance *agricoltori*; in *La Villa* Bartolomeo Taegio provided a reconstruction of its geometry.)

In the sixteenth century the same sentiments recur, though usually transposed on to classical precedents. Taegio praises Diocletian, 'that very wise and very powerful emperor, who, since he well recognized and understood the toils of ruling, retired to private life, and at Salone [that is, Split] in a villa of his in Slavia used to plant shoots with his own hand, and never could be induced by plea or circumstance to depart from that firm and brave resolution, preferring the glorious tranquillity of that private life to the turbulent and stormy greatnesses of empire and command'. In Agostinetti's treatise on agriculture published in the early seventeenth century this commonplace has become particularly silly: 'The Emperor Diocletian, having renounced the Empire, retired to his villa at Spalato, which he had chosen for his enjoyment. When the Roman Senate sent ambassadors to call him back to the throne, he replied, "Did it seem to them honourable, that one who had planted and dug out these tender lettuces should leave them to go back to the uproar of Rome?"'

However, gardening had other implications for a landowner. Cosimo's bid for power in Florence had depended, when it came to a crisis, on the Medici's ability to pack the assembly with men from his fields, and in the struggle for power the holdings in the Mugello that his father had put together had a weight almost as great as that of the Medici bank. It is not altogether surprising that 'in all his "possessions" there were few farming operations not directed by him ... moreover, when the peasants came into Florence, they would ask him about the fruit trees and where they were to be planted'. One wonders whether he followed a tip in Alberti's book

Della Famiglia that the prudent proprietor should plant trees on the edge of his land, so that their shade should impoverish his neighbours' fields rather than his own. Francesco da Porto owned more than 3,500 acres, so also on his part not to have taken some interest in agriculture would have been singularly improvident.

In the 1550s in *Le Ville* Anton Francesco Doni resumes the delights of *agricoltura* both nicely and a little ironically. He looks back nostalgically to the days of Cosimo and Lorenzo de' Medici, recalling, for instance, the Medici villa at Cafaggiuolo, which had served 'both one and the other, gentlemen and writers'. 'The gentleman, tired of the travails he has sustained for the state, leaving his place in government to another, seeks some quiet relaxation, twice or three times a year for a month or two, so as better to be able to tolerate the irritating annoyances, and unbearable toils, which indeed frequently beset him in government. The writer, tired from the reading of sophistical books, lest he should be completely worn out, mounts a hill, walks along a plain, and regains his breath with a book for pleasure in his hand, and under the greenery of some pretty bower restores himself and his eyes, exhausted from the long reading of so many many kinds of books. Both gentleman and writer are able to take delight in making fine grafts, in planting good fruits, or in making some sort of small ornamental garden, with no more effort, however, than should start a sweat, otherwise he will be a complete peasant'.

In contrast to Petrarch and to Taegio, who had mentioned besides Cyrus, Diocletian, Cicero, Pliny and Seneca, also King Attalus, Manlius Curius Dentatus, Atilius Serranus, Cincinnatus, Marius Regulus, Atilius Colatinus and Scipio Africanus, Doni breaks off: 'And if anyone reading *Le Ville*, or hearing them read, thinks that the ancient kings, and this citizen or another, did things with their own hands, and should object about my last remark, then as the day is long I shall reply that when writers overstep probability one should withhold belief. I do not mean to say that the ancients were a different race, because eggs have always been eggs and melons melons. I believe that it was then as I have seen it today, among moderns who do such things, or make a show of doing them: your Duke will pick up a pretty and upright plant, since the mood so strikes him among beautiful gardens; and having first had the hole dug by the peasant, and having had the graft given into his hand by his factor, he will place it in the ground; and then this lord can say with truth, when they bring him fruit to his table: these are my children, I planted these, and had them watered. So one needs to exercise one's judgement in writing and in understanding the way things are put. Most of those ancient heroes must have used the same sort of decorous means – those Cincinnati, those great kings, those stupendous Cirri and others.'

When Doni's contemporary Alvise Cornaro enthusiastically preached what he called 'holy agriculture' to an audience for the most part converted and already practising, he meant by it something less ritualistic than this, but even he did not mean using a spade as a spade. He frankly claimed he had made money from 'agriculture' and that others were doing so, but he never ceased in the same breath to call it 'recreation', and to place it on a par with gardening. He owned several fine gardens, one across the road from his town house in Padua and the others on his country estates — 'my various gardens, with the running water that runs beside them, in which I always find something to give me delight'. At Este in the Euganean hills his estate had 'its fountains and gardens', and he could also hunt; at Codevigo his villa was so beautiful 'because it is full of beautiful roads, which all converge in a beautiful square, in the middle of which is a church ... it is divided by a broad, flowing part of the river Brenta, on each side of which there is a great extent of country, all of fertile and well cultivated fields'. God was always doing geometry; a gentleman was always surveying his acres.

14

Farming Economics

What was the financial base behind the fine show of the Palladian villa? Granted that the villa had many pleasures, was it not also a business? It is not unreasonable to seek the grimier truth behind the excessively pretty picture Renaissance landowners painted or had painted of themselves, but not all of the dirt one might expect sticks at the point of fact. Farming never did and never could make much money in the Renaissance, except in so far as it included 'agriculture' in a rather wider sense of capitalist speculation.

There is a famous passage written by the Venetian diarist Girolamo Priuli just before the outbreak of the Cambrai Wars confirming that there was a paradox in Palladio's patrons' investment: 'Since the noblemen and citizens of Venice had enriched themselves, they wished to enjoy their success and to live in the Terraferma and elsewhere, devoting themselves to pleasure, delight and the country life, meanwhile abandoning navigation and maritime activities. These were certainly more laborious and trouble-some, but it was from the sea that all benefits came. We can judge the damage inflicted by the Terraferma on the city of Venice from the way in which her intoxicated nobles, citizens and people bought estates and houses on the Terraferma and paid twice as much as they were worth. They paid 20 to 25 ducats per *campo* [almost an acre] of land, which yielded less than 3 to 4 per cent per annum, and subsequently erected palaces and houses on these estates which consumed large sums of money ... Nonetheless, there was no man of means, among nobility, citizenry or people, who failed to buy at least one estate on the Terraferma, especially in the Padovano and Trevigiano, for these were nearby regions and they could go and stay and return in a day or two.'

Clearly those who invested in land had already made money, rather than were seeking to make it; and from Priuli's figures it is obvious that trade and finance were a much better investment than land, as far as return on capital went. There is no reason to believe that the yields improved during the sixteenth century: when the banker Andrea Dolfín itemized his assets and their yield in 1570, he accounted the return from his lands still at 4 per cent, which was slightly higher than the rent he obtained from housing (3·1 per cent) but less than that from government stock or from loans (between 6 and 7 per cent). In the 1584 suit over the inheritance of Francesco da Porto in Vicenza the judges discussed the sources of his wealth, opining that he must have inherited it all, for he was not known to have traded. 'If he was rich, those riches had come from his father, and he had become very rich through the deaths of both his father and his uncle. Otherwise the earnings from a small estate could not have produced any noticeable increase in his wealth, and he would have had need of "industry or trading" or other good fortune, which cannot, we believe, be shown.' Priuli with little doubt was a victim of a recurrent Venetian neurosis, which responded to any setback in mainland politics by lamentation that the city had 'abandoned' the sea. It would be more accurate to say that the city had never abandoned the land, and that the city did not effectually 'abandon' the sea until the sea was wrested from it in the 1570s.

What Priuli was not to know, but it might be fair to guess others did divine, was that land prices, far from reverting to 'what they were worth', would continue to rise. Around Vicenza, immediately after its recovery by the Venetians, but even before peace had stabilized, the price of a *campo* was between 30 and 36 ducats, that is, three times what it had been before. Rents rose at the same time. Perhaps they did not continue to rise; Alvise Cornaro was reckoning to get 30 ducats a *campo* in 1540, but that was for newly reclaimed land, not for land of the first quality. However, it is obvious, even where further details of this kind are lacking, that confidence in the value of land never faltered, and that there was always a ready market if one were forced to sell. Land was a large part of Andrea Dolfin's 1570 portfolio, probably because, though less active, it was more secure. The same Priuli, when war broke out in 1509, reported, as I mentioned before, people lamenting that they had not put their savings into land, because, even though the land was in the hands of the enemy, they could expect to get it back once the war was over, whereas government stock was not worth the paper it was written on. Confidence in government stocks seems never to have been restored.

On the other hand, if nobody could lose by investing in land, it is certain that no one had much to gain financially by building fine houses on it. Building seems universally in Europe during the Renaissance to have been a ruinous occupation. In cases where builders were forced soon afterwards to sell, they never recovered their money, and the increase in rental value obtained was widely disproportionate to the expense of building. Buildings, as opposed to land, belonged with clothes, horses, servants and entertainment as items of consumption, and, further, they required maintenance and updating. People explicitly said as much in the case of Francesco da Porto, as I quoted earlier. Buildings much better exemplify the theme on which Priuli elsewhere harps, that hedonism and indulgence have undermined the State; he could not sustain his complaint on the evidence simply of investment in land. If the fashion for buying land and for building villas was a single phenomenon, then it certainly cannot have been profit-led.

If, after the Wars, certain people made money out of land, they made money out of new, that is, reclaimed, land rather than from buying and selling old land in a rising market. Alvise Cornaro, 'spokesman' of *agricoltura*, made his money in this way, as he said himself: 'I have always had since my first youth a natural inclination towards agriculture, and knowing it to be a just, holy and noble profession, I set myself to practise it, and I do not regret it because, by the grace of God, by this means I have brought home a great deal of honest wealth. The reason is that, since the main profit of this science is the conversion of unprofitable land to profitable, the lands that I had that were unprofitable I brought back into cultivation, and buying more I did the same thing. When some of my neighbours saw this, they took me as a partner in a great quantity of marshland they had, where in a short time I made them see that, contrary to the common opinion, which believed it to be uncultivable, it was easy to work, because I recovered part of it and got the rest to such a condition, that in a short time it was recovered. And in truth the agriculture of reclamation is a real alchemy, witness the fact that all the great wealth of the monasteries and of several private citizens has been made by this means.'

Land reclamation, rather than improved yields per unit of land, was all the accent of sixteenth-century agriculture. It was surely stimulated as a result of the Wars, in which much damage must have been done to existing dykes and watercourses. In the flat region of the Po valley, where so many rivers have their outlet, land could easily revert to marsh, but also could be drained without great difficulty. On almost every large estate on the plain there must have been one or more marshy areas. The method used (also by Cornaro) was to erect dykes and to lay drain-traps (*botte*), in which the drained water could be held while the watercourses were high; when the level fell they were emptied, and in this way progress could be made. Other sources confirm that in the region where Cornaro was operating, between Padua and the Venetian lagoon, there was good land, but recurrent problems with flooding. Those had even been compounded by the action of the Venetian government, which, just before the Wars, had dug a new canal to carry the discharge of the Brenta further to the south, towards Chioggia, in order to prevent silting in the central part of the lagoon: the canal tended to flood whenever wind or high tide held back the water, 'to the ruin of Padua' it was said. Under such conditions the land more often than not could not be sown in spring, and only with an inferior cereal when it could. Obviously, if it could be protected from flooding, so that it could be planted with wheat, the land would be worth more or would bring in more. The reclamation Cornaro advocated (which others were already practising, and many on a large scale) had become so widespread that in 1545 the government created a magistracy in order to regulate the new schemes of irrigation everywhere being initiated – certainly among most of Palladio's patrons as well. It was soon after allowed to lapse, but was reinstituted in 1555, and Marcantonio Barbaro, among others, was elected to it.

As I quoted him, Doge Contarini, looking back from the following century, dwells on the benefits of the land improvement achieved in the sixteenth. It is estimated that about one quarter of the Veneto was uncultivated at the beginning of the century, and of that more than half was rendered arable in the course of it. Not all of it, however, was reclaimed by draining: some was deforested, and one of the main reasons for the creation of a supervisory body in 1555 was abusive enclosure by land-owners of common land. In general, Alvise Cornaro's pamphlets vin-dicating land improvement reflect a widespread trend, which took some time to be sanctioned by the Venetian government. It must only be said that sources all over Italy speak of an improvement in prosperity in the countryside in the middle of the century, and if 'the den of some beggar' is found transformed into the 'lodging of a good family', that is largely due not to some new economic ingredient but to the effects of peace after devastating wars.

The second, but a less significant and also more traditional means of improving yields, also practised by Alvise Cornaro, was in one way or another to manage one's tenancies better. The basis for land tenancy was either rental, paid in money or kind or both, or sharecropping, whereby the tenant paid in kind between a half and a third of the yearly produce of the land, including not only the cereals grown in the fields and grapes or wine but also firewood and brushwood; there were often also various *honoranze,* such as hay for the landowner's horses, a ham, a pair of chickens, and so on, and not least the cartage to where the landlord wanted it, which was the tenant's responsibility. It was to store such *entrate,* or payments in kind, that the landowner needed ranges of outbuildings adjoining his villa. It was observed that Francesco da Porto built his new villa at Thiene specifically in order to cope with his enormous *entrate.* Of the two kinds of lease, sharecropping was the more profitable to the landlord: Cornaro, acting for the Bishop of Padua, set out to convert all rentals to sharecropping terms, and many landowners were among those who rented from the Church at less than going rates. A cash rental gave the tenant greater scope, for instance to sell his produce in the city market (if, as a country bumpkin, he could avoid being cheated); it also gave him the means to greater security, because, although he had no other defence against the landowner's right of eviction, if he had made improvements to the property the landlord was obliged first to refund him for them. It was the money Cornaro wanted up front from the Bishop to buy out his tenants' improvements that was the bone of contention between them — and the reason why the tenants remained on their old terms and the returns did not rise.

Although the burden on the sharecropping tenant seems high, the yield to the landlord could also seem low, if it achieved a value of only around one or at most two ducats per *campo,* as seems not unusual. Of course, should the landlord decide to improve the land, the tenant could grow crops of a better quality. Wheat, from which the bread of the rich was made, naturally fetched a higher price than other cereals, such as sorghum, spelt or millet, from which the peasants made either not such good bread, or *polenta;* but wheat required better land. A crop new in Italy in the sixteenth century, and well suited to the watery plain of the Veneto, was rice, to which, among Palladio's patrons, Marcantonio Sarego decided to convert, first having the entails annulled and then selling one of his four estates (to a Venetian) in order to invest in another which had the necessary water. (Maize, which is or used until very recently — until soya — to be ubiquitous in the Po valley, was hardly known at this date; though first recorded under cultivation in the Veneto in 1554, it was established as the ideal crop for the Po valley only in the seventeenth and eighteenth centuries.)

Landlords would also achieve higher yields if they could ensure that the size of the tenant's parcel of land was the optimum for his own and his family's labour, and if they could put in so-called 'good' tenants. Cornaro wanted to get rid of 'very poor' peasants, above all because they had no animals with which to work the land, but also because their plots were unworkably small: there was little scope to vary or rotate the crop and such tenants would tend to die of diseases induced by malnutrition in bad years. 'Good' tenants, however, were not so easy to find, and would not be attracted unless, again, the landlord contributed in order to keep the estate in good order. Cornaro's near neighbours, the brothers Garzoni, in their villa at Pontecasale, complained that 'because of the great damage done by the water the wretched labourers have been unable to achieve anything or find any way to work, therefore we have been forced to make courtyards and barns and to divide up the land into small allotments, through not being able to find good workers'. It was pointless simply to

Plate 45
Autumn: the vintage, drawing by Lodovico Pozzoserrato (Fitzwilliam Museum, Cambridge). While Bacchus, against the tree in the foreground, presides, life in the villa proceeds behind him: the *entrate*, the vintage, are brought in to be processed (the grapes are being trodden) and stored (vatted) in the landlord's porticoes. The landlord comes down to pay a visit; an underling doffs his cap.

grind down the workers: the ideal tenant was healthy and prosperous, a point upon which the agricultural manuals insist.

Thus the landord had to reckon with the tenants' demands for the maintenance and improvement of the fabric or property, so that money was always going out as well as coming in. However 'good' the tenant, between landowner and those who doffed their caps to him there must have been suspicion: according to some, the landowner must always be alert against 'robbery', and he could seldom afford to trust even his factor. On the other hand, others like to paint a picture of cosy co-existence, and the manuals suggest that his staff should be induced to become well disposed as well as respectful towards the baron, whose nobility anyway demanded that he be 'always kind, loving and generous', as Agostino Gallo has it – while remaining of course remote, never familiar, and never lax. There were obvious advantages in having loyal able-bodied men around you, should you wish to settle a dispute by violence, for instance, or smuggle (avoiding *gabelle* or city-gate taxes), a constant practice of the nobility.

In practice, most landlords' intensive *agricoltura* was probably limited to the land of their own residential villa, to a holding of perhaps 40 acres like that of the Barbaro at Maser. Only there could the owner see the crop through from seed to fruit personally; otherwise, although the landlord registered what he was doing, it seems generally to have been up to the tenant to take the decision and act, so long as all were well. The landlord would make his presence felt only at harvest time. Agostino Gallo in his manual has his protagonist recommend that the patron give the tenant his seed, and stipulate in the contract each thing the tenant should do throughout the year; but his interlocutor says he has never heard of such detail in contracts, though, yes, it seems a very good idea. In fact it might simply have created trouble, disturbing much of the leisure in which Gallo's dialogue is rosily set.

With little doubt, the most effective means to increase returns was believed to be to speculate, though here the manuals fall silent. Speculation, according to many, was the direct cause of the famines recurrent throughout the sixteenth century, and it was extremely widespread. The landowners, as a more or less coordinated body, would withhold their grain in order to drive up the price. Although the Venetian government soon made it illegal to withhold more than a proportion of the harvest, imposing quotas, most proprietors were prepared, nonetheless, to underdeclare their harvest, to fail to fulfil their quota, to ship their grain across country to other markets where the price had climbed (chiefly to Venice, but also outside the state altogether, which was doubly illegal) and in every way do all they could to thwart and defy the Venetian governors' attempts to ensure an adequate local supply and to prevent inflation. The *podestà* of Verona in 1558 had to recuperate at a spa after his term of office, 'principally by reason of the grain, about which matter I have had so many impediments and obstacles from the wicked citizens of Verona; I had to have their corn brought into the city by force of arms'. This was after two successive bad harvests, when there was such great shortage that he feared riots. His experience was typical: what the landowners would like is 'perpetual famine', commented another, and their resistance to the rectors' attempts to prevent starvation in the region under their command was callous and bitter. In times of bad harvests, which were frequent enough, prices would rocket. On the other hand, the nobleman would not make a killing unless he had achieved, against the trend, a good harvest, and to that, it is quite clear, his art of *agricoltura* did not extend.

The motivation to undertake 'agriculture' in the sixteenth century seems simply to have been the pervasive idea that money should 'work', but applied now to land. From immediately after the Wars, there was a long period during which the economy was put back where it had been, and then that seems to have continued, invisibly, into an attempt to make everything more efficient. To squeeze a better percentage from the land would mean a heavier input of management. Andrea Dolfin's 4 per cent from land was a banker's money, unmanaged; perhaps if he had gone to the farm himself he could have got more. He might have believed he could, anyway. The proverb that 'the eye of the owner enriches the soil' or the equivalent was endlessly quoted. It was perhaps true only up to a point. Many of course turned to *agricoltura* not because they thought it, objectively, a good avenue of profit, but because they had nothing else they could so well exploit. 'They have no "industry" of any kind, and those that are gentlemen even consider trade shameful', wrote the Venetian *podestà* of Padua in 1548; 'the only "industry" they have is to hoard their corn in their granaries as much as they can, and to yearn that they could get a *scudo* [coin] for every grain, and this is one of the things that makes the people hate them'.

No wonder that Palladio recommends (QL II, xii) that his patrons build beside a river, 'because the *entrate* can be transported at any time and at little expense into the city on boats' — putting first things first; he goes on to add, of course, that the water will be useful for other things, for the animals to drink, for the staff to use in the house, and for the peasants and labourers to irrigate the fields, gardens and *brolo*. One may doubt that 'agriculture', as Cornaro claimed, always brought an 'extremely honest income', even by his own comparison to making war, or that, with all its conspiracies and evasions, not to say problems of management and worries about the weather, or crop disease, or locusts (in 1545), it was less stressful than trade over sea. For the Venetian Garzoni at least farming was a ceaseless struggle, taking up, they imply, much more of their time than was desirable; requiring them to keep a house in Padua, so frequent was the call on them even out of season; they speak of the 'travails' their *possessioni* cause them. Ideas that farming led, by contrast to other means of making a career, to a long, peaceful and satisfying life derive more from Horace and other classical authors than from reality, although for many it may have been a matter of pride to believe them.

15

Splendour and Magnificence

The attachment to agriculture became stronger as the concept of nobility hardened and its rules and taboos became codified, and as conversely there came into being a palpable prejudice against 'merchants', that is, anyone involved directly in manufacture, shipment, retail and shopkeeping. That did not prevent the assimilation of such people into the nobility or ruling class but no doubt it slowed it and required them to relinquish the means by which they made their fortune. By the beginning of the seventeenth century both the Venetian and Terraferma nobility crucially lacked first-hand, 'shop-floor' (or ship-deck) experience (several knew it and said so). They no longer owned the ships, warehouses and industries at home and abroad which their fathers may not have created but had inherited and continued to manage; what they had was now entrusted to others. Agriculture became the only 'art' and sometimes the only occupation of a *rentier* class. More and more the nobility became like those described in Padua in 1548, who had no 'industry'; nobles like those in Vicenza at the same period, 'extremely rich both in property and in cash, which they do not leave idle, but keep employed in various businesses ...', became fewer. Vincenzo Scamozzi in his *Idea dell'Architettura* of 1609 advances no other motivation for building villas than the inducement they provide to the owner to visit his land, and so obtain a higher yield. But there was rather more to Palladio's villas than the task of overseeing.

Palladio's villas were built as an extension and manifestation of their owners' nobility, as honorifics. The 'frontispiece' that distinguishes Palladio's villas was designed to express 'magnificence'. Palladio remarks (QL II, iii) that the very worthy knight Giulio Capra, gentleman of Vicenza, was preparing to build a palace not out of any personal need, but to provide 'an ornament for his city'; and the result was to be as honourable and magnificent as the gentleman's 'spirit' deserved. That was for a town house, but the idea that a man's house reflected his *animo* was commonly expressed (Doni had said it of Federigo Priuli), and town and country houses were alternative residences, equally gentlemanly.

The expression of magnificence on the one hand and the avoidance of demeanment on the other were two sides of the same coin. Both ideas are humanist, having been found in Aristotle: somewhat reinterpreted, the Aristotelian distinction between 'free-born' activity and the work appropriate to slaves underpinned the Renaissance belief that 'mechanical' work was ignoble. Both attitudes were partly at least newly crystallized, and are an aspect of what is called the 'neofeudalism' of the sixteenth century. Although the gentleman in the country might like to pretend to live the simple life, piping beneath the broad fronds of a beech like Tityrus in Virgil's *Eclogues*, he would no more do so in reality than he would plough a field with Cato or Cincinnatus. His homes were as much a part of his external dignity as his clothes, his table, his plate, his feasts, funerals and weddings, his animals, and the gifts he bestowed. And his external dignity was all his dignity (for which the age has been condemned). Just how much so is vividly revealed by the large dossiers in which persons wishing to gain entry to a city's Great Council (that is, gain noble rank) or even defend their place there were minutely scrutinized. The kind of damning evidence adduced might be, for instance, that a man's grandfather had been seen handling the cloth in his shop (which a gentleman might own – but he was not to work in it) and, most ignobly, serving someone, even if it was only while his staff had their lunch-break. Or, in another case, that an ancestor had demeaned himself and his blood by himself taking out their lunch to the peasants working in his fields. In a third, still more extreme case (though it dates from late in the seventeenth century), it was debated whether a branch of the Sperandio, an undoubtedly noble family of Padua, had permanently infected themselves in the previous century when they had become not merely impoverished, but reduced to working their land themselves. It had once been recorded that Giovanni Antonio Sperandio had 'walked behind his horses and animals', and the judges summed up: 'Can one better describe a peasant in vile exercise? Here is the proof that Giovanni Antonio senior was ... a peasant. If he had said, "Because I was going to see my horses and animals", one could give him the benefit of the doubt, assuming that he had gone to inspect them to see how they were treated by the hind or servant to whose custody they had been entrusted, but he says, "Because I was walking behind the horses and animals" ...' Giovanni Antonio's grandsons were therefore denied a place in the Great Council.

Social position and status were intimated not so much through 'symbols' as directly and instantly, not only by numerous appurtenances but by gesture and behaviour, and by clothing, for instance. In yet one more case it was held against a claimant for nobility that his forebear, as an artisan, had had alternative 'Sunday best' and ordinary clothes, which would be quite unbecoming to a nobleman, who dressed in finery on every day of the week. It was not, therefore, merely a scholastic habit of mind that made architectural writers, including Palladio, begin by categorizing houses according to the rank of the habitant. When Palladio and other writers talk of the 'magnificence' which is appropriate to a nobleman, they mean something as essential to his status as a uniform – even if sensitivity to architectural magnificence was particularly quick in Vicenza.

Behind the expression of magnificence lay long tradition. Ultimately it goes back to that essential quality of any claimant to chivalry, generosity. It was ignoble to be stingy – though it was foolish to be prodigal, and prodigality was further censured (particularly by merchants in communes, who tended to be 'anti-feudal') as luxurious and wasteful. The Florentine chronicler Giovanni Villani, describing in the fourteenth century a phenomenon just like that described by Priuli at the end of the fifteenth, and again alluded to, less ingenuously, by Contarini at the beginning of the seventeenth, took the dim view: 'There was no citizen,' he says, 'noble or common, who did not have a "possession" in the countryside, and who had not built or was not building at great expense much bigger buildings than in the city; and everyone sinned in luxurious expenditure, so that they were held to be fools'. Priuli also believed his contemporaries were throwing their money away, but this, if one took the other view, is what magnificence was, conspicuous, pointless and luxurious expenditure. During the fifteenth century, whether or not under the sway of the pendulum setting back towards 'neofeudalism', luxurious expenditure gradually found defendants, who took their cue from Aristotle: a great man should have worthy state, that is, conspicuous consumption was a sign of inward quality. Alberti, whose *Della Famiglia* belongs to the first half of the fifteenth century, is either softening the ground or skirts cleverly around ground already soft: he divides expenditure neutrally into 'necessary' and 'unnecessary' expenditure, and the latter in turn into 'reasonable' or 'foolish'. It is reasonable but unnecessary to spend on pleasures, and he lists 'painting the loggia, buying silver plates, magnifying yourself with pomp, clothes and giftgiving' and 'gentle' pleasures such as 'beautiful books, noble horses and such like desires of a magnificent and generous mind'. Suchlike desires would surely include rebuilding the loggia – such as the loggia Rucellái by the Rucellai palace in Florence, which Alberti himself designed? For Alberti expenditure both unnecessary and 'foolish' (under which Giovanni Villani, earlier, would have included building) was to keep at home snakes and even worse animals – meaning tigers, asks an interlocutor, as if keeping a menagerie, an amusement that only princes could afford, were meant. No, vicious and lying hangers-on and calumniators, is the reply, presumably a veiled reference to priests or friars.

At the end of the fifteenth century the Neapolitan humanist and courtier Giovanni Pontano, writing an essay *On Magnificence,* significantly refined the concept, declaring that true magnificence, as opposed to mere expenditure, should have something permanent about it – like the remains of antique Rome. He felt that 'in our age' Cosimo de' Medici 'had imitated antique magnificence, by building churches and villas and by founding libraries'. He also mentions the Medici town house but gives preference to the Medici villas for their 'singular magnificence'. Though he lists other modes of magnificence, including weddings, funerals, giftgiving, hospitality and keeping fine animals, architecture has taken on particular importance. Pontano also wrote an essay *On Splendour.* Splendour included two favourite Renaissance pastimes, collecting gems and precious stones, and making villas and gardens, about which Pontano is particularly revealing: 'We also want [the prince of a state] to have gardens, in which he can take exercise by walking, and in the right weather hold banquets. These gardens will be laid out ingeniously and becomingly with exotic and rare shrubs (among which topiary work in myrtle, box, citrus and rosemary is recommended), and not at all in the same way as the garden of a thrifty merchant. A great addition to such splendour will be villas, not those, however, of "rustic" type, but "urbane" and magnificent. For it is important that a great man's furnishings should be splendid not only in the city but also in the country, lest, whenever he should wish to withdraw from city business, he should seem to move as it were from light into darkness. Since furthermore he will even in withdrawal require amusements and spiritual refreshment both for himself and for his companions, and for any who, on a visit or for any other reason, come to stay, to avoid any diminution of his splendour, he will make provision beforehand of fish and game, and also flocks of peacocks, pheasants, partridges and other birds, not to mention nets and hunting dogs, and anything else which can affect the mind with decent pleasure, and restore flagging spirits. He will not only feed his household well and splendidly, but he will also have, as the phrase goes, many from the highways and by-ways to share his table, and just as stale broth ill becomes silver dishes, so the bowl of a prince spurns common cabbage. Therefore, as his table must gleam with silver and gold, so it should have a splendid dinner on it. And let it seem that he has prepared all this more for his guests than for himself, although he should keep within limits in this as in other matters (lest we should appear to bring everything down to carnal pleasure).' Pontano goes on to allow the prince himself to dine rather modestly while others feast, so long as he does not do it grumpily, and tells a story of Lucullus, that byword for

Plate 46
Villa dei Vescovi, Luvigliano, Padua. Though it lacks a temple front, it has
pompous staircases, and there is no doubt about the grandeur of the villa, an
imposing building on an imposing site. In the courtyard there are also
magnificatory triumphal arches. The site was already the country seat of the
Bishop of Padua in the fifteenth century; Alvise Cornaro undertook its rebuilding
about 1535. The design seems to have been Cornaro's, although he employed
a supervising mason, Andrea da Valle, who continued work there after Cornaro
had left the Bishop's service.

extravagance, who ate magnificently even when alone: when that was
queried by his steward, he replied, 'What? Is not Lucullus coming to dine
with Lucullus?' Thus, even purely selfish indulgence could be justified as
noblesse oblige.

Pontano distinguishes between 'rustic' and 'urbane' 'villas'. In his *Della
Famiglia* Alberti similarly distinguishes between a modest kind of country
holding, but entirely adequate – where, as he says, if you bought a quarter
of salt you could feed your household all year round – and grand country
houses, 'which are rather lords' palaces, and have the form more of
castles than of farms ["villas"] ... superb edifices, and excessively "ornate"'.
Palladio's villas (so called) belong to the 'castellar' tradition, being primarily
the country palaces of lords, and only secondarily farms – of course castles

have always had farms attached, too; that is, his villas were pretentious buildings. They are not always understood in this way, however, for the matter is complicated by an alternative tradition, that the countryside was 'humble' as opposed to the 'pomp' of town. Therefore Pontano and many others insist as it were against the drift of expectation that country villas were not rustic huts, but palaces.

In the Veneto, there was immediate precedent for Palladio's buildings in the villa at Luvigliano remodelled by Alvise Cornaro for the Bishop of Padua (Plate 46). Luvigliano was hailed in 1544 as a model of its kind: 'Who wants to build a palace fit for a prince, though outside town, let him go to Luvigliano, where he will gaze upon a lodging fit for the habitation of a Pope or an Emperor'. It was, as I say, built for a bishop; Palladio's villas, which are not smaller, were built by the same rate of inflation for the nobility but in princely style. The model for the villa at Luvigliano was the villa built by Cosimo's grandson Lorenzo the Magnificent at Poggio a Caiano, though Luvigliano lacks the temple front which appears for the first time at Poggio (Plate 47).

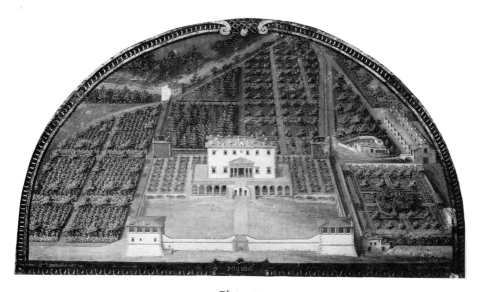

Plate 47
Villa Medici, Poggio a Caiano, Firenze, painting by J. Utens (Museo Topografico, Florence). Giuliano da Sangallo's design for Lorenzo the Magnificent was an entire rebuilding, more thoroughgoing than Cosimo de' Medici's villas, which were by comparison adaptations. He combined the exterior temple frontispiece (housing the Medici arms) with an interior central great hall soon decorated with classical antetypes of Medicean achievement.

Contemporary proof that Palladio's villas expressed noble magnificence is the categorization of Anton Francesco Doni's *Le Ville*, written shortly before 1557. Doni divides his country houses into five kinds, 'villas', holdings, 'possessions', houses and huts, respectively for princes, who take pleasure in them, gentlemen, who own them, merchants, who buy them, artisans, who rent them, and peasants, who work them. Merchants buy them with cash when they make a coup, to take their days off in them; only artisans, according to Doni, have villas for another reason altogether, that is in order to save them money and feed their family. The thrift of Alberti's prudent Florentine businessman, extolled in *Della Famiglia*, and the uncastellar villa have been demoted. Doni explains: 'Our princes, in order to be able sometimes to withdraw from the roar of the crowd, make for themselves "in villa" fine "villas", as for example, the Duke of Tuscany's villa Castello, the Coppare at Ferrara, Marmirolo at Mantua, the villa Imperiale at Pésaro [for the Duke of Urbino], and many others. These villas are situated far or near to the city, as their lords may decide, and they are made so fine, rich and convenient out in the countryside that there is no difference between them and palaces or town residences.' Doni adds acerbically that he has nothing to say about the villas of the ancients, 'which many talk and write about in confusion', and which are so much air; and anyway, he jibes, they are not comparable to lordly villas of today because the owners of ancient villas would dig with their own hands. Nevertheless withdrawal from the roar of the crowd is a classical sentiment, if also a 'neofeudal' one: the Horatianesque 'PROCUL ESTE PROFANI' (stay hence uninitiate) is written above the door of Palladio's villa Godi.

Doni's specifications for a first-class villa are as follows: 'The first, the noble villa, is for a king, duke, or powerful and mighty lord, and there is no difference between this "outdoors" house and his "indoors" [or town] house, as the following model will show. Imagine with your mind's eye a space a hundred yards or more across and long, a square like a piazza, but longer, the size of a racecourse, to make a good jousting run, with room for spectators, or a football pitch: that, I think, ought to be the plot for a lordly building.' (It may be difficult to imagine a racecourse for horses only

Plates 48a and b
Villa Badoer, Fratta Polesine, Rovigo: views of the front overlooking the court and of the back overlooking the enclosed garden. For the back in the *Four Books* Palladio designed a second temple front and set of threefold steps, which are missing, but otherwise the villa as built corresponds closely to the woodcut. A high wall divides the garden from the *brolo* and the fields that stretch away in this flat land at the mouth of the Po; the main front of the house still looks on to the canal before it.

a hundred yards long, but Doni is alluding to Pliny, who had a hippodrome in front of his villa; tournaments, however, were popular in the Renaissance.) Doni continues: 'At one end I would like a fine palace to which one mounted by a stair of three sides, all of the same breadth, in a good style and showing variety, like that in the Laurentian Library [by Michelangelo]; from this people would arrive at the top beneath a stupendous colonnaded loggia, and walking or sitting there they would oversee the entertainments and games which would take place at the ground. From this first space, to which one mounts by eight or ten broad and convenient steps, there are to be at the side the apartments, consisting of honourable rooms, magnificent halls, *anticamere* and convenient studies, all a joy to see — rooms, I mean, that are absolutely what they ought to be, and according to the design of a prudent architect such as Palladio of Vicenza.' Even if Doni had not mentioned Palladio, a villa of Palladio's maturity, such as the Badoer, would spring to mind (Plates 48a and b): the Badoer has similar steps, the space in front and of course the 'stupendous colonnaded loggia'; the Badoer, being built, is a little smaller, but other designs in the *Quattro Libri* could match Doni's dreams also in scale.

As Doni goes further inside his ideal princely villa he continues to recall Palladio: 'Below this first floor there are to be wine store, kitchen, wells and storage rooms, with "secret" steps for the coming and going of the servants administering to all and to the lord who lives there. In the middle of the loggia I mentioned there will be a great portal, leading into a vaulted hall, which portal is matched by another similar door, through which one arrives beneath another similar loggia, behind, where one can withdraw in the greenery [looking out on the garden], dine, sup, and walk about.' In the Badoer one passes through the hall to look out on the garden, though it has no temple front at the back — in reality; it has in the *Quattro Libri*. For what Doni goes on to say the villa Barbaro provides a parallel: 'Then in line from the door matching the first there will be a high trellis, thick with delicate grapes of every kind; this will be "barrel-vaulted" rather than flat; beneath it a man walking in the shade will be led, along a path of a decent length, that is appropriate to a lordly garden, till he arrives at a little hill, covered over, like a secret wood of trees and fruits.' In the Barbaro, the garden interlocking with the house and the 'barrel-vaulted' trellis (in Veronese's lost frescoes) correspond. Doni goes on to describe at length a garden with an extraordinary variety of sweet-smelling plants, with a maze, a grotto, two fish ponds (one for big fish, the other for little) and *giochi d'acqua*.

16

The Villa within the Villa

The countryside was where peasants lived, and the kind of building 'appropriate' to the countryside was a hut. There was undoubtably a paradox in having a countryside house that was not rustic. Furthermore, going to the country was strongly associated with withdrawal from 'civil' things, therefore with moving from pomp to simplicity, from business to pleasure, from society to solitude. Going to the countryside looked like retreat, for which almost invariably in the fifteenth century and still in the sixteenth people would apologize and find justification. Even Doni has to say that 'these [regal] villas are made so fine, rich and convenient out in the countryside that there is no difference between them and palaces or town residences [such as one might expect]'.

The paradox was the reality, but I do not mean to ignore what amounts to a double paradox, the pretence made by noblemen of 'going rustic' when in the country. It has been seen that in the *Four Books* Palladio implicitly transferred to villas certain values and virtues that were properly 'civil', and that Annibale Caro's 'leisure with dignity' involved a similar transference. Each had their own reasons: Palladio was introducing stately architecture though in the country, Caro was justifying an alternative way of life outside institutions. Others, however, for instance Bartolomeo Taegio, defended spending most of their time on their estates more simply and less truthfully by direct attack on the 'evils' of 'the city' or by stressing their opposite, the value or pleasures of rusticity. For both of course there was abundant classical precedent, for the former chiefly the Roman satirists, Horace, Persius and Juvenal, for the latter Horace again and Virgil's *Eclogues* and *Georgics*, or Ovid's lines *'Beatus vir qui procul negotiis ...'* (Happy the man who far from *negotia* ... ploughs his father's land.)

For noblemen who were still noblemen (unlike the unfortunate Giovanni Antonio Sperandio of Padua who walked behind his animals), to pretend to be living a life of rustic simplicity in the country was simply a lie. In practice few quite lied, but rather took the Horatian line of moderation, eschewing the luxury and perturbation of 'the city' but permitting them-

selves a few choice comforts, above all their books. There is a representative
example in a letter from the aged Bartolomeo Pagello, a leading Vicentine
intellectual of the later fifteenth century, addressed to the Great Council
and declining to take on the kind of embassy that Giangiorgio Trissino,
too, in his old age, would find irksome. Pagello writes: 'I hear that there
are some who disapprove of me because I stay in the country and till my
fields, although agriculture has always been valued and held in the highest
honour, and many great men, Hesiod, Virgil, Cato the Elder, Marcus
Terentius Varro and Diophanes in a letter to King Deiotarus [quoted by
Varro] and others have studiously written about it and extolled it. This
was the life led by the first men, before cities had been founded, with
country simplicity and pure habits. This same life was that of the earliest
Romans, when those who, often, were to be great, having been elected
generals, consuls or dictators, were summoned into the city from the fields
to take up their magistracies, which finished, and justly and vigorously
executed, they hastened to return to agriculture. Again to the tranquillity
of this life King Attalus and the Emperor Diocletian resorted, abdicating
kingdom and empire. Therefore without envy I bid farewell to you with
your problems and worries and ambition and your civil, that is to say,
uneasy duties; leave me to this happy and blissful life, which you like to
call lazy and inactive.'

He says more of the context of this happy and blissful life in another
letter, written to a friend in Padua: 'I beg you finally for the sake of our
friendship that you permit me to build a villa at my beautiful Monticello —
I do not mean with the great expense Pliny the Younger went to in his
Laurentinum ...', and he describes Pliny's villa's more extravagant and
polysyllabic appurtenances, 'But that I should build the villa which suits
my state and provides honest pleasure. It is enough for me, if a single
portico rising only two steps leads out from the courtyard to my pleasant
orchards. On each side there should be rooms, nothing elaborate, but only
as convenient as they need to be, and beside the part where I sleep let
there be a choice enough collection of books.' What is revealing, is that
Pagello also models his modesty on the younger Pliny, at the point where
Pliny, having described his evidently vast villa at Laurentinum, says that
his 'true rapture' in it is a garden apartment 'where I seem to retire even
from my villa'.

The nature to which the Renaissance nobleman retreated was similarly
a kernel in the centre of a much larger nut, the apparatus of his rank,
status, duty, position. His 'simplicity' required a trained household, his
'tranquillity' depended on the smooth running by others of his estate. That
was all the evocation of primitive man or of Adam — who, delving, first
practised *agricoltura* — amounted to. Pagello goes on to confess in the same

Plate 49
Casa di Petrarca (Petrarch's house), Arquà Petrarca, Padua. Petrarch was given
the house by Francesco Carrara, ruler of Padua, to enjoy for the last six years of
his life (he died in 1374). While Petrarch's more celebrated country retreat at
Vaucluse near Avignon is lost, this house (and his tomb in the church down the
hill) was not forgotten in the Renaissance period; nor were Petrarch's attacks
on 'the city' and praise of a life of contemplation, ideally in a quiet
country retreat.

letter that he could not be content 'with the barrel of Diogenes the Cynic or such a meagre diet as his'. The 'natural' was simply what he found to be enough.

Another tradition which Renaissance landowners liked to usurp was that of the ascetic in the wilderness. Had not Plato withdrawn to Academia outside Athens, where he had conversed in the groves beside the river? Citing Plato's example St Jerome had retired to the 'desert' and after him numerous 'desert fathers' and western Benedictines, and then in the rising Middle Ages the Cistercians and Carthusians, Abelard, St Francis of Assisi and Petrarch. The 'desert', it should be understood, though it might encompass a few token rocks, was a wilderness or uncultivated place rather than an arid one in medieval and Renaissance interpretation. Petrarch, as he wrote from his 'desert' which was also an orchard at Vaucluse near Avignon or later from the vineyard given him by the lords of Padua at Arquà, was conscious of both traditions, classical and Christian, religious and secular. Christian hermits and pagan philosophers both rejected world-liness, reverting to simplicity, and both lived in caves or huts or at least modestly and soberly. What both sought in the countryside and found was solitude, or what today would be called privacy. There was a close connection established in classical times, continuing unchanged through the Middle Ages, and hardly broken during the Renaissance, between hut and study, between cabin and cabinet, between the inner rooms or sequence of rooms where the great could withdraw and the only privacy the poor man could find, in the open countryside. Simply by being alone, a Renaissance nobleman could envisage his villa as a study and his landscape as a desert, and himself as a sage.

According to yet another convention, nature was a woodland alive with satyrs and nymphs. Petrarch again and Boccaccio had given glimpses of such a visionary countryside, animated sometimes fleetingly, sometimes for longer, by figments of their eroticized imagination. They had begun to combine or to substitute for medieval conventions of sexual fantasy the country gods or 'half-gods' of classical mythology, which occasionally became the protagonists but more usually formed the chorus of Renaissance pastoral stories. Renaissance pastoral was generally informed, not by classical pastoral such as Virgil's *Eclogues* but by the figures of Ovid's *Metamorphoses* and the entourage of such gods as Bacchus and Diana, as they were incidentally mentioned in literature or represented in art. Sannazaro's *Arcadia*, the story of a visit to a place where all these creatures lived, definitively transformed the Petrarchan tradition in which the lover sobs and dreams alone with his visions in the countryside into a kind of a peepshow, in which the lover has only to sigh to be surrounded by a host of fluttering and dancing nymphs and lascivious fauns. Something of the compulsion of the fantasy is conveyed by the celebrated *Concert champêtre* traditionally attributed to Giorgione in the Louvre (Plate 50). It represents, in the twinkling of an eye, the appearance of two nymphs to two youths singing and playing, youths who may be shepherds in pastoral convention but not shepherds like the real shepherd who appears in the backdrop landscape bottom right, actually driving sheep. The hirsute appearance of the youth without an instrument perhaps shows him to be distraught; if so, it is surely from love. One of the nymphs, pouring water into a well, is a water-nymph, a Naiad, like those declared so frequently to inhabit the rivers beside villas and grottoes in their gardens; the other, joining in the shepherds' music, may be a Dryad, a forest-nymph, representing the murmur of leaves in the sylvan wind as they respond to

Plate 50

Concert champêtre, traditionally attributed to Giorgione (Louvre, Paris). The music the young men play and sing is so beautiful that the nymphs come out to listen or join in – that is the principle of this pastoral allegory painted in Venice probably about 1510–15. It seems to convey perfectly the enhanced sensibility which poetic Renaissance gentlemen liked to feel in their gardens and orchards throughout the sixteenth century.

the sentiments flung abroad by a desperate lover – or perhaps an Echo, the would-be suicide's constant companion. Both have been evoked, or allegorically made material, by the feeling in the music the youths play. In the same way, poems often assert that the nymphs rejoice in the villa they visit, and precisely such figures, in stone, physically inhabited gardens.

Easily the villa could take on the charm of a little room that is an everywhere, just so long as it is a small room. It was essential to the pastoral convention that it was a 'lowly' genre, and its 'humility' was so closely interwoven into the formulae of incantation that it had to be protested time and again to make the poems efficacious. But they were no more than a spell, a game like the game of pastoral itself, which involved no change into realistic costume by its shepherd performers. On the contrary, they strutted and swooned in silks. Similarly, Palladio's villas were a benign refuge, kind to fantasy, soothing to the nerves and delightful to the senses, but palaces nonetheless.

PART 4

Architecture

17

The Anatomy of a Villa Farm

Exerting that particular charm that belongs to the Venetian Early Renaissance, unique, intact and fascinatingly transitional, stands the villa, or Castello, Giustinian in Roncade. Roncade is in the Trevigiano, about 12 kilometres east of Treviso and 20 kilometres due north of Venice, by mills and a bridge over the river Musestre. The village, though still overshadowed by the mighty villa, or castle, has suffered in the twentieth century: there is a roundabout where once there was the market square, and some of the Renaissance porticoes which lined its main street were recently destroyed. Most of it remains, however; furthermore, the gaps among the buildings that have survived can be blocked in, and the plugs flushed out, by old maps and photographs, in particular by an informative map dating from 1536, soon after it had been completed (Plate 51).

Probably early in the fifteenth century, a branch of the ancient Badoer family of Venice, who owned considerable property and the mills in and around Roncade, built a house overlooking the heart of the village. How long they had been there is not known: someone else had owned the castle reported there in the Middle Ages, and Venice had annexed the area only in 1389. In the 1490s, Hierónimo Badoer's inheritance passed to his sole surviving offspring, Agnesina. She had earlier married another Badoer, who had died some time before; then she married, in 1497 or 1498, Hieronimo Giustinian, whose family was no less ancient and who afterwards became a Procurator. It was surely the influx of money occasioned by the union of these two families already well endowed that encouraged the pair to undertake a new villa. Agnesina's arms appear as proudly on one side of the main gate as Hieronimo's on the other, and of the two she was the richer. They did not adapt the existing house, which still stands beside the villa, though it has been refurbished; once the villa had been built it was let and became an inn. Instead they built the villa on the adjacent land to the south (Plates 52a–c). More than possibly this was where a castle once had been, but at this date it can only have been a ruin, long uninhabited, and not enough to inspire or influence the form of the

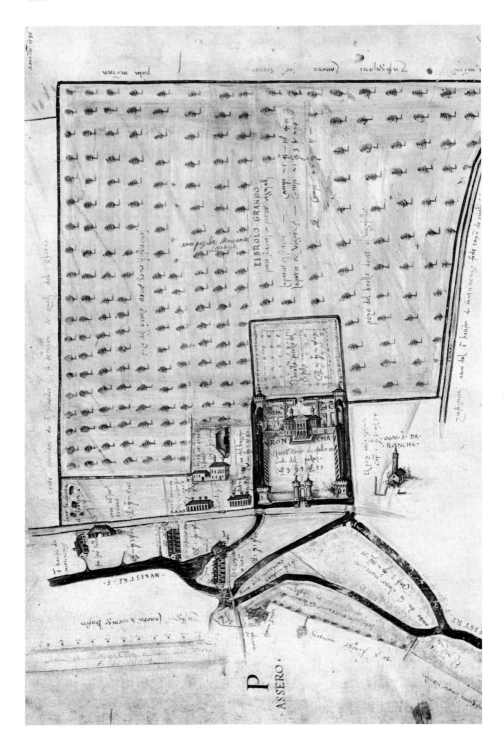

Plate 51
Map of the village of Roncade, Treviso. The map dates to 1536, when the villa
had just been built, but the topography it reveals is virtually unchanged today.
Both the villa Badoer-Giustinian with all its towers and walls and (beside it) the
former house of the Badoer family (in 1536 an inn and today an ironmonger's
shop) survive; so also do the porticoed outbuildings of the old house, which are
detached in the medieval way but are ranged before it symmetrically in
Renaissance spirit.

new villa, or castle. It was considerably bigger than the old house, as one
can see from the 1536 map, showing beside the new building and its court
the original house and its own court. It is not certain when the new house
was completed. In 1514 Hieronimo Giustinian and his wife were still living
in the old house, while 'next door the court (*cortivo*) with its different
habitations is still not yet half done'. The continuing wars can hardly have
hastened the building works. We hear that in the summer of 1522 their

Plate 52a
Villa Giustinian, Roncade, Treviso, seen from the front gateway. It is one of
many buildings of the period for which no known architect can even be
suggested, though generically it belongs to the tradition established by
Mauro Codussi.

Plate 52b
Villa Giustinian: view of the court (*cortivo*) from the upper loggia, looking
straight down towards the entrance gate.

son Leonardo spent a period of quarantine at the villa after a trip to Africa,
but we are not told whether he stayed in his father's old house or his new
one. However, the villa was definitely finished by late August 1529, for
then Cardinal Francesco Pisani, Bishop of Padua, had called in on his way
at the 'villa, or castle, of Hieronimo Giustinian the Procurator'.

It emerges from the 1536 map that the village was virtually an adjunct
of the house: the blacksmith, for instance, was living in one of the porticoed
buildings in front of the old Badoer house, and which must have been
built for it, since they are symmetrical to it. The map shows nothing else
except Badoer-Giustinian property, though notice is given round about it
of neighbouring landowners and tenants. Groups of buildings are marked,
for instance 'seven little houses and plots' and their measurements; also
some of the mills; a sand quarry; marshy land; the blacksmith's house; the
house, orchard and plots given over to the wheelwright; south of the
castle, the 'piece for the church' and the church. Later in the sixteenth

Plate 52c
View of the court (*cortivo*) from the upper loggia, looking to the right (towards
the former Badoer house): the tower serves to this day as the factor's house,
and the grapes were being crushed in the portico beside it when the photograph
was taken. Also the little garden corresponds to its position on the 1536 map.

century, if not earlier, the parish priest was living in the tower of the castle
nearest to the church, and there are remains of a pious fresco, of the
Madonna, still in the tower. The former Badoer house with its orchard
and plot of land is now marked as an inn; close by, between the inn and
the castle, is a 'yard [*cortivo*] for baggage', presumably connected with the
large tent behind the inn – a military installation?

The map also gives a little anatomy of the new house itself, which
consists clearly enough of a villa in the middle, but is called a castle since
it is surrounded, as it remains to this day, by battlemented walls and four
large towers. In front of the villa, facing the road, is the courtyard or
cortivo, though it is not called that on the map, but only 'the plot where
is the Castle and the farm of the palace', with its measurements. Though
no more than a wall runs between the gates and their flanking towers,
along each side there are outbuildings, or *barchesse*, with open porticoes.
The garden is also marked, beside and behind the *palazzo*, and divided

from the *cortivo* by a low wall. From the back gate one passes into the *brolo piccolo*, an area about the same size as the *cortivo* in which the villa stands; this in turn opens on to the *brolo grande*. The *brolo* or *bruolo*, the plot of land that directly serves the house, was commonly given over as an orchard, but fruit trees, according to the map, occupy only the northern part of the *brolo grande* of the villa Giustinian; the other part was under vine. It would not be let, but worked by labourers. Not here, but in many cases it would be surrounded by a wall, which usually would also run all round on either side of the house to the portal giving entrance at the front.

These then are the main elements of a villa, recurring time and again: the house (*casa* or *palazzo*) with its court in front and its garden and *brolo* behind; then also varying other buildings, often called 'habitations' generically, which may be houses or *barchesse*. Houses range from unspecified *case* to little houses, *casette*, which would be for labourers, and bigger houses, *casoni*, which would be for the steward and the factor. Labourers, tenants or staff also commonly inhabited one end of a *barchessa*. *Barchesse* are long buildings resembling barns, blind on one side but open in part on the other; for much of their length they simply roof a large area, to which there is access through a high portico, but at one or both ends they will be divided into two or sometimes three storeys, in order to provide living accommodation, or storage for material that must be kept dry, or both. Thousands exist in the Veneto, many of them built during the Renaissance period, though few are earlier; they are a necessary adjunct to any villa, but many were built far from the villa, beside the fields they serve. Some that formerly belonged to the Giustinian have survived, a few miles away out in the country in the fields the Giustinian owned: these outlying pieces of land were more usually scattered than not, in a variety of tenanted units. In 1536 the Giustinian owned nine such holdings, seven of them within the parish of Roncade, two outside.

There were also other kinds of farm buildings, such as a *teza*, deriving from Latin *tectum*, a roof, and meaning a building for dry storage, for instance hay, wood or grain, though there were the words *granaio* and *fienile* for buildings to store grain and hay respectively. *Teza*, unlike *barchessa*, can be translated as 'barn', but the attic storeys of a villa, which very commonly served for the storage of grain (Plate 53), could also be called *teze*. Both *teze* and *barchesse* could house animals, though the stable-block, *stalle*, of a larger establishment might be differentiated. The *barchessa* could also contain a canteen or *caneva* for the wine — or two, one for vinification and the other for the storage. All these buildings or part-buildings, including the main house, constituted the *cortivo*, which meant therefore rather more than the court in front of the house: hence Hieronimo

Plate 53
Villa Pojana, Pojana, Vicenza: the upper storey, serving in the first instance as a
granary — the windows are flush with the floor — but in the second as
accommodation: notice the fireplaces. From the windows one looks down on to
the farmyard beside the villa and its *cortivo*.

Giustinian declared in 1514 that his *cortivo* was not yet half built, meaning
the whole villa complex.

The *cortivo* was the nub of the villa. As the area round which the
'habitations' were ranged, whether loosely or symmetrically, it was a yard,
but a court rather than a yard, and certainly not a farmyard, which is a
more lowly, not to say muddy and smelly place; the expectation runs from
Vitruvius through Petrus Crescentius's medieval work on agriculture to
Palladio that the patron will wish to avoid any such indecorousness. The
cortivo had also to serve as a place of reception: the visitor would dismount
or the owner mount in the court before the house. One would attempt to
keep it clean (Petrus Crescentius recommends that the gate to it and path
through it are not set central but to one side, in order to minimize muck,
and the advice was followed). Since keeping it clean was probably not so
easy, there is a separate raised paved area in front of the villa Giustinian
which would serve as an island or pontoon; similarly Sansovino's villa
Garzoni and Palladio's villa Emo have a long shallow ramp in front instead

of steps, on to which one could ride and then dismount on the dry. Next, since the owner had to manage and check the rent in kind due to him from his many tenants, the court had to receive the *entrate* and its buildings had to house them, and often also to process them. The grapes had to be crushed, the corn to be threshed, and the owner would like to oversee that, but the threshing-floor, though within sight of it, should not be too near the house, for fear of the dust, as Palladio acknowledges (QL II, xiii). The Giustinian perhaps used the court of their old house, when the tent had gone; usually in Palladio's and other contemporary villas there is a second court, with a threshing-floor or serving as a farmyard proper, where the animals might be brought. There is a second court, for instance, at Palladio's villa Badoer at Fratta Polesine; according to Palladio's commentary (QL II, xiv) the porticoes and outbuildings of the *cortivo* were for houses for the factor and steward, for stables and for other appropriate things.

According to Vitruvius and to Renaissance writers, including Palladio, it was important that provision for storage and for the keeping of animals took account of the sun and of the winds. The patterns architectural writers created in disposing the different buildings round the compass seem to fall somewhere between common sense and an ideal and unnecessary neatness; Palladio himself keeps his injunctions to a minimum, to keeping the grain and hay out of the sun and open to a cooling wind, and more recurrently to diverting unwanted smells away from the manor house. He does not give the points on the compass on his woodcuts or remark on orientation on his notes to his buildings.

Both the older Badoer house at Roncade and the newer Badoer-Giustinian 'castle' already show the tendency towards symmetrical organization that would become so important a feature of Palladio's and Palladian villas. Its pivot was not the manor house itself but the *cortivo*, the interface between the owner and the world. That fact seems to me to make a little more intelligible Palladio's statement that 'the buildings for the matters of the farm should be constructed having in mind both the produce and the animals, and should be conjoined to the owner's house in such a way that he can go everywhere under cover'. He would wish to preserve his noble dignity even while undertaking the necessary tasks of managing and checking. Otherwise Palladio's villas, however imposing, hardly dominate their *paese* or village more than the villa Giustinian dominates Roncade, or other earlier villa complexes their villages: the Porto villa at Thiene is located even more centrally in what is rather a small town. The villas Porto and Giustinian, of course, are castellar, while Palladio redesigned the *cortivo* under the inspiration rather of classical temple or bath complexes; but its walls obviously anticipate what Scamozzi called the 'arms open to a complete body' to left and right, where they were best disposed, according to him, for surveillance. Certainly at the villa Badoer in Fratta Polesine the factor and steward were prompt at the gate.

18

The Anatomy of a Villa House, before Palladio

The main house of the villa Giustinian is again an illuminating as well as beautiful example of the elements and the pre-existing order which Palladio took over and further rationalized. Its plan is remarkably simple, but its symmetry and simplicity were new, replacing something less clearly conceived and less constant, though one can pick out recurrences in earlier building. Subsequently during the sixteenth century, though remaining symmetrical, villas developed in more complex forms.

Some writers have attempted to trace back the morphology of the northern Italian Renaissance villa to a nuclear form, the so-called 'Venetian house', consisting of supposed twin 'towers' flanking a loggia in between. The classic example cited is the so-called Fondaco dei Turchi (Turkish trading-house) on the Grand Canal in Venice, originally however a private palace. But there was no 'model' form on which the builders of Renaissance houses made variations; instead, practical considerations created what amounted to a common bias or standard solution – a few recurring functions and a few recurring building practices were coordinated in a few typical arrangements.

Instead of 'tower' and 'loggia', it would be better to distinguish two kinds of room, respectively open and closed, cool and warm. In Italy, it is pleasant to have a broad, cool space, providing both shade and air, but it is also necessary to have a room or rooms immune from the elements, capable of being heated and of being kept dry. Such rooms have to be small, and, as a protection against damp, on the first floor rather than the ground. Or, to put it in Palladio's words (QL II, ii): 'Another thing that makes houses "convenient" is that the rooms for use in summer are large and spacious, and turned to the north; and those for winter should face south or west, and should be smaller than the others, because in summer we seek shade and breeze, and in winter sunshine, and small rooms are more easily heated than are large ones.' Combining the two requirements, one arrives at a narrower more vertical building resembling a tower and an adjacent more horizontal portico or loggia or gallery. In fact these are standard constituents equally of the town house, the villa and the *barchessa*. Small establishments amounting to no more than this existed and a few still do; very thick walls and the remains of a Romanesque window in the masonry of one wing of Palladio's villa Gazotti suggest it incorporated an older lodge or tower, while the matching wing was entirely new. If the smaller rooms are arranged on each side of the gallery, one has the so-called 'Venetian house' type — but that is only one possible precipitation of a more nebulous, less specific requirement; it does not mean that all other permutations derived from this one.

Houses suitable for a gentleman's habitation, whether constant or inter-mittent, as opposed to the dwellings of servants, factors or tenants, were called *di stazio* or *per stanzare* in Renaissance documents: that is, they were houses for staying in, as opposed to other accommodation less suitable. The term suggests the presence of at least one *stanza*, a room larger than a *camera* but not a hall. It is a loose term, but *stanza* may be defined as a gentleman's living room: therefore it would not be encumbered or degraded by any function, such as sleeping or eating, and would be suitable not only for the daytime residence of the owner but also for any company he might have. Whether or not it was the only such room, it would be flanked by smaller rooms, some, such as the oratory or kitchen or lavatory, with predetermined functions, others, the generic *camere*, for varying use, as bedrooms, lumber-rooms, study, anything. A *stanza* would be well lit and well positioned, therefore set on an upper floor, for two reasons — for greater coolness, light, cleanliness and generally insulation and withdrawal, and so that the owner might observe the street, landscape or courtyard and be informed or diverted by any movement in them.

Granted the provision of such a *stanza* on an upper floor, basic statics demand the equivalent below, so that the upper internal walls can rest on lower internal walls and not on a void. One could divide up the space underneath with cross-walls, but there were advantages in having a second large room below, for vestment and divestment, carrying in and carrying out, receiving groups of people, depositing things. It was a hall. It could also serve as a dining room in the event of a large indoor gathering. One could transact business in it with visitors of a lower class whom one would not wish to invite upstairs or into a private room, or one could mix in it with the rest of the household as one would not do upstairs. Of course it would need an entrance, which statics or symmetry would align with whatever opening there might be above. So again these requirements would gel in the so-called 'Venetian house', as a typical solution, not as a necessary form (Plates 54, 55 and 56).

In the course of the sixteenth century palaces grew larger and more spacious, and one finds a large *sala*, then several *stanze* also quite large and

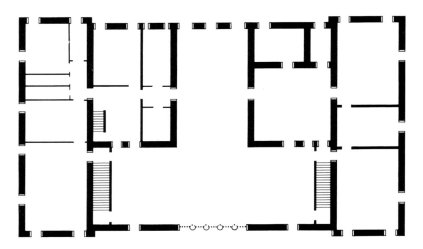

Plate 54
Plan of the villa Porto, Thiene: both downstairs *entrata* and upstairs *sala* are T-shaped (see Plate 4 for the exterior and Plates 59a and b for the interior).

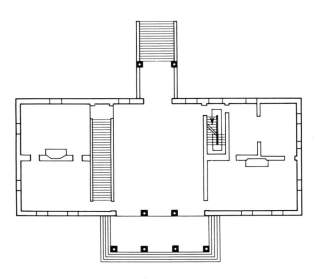

Plate 55
Plan of the villa Giustinian, Roncade: both downstairs *entrata* (almost completely unenclosed at one end) and upstairs *sala* run straight through the house.

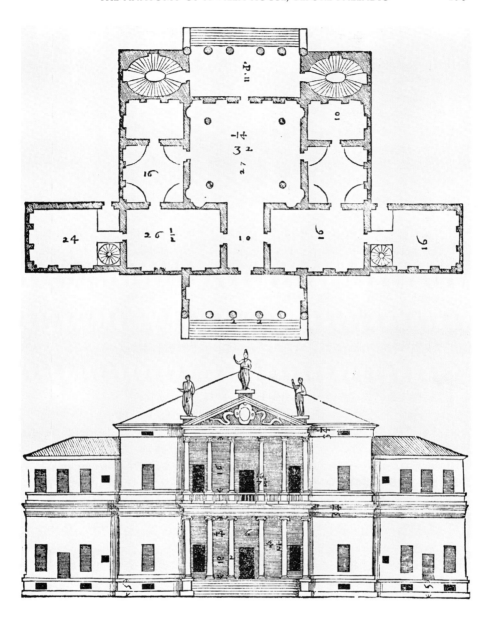

Plate 56
Plan of the villa Cornaro, Piombino Dese (from the *Four Books*, II, xiv). Palladio's
interiors are in one sense merely so many variations on the 'Venetian house' T-
plan. A diaphragm wall divides the *sala*, which in earlier houses had
communicated directly to the outside, into vestibule and atrium.

Plate 57
Palazzo Pisani (Fondaco dei Turchi), Venice, in an old photograph taken before
restoration. The building is assumed to date to the middle of the thirteenth
century. Its cramped arches with their heavy archivolts are of Byzantine
derivation.

then *camere* and still smaller *camerini*. The development antedates Palladio
but he pushed its evolution forward and codified it. Before the sixteenth
century there was usually a single *stanza* above, a hall or portico below,
and then smaller rooms. The greatest variable was the way the main room
opened on to the world. It could be lit along one long side, and backed
by smaller rooms; smaller rooms could also be provided abutting one or
both ends of the loggia or gallery. Alternatively, the main room could be
lit at each small end and be flanked along its long sides by smaller rooms;
it would be correspondingly darker and cooler and less airy though no
less spacious. From early on the alternatives were combined in a T-shaped
plan, in which the bar of the T opened out into a loggia or large, multiple-
light window, while the stem ran back into the house, opening at the other
end in a smaller window.

    These various dispositions occur, of course, in both town and country.
The Fondaco dei Turchi (Plate 57), of the thirteenth century though heavily
restored in the later nineteenth century, is an example of the 'loggia' plan,

uncommon in the city, though others of later date exist in the country. Where the main room, extending across almost the whole façade, gave way at each end to smaller rooms, there is visible a slight interruption in the rhythm of the windows, marking the abutment of the cross wall inside. It preserves its original two storeys (the usual height of palaces until the Renaissance) except at the corners where 'towers' were added in the 'restoration'.

The Fondaco dei Turchi, incidentally, should not be associated with the Fondaco dei Tedeschi, which was purpose-built from 1505 as a *fondaco* for German traders in Venice and resembles a palace not at all. The place is massive, resembling instead the corn exchanges of northern Europe. Its largest rooms, which served as dining rooms, were placed in the wings, not in the centre; most of the rest of the building consisted of goods units, *botteghe*. The wings, as it happens, were once topped by little towers, known not as towers proper but as *torricelle*; they had no known purpose except to display the Lion of St Mark, and have no correspondence to palace design since they are smaller than the wings (the cross walls do not run up into them). However, before they were demolished they seem to

Plate 58

Palazzo Valier, Venice (now lost), in an early eighteenth-century print by Luca Carlevarijs. The long window frontage is unusual; it may be relevant that the palace was situated on the outskirts of the city, in the then largely undeveloped Cannaregio district.

have inspired the spurious, nineteenth-century towers on the Fondaco dei Turchi.

But the Fondaco dei Turchi may be compared with the lost palazzo Valier in Cannaregio in Venice (Plate 58), of which Francesco Sansovino remarked in his guidebook of 1581: 'The *salone* is numbered among the largest in the city'. Presumably it ran all the way across behind the fourteen lights of the central window, and perhaps extended back into the house in the centre as well. The central upper attic with its gable and volutes was obviously added later, but since all the other windows are Early Renaissance, the palace may be no earlier than fifteenth-century. It may also be compared with the Porto house at Thiene, built between 1441 and 1453. The Porto house also originally had only two storeys, except that the wings rose to three, making 'towers'. The upper part of the house was crowned by battlements (still visible beneath the rooflines added in the sixteenth century); similar crenellations top the walls that enclose the house and its *cortivo* and gardens. The building altogether was meant to have a castellar air, and therefore the wings were made to resemble towers – a new fashion, not a conservative medievalism. The later, Early Renaissance palazzo Negri beside Palladio's palace for Marcantonio Thiene in Vicenza also has battlemented towers.

Inside, the villa Porto has an enormous *sala* upstairs and a corresponding hall downstairs both in T-shaped plan (Plates 59a and b). The hall opens into a five-arched portico, but the central windows above are only as wide as the stem of the T behind them. At the back, the house was not quite so symmetrical, since the flanking windows on the first floor differed on each side. That has been compounded by sixteenth-century alterations, but was probably there originally and was due to the different functions of the two halves of the building: on one side were the owner's private apartments, on the other offices, storage and utility rooms. One can find similar asymmetry elsewhere: the late fifteenth-century Casa dall'Aglio at Lughignano sul Sile, Treviso, has mezzanine floors and corresponding windows on one side and not the other, and hall below and *sala* above, though they align with each other, are not placed in the centre of the building.

Plates 59a and b
Villa Porto, Thiene: *entrata* and *sala*. Both rooms have the same T-shaped plan. The *entrata* below is open through an arcade to the garden, and is closed at the rear (the stem of the T). The *sala* above is lit by a large window at the front and a smaller one at the back. Behind and above the pictures now hanging traces remain of frescoes, which should be those said to have been painted by Veronese but are evidently not: here the remains of a frieze of playful putti can be seen.

The system of a *sala* over an *entrata* (as Palladio calls them in QL I, xxi) flanked by smaller rooms is a significant common denominator of fifteenth-century houses in the Veneto. It not only creates a formal symmetry, increasingly desirable as Renaissance ideals took hold, but also was produced by a straightforward building procedure: the house is divided inside by two cross-walls, running from front to back. The cross-walls determine the point where the façade divides into middle and sides, or block and wings (or 'loggia' and 'towers'); the caesuras of the external façade invariably correspond to the internal abutments of the cross-walls. (Where the *sala* is T-shaped, they align with the outer ends of the bar of the T, not with its stem.) It could reasonably be claimed that the main function of palace façades was to inform the onlooker of the size and nature of the owner's great room, the essential constituent of a house *per stanzare*.

The *sala* or great room seems to have become notably greater in the Renaissance. The *sala* for instance of the villa Porto at Thiene is truly enormous, larger than would be comfortable to live in. It was patently a reception room, for 'representance' and, as Palladio says of *sale* (QL I, xxi), 'for entertainments, for banquets, for the staging and recitation of comedies, for weddings, and similar recreations; and therefore these rooms should be much bigger than the others'. Whether or not Serlio built a stage within the house in 1539, both the hall below and the *sala* must have been thronged with guests; the *sala* had in fact to serve as what later would be differentiated as the ballroom.

Except that it has no towers (though still plentiful battlements) the villa Giustinian has a similar disposition, modified in two respects which herald sixteenth-century developments. Neither *entrata* nor *sala* is T-shaped, but both run straight through the middle of the house, flanked on each side by two large rooms (*stanze*) placed one behind the other. Instead, both the main and garden fronts had protruding loggias (of different design; that behind has long since been removed, but traces are clearly visible). They are nonetheless still close to the old type of plan, since the width of the loggia is governed by the internal cross-walls, even though rather awkwardly as a result an extra balcony has to be provided in order to give access to it from the stairs. The projecting loggia of the villa Giustinian seems to be the earliest such to survive in the Veneto; it obviously anticipates Palladio's temple fronts, since it is crowned by a pediment. Also the basement on which the Giustinian stands is one of the earliest to appear in the Veneto, but was to become standard in Palladio's villas. The combination raises the question whether there may not be some influence from central Italy, where earlier villas, like that at Poggio a Caiano for the Medici, had previously had temple front and basement. The Giustinian has further not only a basement but also a third floor, of the kind that was subsequently introduced at the Porto: both loft and basement, surely, were provided in order to free the *entrata* floor, as well as the *sala* floor, for the exclusive use of the owner. This is something that Palladio later stated to be desirable (QL II, ii), but evidently did not invent.

The provision of a basement had important consequences affecting the whole of the rest of the building, and not least differentiating country houses from town houses, for which an entrance and hall on street (or canal) level remained indispensable. In town houses in the sixteenth century the system of dual *entrata* and *sala* was generally maintained (even though mainland houses commonly also had a basement or semi-basement serving as a wine-cellar). In villas, the *entrata* often disappeared, and steps that spread out before the entrance would convey the owner or visitor over the utilities straight into the *sala*. However, since it was the first room one entered in the house, the *sala* had also to take on some of the functions of the *entrata*, but this it easily could do, since the number of large residential rooms, or *stanze*, at the same time multiplied. So it was that the 'Venetian house' system, consisting of an *entrata* giving access by stair to single main room or *sala* from which one entered smaller *camere* usually only for domestic use, gave way to a new dispensation, consisting of a stair giving direct access to a *sala*, from which one gained a series of rooms *per stanzare*, off which there were then also smaller *camere*. In a word country houses ceased to conform to the 'Venetian house' system in the sixteenth century, though it remained the best solution in the town. It may be added that as a corollary the entrance staircase took on new importance, epitomized by Doni's idea of installing Michelangelo's Laurentian Library staircase before his ideal princely villa. Through Serlio and Alvise Cornaro Bramante's staircase designs, particularly the alternative concave and convex stairs he had used in the Vatican palace, had been disseminated; Palladio used them in the designs for his early villa Pisani at Bagnolo, and later he experimented with various schemes closer to those of Michelangelo.

Alternative dispositions began to supersede the 'Venetian house' type, still clear in the Giustinian, before Palladio's career began. Few villas were built or substantially rebuilt in the 1520s, or even in the 1530s. However, at Treville near Castelfranco, Treviso, the villa belonging to Federigo Priuli, described as new in 1533, now lost, is recorded not only by Doni but also in a plan and elevation by Vincenzo Scamozzi. Like the Giustinian, it had an attic and a basement, and two large rooms on each side of the central *entrata* and *sala*; but the *entrata* and *sala* were T-shaped after the old fashion, the *portego* opening out into a broad arcade of nine arches, and therefore there was no projecting loggia. The whole house was correspondingly broad, and no deeper than the short sides of two rooms.

Another, surviving example is the broad-fronted Garzoni at Pontecasale, Padua, designed by Jacopo Sansovino (Plate 60). So imposing as almost to be bleak, the villa is set on a high basement with a batter; the equivalents of *entrata* and *sala* are both set broadside, opening on to *stanze* on either side but behind on to a courtyard, above the basement. The courtyard is really the *sala* of the villa. It is enclosed on two flanks by wings and on the rear by a pierced wall. Except at the rear, it is lined by a portico, off which rise the main stairs; the stairs give on to a terrace above the portico, overlooking the courtyard and providing the only access into the upper central front room. Since the villa was designed by the Florentine Sansovino probably early in the new career he began in Venice in 1527, its unprecedented (and unrepeated) features can reasonably be put down to the influence of central Italian palaces (perhaps the Medici villa at Careggi, or the cloister-like garden, now lost, formerly attached to the palazzo Venezia at Rome, or many town houses with internal courtyards); however, evi-

Plate 60
Villa Garzoni, Pontecasale, Padua. Half of the house is either in the open or unenclosed – though this is perhaps more striking today since so many doors, windows and arches in villas that were originally open have been glassed or otherwise closed or made closable.

dently the brothers Garzoni who commissioned him already felt the 'Venetian house' type inadequate, and in particular required much more space for 'representation'. The Garzoni had no great influence on Palladio's villas, although Palladio's late villa Sarego at Pedemonte, Verona, similarly has or was to have porticoes and galleries round an enclosed courtyard and correspondingly no very dominant *sala*.

Though its site and plan are different, Alvise Cornaro's villa for the Bishop of Padua at Luvigliano, Padua (Plate 61), has similarities to San-sovino's villa. Unlike the Garzoni on the plain, the villa 'dei Véscovi' (of the Bishops) is delightfully situated on its own hill amid the Colli Eügánei, but its massive basement and several open terraces and loggias are com-parable, also its style of heavy piers. Both houses have a *cortivo* before them while the farmyard and its outbuildings are clearly separate beside it; the *cortivo* at Luvigliano is further adorned by inscription-bearing triumphal arches, one of which leads nowhere but to a vision of the valley towards Padua. On Luvigliano there is more clearly Tuscan influence, from

Plate 61
Villa dei Vescovi, Luvigliano, Padua. This is an important early use in northern Italy of multiple staircases in order to impart grandeur to a building, though the stairs were partly dictated by the site. The building is very much a viewing platform.

Plate 62a
Villa Godi, Lonedo di Lugo, Vicenza: side and front. Although the long front
contains the loggia and bears the owner's coat of arms, the entrance at the side
was also for the owner and visitors, since it opens to a staircase that delivers
the visitor straight to the *sala* (contrary to what appears in the *Four Books*). The
stanze are of uniform height and have flat ceilings, but are enlivened by an
extensive series of frescoes.

Poggio a Caiano, the villa built by Giuliano da Sangallo for Lorenzo the
Magnificent (see p. 169). Otherwise it has, inside, a 'Venetian house' plan,
but the existence of the central hall running through the building is not
apparent from the outside; it opens at each narrow end into two great
loggias that run the full width of the building, unfolding its delightful
views.

 The villa Godi, which Palladio designed probably about 1537, more
closely resembles villas from before the Wars than any of these just
mentioned (Plates 62a and b). It is also quite distinct from the main series
of villas on which Palladio began work about 1540. It still has the bare
walls and unframed lines of a fifteenth-century villa, as if it were to carry
painted friezes or even frescoed pictures between its doors and windows.
Its mass is unarticulated: it has, for instance, no entablature-like band
running along the top of the façade 'like a crown', as Palladio himself puts

Plate 62b
Loggia in the front of the villa Godi. The loggia with the Godi coat of arms
above (on which the imperial eagle reveals the owner's rank of count) constitutes
the villa's 'frontispiece'.

it once, or any classical order applied. To the mature Palladio, that was evidently a defect, for he introduced into the *Quattro Libri* woodcut an emphatic string-course delineating the basement (Plate 62c). He also altered the proportions, and in a later design some of the services and offices which such a large basement provides would perhaps have been extruded into the outhousing, so that the main block could be more vertical and more compact as it is made to appear in the woodcut. However, in keeping with the tendency shown by the villa Priuli or the villa Garzoni, the villa is divided nonetheless into basement and *piano nobile*, and it spreads, in order to provide not only a *sala* but also a large number of *stanze*.

Its major novelty is the *sala*. The whole house centres on it: not only the front steps lead up to it through the loggia, but also an old-fashioned

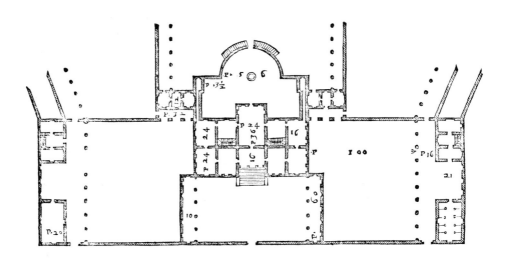

Plate 62c
From the *Four Books* (II, xv): the transformations Palladio has introduced thirty years after the villa was built serve chiefly to simplify and emphasize the different elements making up the building.

long tunnel-like straight internal stone staircase gives straight on to it from a door at the side (as well as probably, originally, a wooden servant's staircase on the other side). As in other houses, the *sala* runs through to the back and here even protrudes slightly, by the same measure as the setback of the front loggia; uniquely, though the arrangement would become standard in Palladio's work, the *sala* rises above the height of the surrounding rooms. It was originally lit at the back, above the present 'Palladian' window or *serliana* which was installed later, by a semicircular 'thermal' window. Before it was blocked out (in order to give scope to Zelotti's frescoes) the upper window must have filled the room with light, air, amplitude in an effect then novel. There is, however, no variation in the rooms which flank the *sala*, of the kind Palladio later introduced, each being the same height, and all middling.

Concatenations of such innovations profoundly altered the design specifically of villas during the first half of the sixteenth century; town houses continued along more traditional lines, although their aspect, particularly their façades, also altered. By 1550, although it had continued vigorously until then (for instance, the villa Querini, now Tiozzo, near Dolo on the Brenta river), the 'Venetian house' stereotype had virtually expired. However, it bequeathed a heritage, though not a constant or an absolute one: a tripartite division of the house, imposed by the walls partitioning the central *sala* from the flanking *stanze*, remained a ready solution — just as it had done, and for the same reasons, before the 'Venetian house' system had become universal. Palladio, it is true, is inconstant to it, but such a sound structural principle was integral to his philosophy, and he never strayed far from it. Most of his palaces, whether town or country, have two partition walls running through straight from front to back.

19

Palladio's Plans and Elevations

At some time while he was under the tutelage of Giangiorgio Trissino, perhaps after his first, brief journey to Rome in 1541 and certainly before his longer stay from 1545, Palladio produced a series of drawings which look to have served as a kind of presentation portfolio. Most show villas; all have the same format, showing the front elevation above and the ground plan below, in the manner adopted by Serlio for the series of books on architecture which he had begun to publish in 1539. Although none of the drawings corresponds exactly to any one of Palladio's villas of the 1540s, the villas built closely relate to the villas drawn. The likely patrons to whom Palladio circulated the drawings might have chosen an appealing design, which Palladio subsequently adapted in response to the exigencies of the site or to their preferences. These patrons ranged from the members of the Vicentine nobility with whom he was or would be most closely connected, such as the Thiene, to Venetian patricians, such as the Pisani, to ambitious men of lesser family such as Taddeo Gazotti (see p. 53); all the villas, however, went up in the immediate vicinity of Vicenza and Palladio's portfolio would have circulated no further.

The moment was well timed, not only because confidence and the economy were picking up, and there was interest in agricultural improvements, but also, surely, because there was a need felt for new forms. The old, Early Renaissance style of northern Italy was clearly exhausted: only greater bejewelment could enliven it, and even so it failed to provide scale and grandeur. New standards were being set by Jacopo Sansovino's Library in St Mark's Square, which was begun in 1536; around this time Serlio and several other central Italian artists, including Vasari in 1541, had travelled up and found commissions in Venice. 'Classicism', so to designate the style forged in Rome before its sack in 1527, was felt, however dimly, to be required. If there had not been that wind of change, it is unlikely that Palladio's radically untraditional designs would have been taken up; even so, while their monumentality was welcomed, there was a tendency to moderate their bolder effects.

In his designs for villas Palladio retained, indeed emphasized, the basic hierarchy of the old dispensation, the old units of habitation. There was a *sala* at the centre of the house, and *stanze* opened off from it symmetrically. There was a clear sequence of more public, central rooms, from which more private, smaller rooms led off. But if the formula of the 'Venetian house' type persists, its variables vary greatly: the rooms are of different and novel shapes and sizes and vaulting patterns, the *sala* is a lofty and echoing 'thermal' hall, and the typical central large window of the first floor has been made into a classicizing frontispiece. There also appear such consciously antique devices as the use of apses to close off the short sides of a room. In earlier examples, including his own villa Godi, the *sala* had been preceded by or opened on to a loggia; Palladio habitually came to provide a vestibule or corridor preceding the central *sala* proper also because, again, it made the house seem more Roman. Vitruvius describes a Roman house as an arrangement of so many parts corresponding to different functions, some of which – such as the *palaestra* or exercise-ground – might easily be left out; but the core of the house was not one room but a sequence of three rooms, the *vestibulum*, the *atrium* and the *tablinum*. Though Palladio does not reproduce that sequence, he reproduces Roman sequentiality, so to call it, imitating if not the individual units of the transition at the least the transition.

Daniele Barbaro translated Vitruvius's *vestibulum* (VI, v) in Italian as *entrata*, and he explains it as follows: 'In ancient times those who wished to build with greater splendour used to leave in front of their doors an open space, which was not part of the house, but which certainly led into the house. In it "clients" and those who had come to pay their respects to the great would stand until they were admitted; there, one could say, they were neither inside the house nor outside it. This place was called the vestibule, and was of great dignity and adorned with loggias and "spaces". Its virtue was to be a thoroughfare, its use to be somewhere commodious to wait, and its delight that the young, while awaiting their elders, could play with a ball, or wrestle, or skip, or other such juvenile activities.' In so far as it was a play area, the vestibule resembled the Renaissance loggia (which was for taking the air and passing the time, according to Palladio); it was also customary to do business in a portico or loggia, as is proved by legal documents from the Renaissance stating that they had been drawn up in such places. In the *Quattro Libri* (I, xxi) Palladio explains 'of loggias, *entrate, sale* and *stanze*' that 'these loggias serve many conveniencies, such as taking the air, eating and other recreations ... Apart from that every properly designed house has in the middle and best part of the house certain rooms on to which and with which all the others open and communicate. Those in the lower part of the house are usually called *entrate*, and those above *sale*. They are like public places, and the *entrate* serve as the place where people wait for the owner to come out for them to greet him, and do business with him; and they are the first place (other than the loggia) that presents itself when one enters the house.'

Both after Vitruvius and following tradition, Palladio's houses invariably have public and private areas, and were designed with the idea that one passed through the former to the latter. The intended sequence is almost always revealed in the details of his plans, for habitually he marked in the jambs of each doorway on which side the door would hang and therefore which way it opened: it hung on the wider, cut-back side (the narrowing of the jamb on the other side prevented a draught), and naturally would open into the room one was entering, while one had to pull the door towards one to go out again. One finds invariably that all the doors of the *sala* open off it, and that the doors from these adjoining rooms open again into other ones. Since Palladio's houses are usually tripartite, on entering centrally one would expect either to proceed through the house, or to turn to the left or the right into one or other of the two sets of private apartments. It seems to have been normal, though Palladio says nothing about it (but Doni, for instance, states it as a desideratum, and it was certainly an old aristocratic custom), that husband and wife had separate apartments. Other things being equal each would have one side of the house. Quite frequently, however, Palladio's houses (if only the larger ones) were built for two brothers and therefore for two households; even more frequently they were begun for a father and finished for all his sons together; at any rate the use of individual *stanze* was not, as it only came later to be, preordained. One cannot subdivide the functions of a Palladian villa much further than into 'public' areas (*entrate, sale*), 'private' areas (*stanze, camere, camerini*), and servants' quarters. Thus Barbaro (on Vitruvius VI, x) urges the modern commissioning paterfamilias, recognizing what he needs, to tell the architect, 'I want so many rooms and "habitations", so many for me, and for my wife, so many for my sons, so many again for the servants, and so many for "conveniency"'. The architect would not then go away and design so many sitting rooms, so many dining rooms, so many bedrooms: he would provide one or more *sale*, so many *stanze*, and so much space for the servants, probably in outbuildings.

Although functionally quite rudimentary, the principle for which I ventured the term 'sequentiality' is fundamental in many ways to Palladio's architecture. The principle could also be called spatial variety: the villas sustain a subliminal interest as one enters from room to room because in each the environmental change is so complete. Or one might say that by contrast to the architecture of his predecessors, which was static, Palladio's was transformational. Basically, he operated a system of large, medium-sized and small rooms, so that as one went from room to room the light and sense of enclosure was constantly modified; the different ways in which the rooms are vaulted, and the fact that they have curved covings, rather than flat ceilings rectangular to the walls, contribute greatly to the effect. The different vaults are each noted in these drawings, as they are again later throughout the woodcuts of the *Quattro Libri*. It was also important that the contrasts between the rooms, as one moved from one to another, were not too striking, that the sequence was not too violent, lest one become disorientated, losing one's sense of a continuity; and that within any one room relative height, length and breadth did not vary too extremely. That devolves to Palladio's insistence on the proportional relationship within and between the parts of a house. His insistence on proportions is in turn inseparable from his classicism as a whole, since the rules of classical architecture are all rules of proportion. So, too, the relative and internal proportions of the rooms of house are another important aspect of Palladio's 'sequentiality'.

However, Palladio does not make so much of proportions as is often assumed. They had for him no symbolic force (except what they might take on in the special context of a church), and it was not important to him what exactly the proportions of a building were, so long as it had proportions, or seemed to have them. Obviously when the classical orders were applied they were to be applied correctly and without distortion or 'abuse', but literally the orders were applied, on to a predetermined spatial disposition. When it comes to ratios of height to length and breadth, Palladio in the *Quattro Libri* (I, xxiii) gives several different figures, and does not say that any one is intrinsically preferable to any other: instead, he refers to the architect's 'eye', his judgement, and to necessity. He surely agreed with Daniele Barbaro, who in his commentary had delved at longer length into the rules given in Vitruvius, and had stressed that the architect must know geometry and 'perspective', but at one point (VI, ii) takes to task 'the arrogance of many, who measure many members and many details in the ruins of Rome, and finding them not to correspond to the measurements given by Vitruvius, deprecate those, saying that Vitruvius did not understand the matter. But they, reproducing the details they have measured in what they build, out of their place, and proceeding always in the same way according to their strict rule, have no consideration for what Vitruvius said ... that is, that one should not always obey the same rules and proportions, because the nature of the site often requires a different set of measurements, and necessity forces us to give or take from what we had in mind. Therefore Vitruvius says that an architect shows great skill and judgement if he gives or takes a little in his ratios in such a way that he gives a rôle to the eye, and allows the eye to manage necessity

with fine and subtle reason. And if we find that the entablature of the
Theatre of Marcellus [in Rome] differs to a degree from Vitruvius's precepts,
but the rest is very well handled, we should not blame the great architect
who built that theatre. One who had seen the whole work in one piece
would perhaps have been in a better position to judge. And so Vitruvius
tells us that although measurements and proportions are an architect's
greatest concern, nevertheless an architect greatly increases his worth
when he is forced to depart from his intended ratios, and yet does not
spoil the beauty of the building's appearance.' It is well known that
Palladio's built buildings often depart from the measurements given in the
woodcuts of the *Quattro Libri*. Even so, only some of the measurements
he gives in the woodcuts produce whole-number ratios; his proportional
system does not extend far beyond the rule of thumb that the long sides
of small rooms should equal the short sides of larger rooms, and that the
heights of rooms should be greater than their short sides but less than
their longer. Or, to put it another way, the proportional systems he gives
(QL I, xxiii) to determine the height of a room are so many tricks of the
trade to ensure that no oblong should stray too far from the square.

A building like the Theatre of Marcellus, with its three tiers of orders,
was greatly influential on the design of the street fronts of Renaissance
palaces, but for these early drawings of villas Palladio had turned rather
to the great Roman baths, those of Agrippa beside the Pantheon, those
of Titus above the Golden House of Nero (with which they were confused),

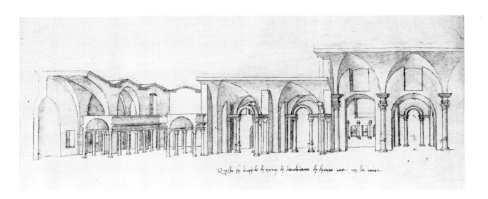

Plate 63
Drawing by Palladio of the Baths of Diocletian in Rome (Royal Institute of
British Architects). Palladio came later to prefer to such comprehensive views
a stricter elevation accompanied by a plan, as in the *Four Books*. Roman
baths offered conspicuous examples of rooms in sequences of different
shapes and sizes.

Plate 64

Drawing by Palladio of a villa (Royal Institute of British Architects). It does not
correspond closely to any built design but may be taken as an early stage in
the evolution of the palazzo Chiericati (see p. 50). The differing vaults of the
different rooms are clearly marked. On the exterior, the gables resemble those
on the left of the drawing of the Baths of Diocletian (Plate 63). Notice also the
straight tunnel staircase, like that of the villa Godi or the villa Giustinian
at Roncade.

those of Trajan, Caracalla, Diocletian (now the Museo delle Terme) and
Constantine – among others, such as those at San Germano mistaken for

Varro's villa. The baths, with their *enfilades* of numerous great rooms of different design, were the main inspiration for the spatial variety and 'sequentiality' of Palladio's architecture; Palladio also believed that the *serliana* window (or 'Palladian' window as it is known in English) which is a recurrent motif of these early villas had been widely employed in them. Again, Palladio's large central rooms rising up above the *stanze* beside them, in the way he had already tried in the villa Godi, were inspired in general by the domed spaces of the baths and were lit in particular by the same kind of semicircular aperture as the baths, the 'thermal' window. Even his handling of the villas' roof gables closely corresponds to what his reconstruction drawings (Plates 63 and 64) show him to have believed to have been originally the scheme used in the baths (notably in the much ruined baths of Agrippa by the Pantheon). Last but not least, in so far as Palladio sought grandeur, he was influenced by the baths.

One of the first to have taken up one of Palladio's projects was Giuseppe di Bernardino Valmarana — not one of the leading members of that prominent family, and of him little is known. But his intentions seem fairly clear: in 1541 he began building the villa, in the village of Vigardolo outside Vicenza, beside a house already on the site but suitable only 'for labourers'; soon after, in 1543, he had bought from another family and from the Bishop of Vicenza the right to the tithes of the village, and the completed villa is consistently called a 'castle'. The villa, as it were, was the robe of his investiture in the fief. Compared to the proposed design (Plate 65a), the great central *sala* was never or is no longer vaulted, and the gable-pediment as it exists is much too high (Plate 65b). Perhaps the owner declined the extravagant rusticated window surrounds in the drawing, but I think one can say that, if so, his meanness shows; they were needed for balance. Later Palladio would much reduce or control his use of rustication, but it features richly in his contemporary town palace for the Thiene, and still in the villa Caldogno at Caldogno (Plate 66).

Palladio's villa Gazotti (Plate 12), though smaller, is a more advanced work, and has a grand, though not very large, cross-vaulted *sala*. Since nothing very much has transformed the quiet Vicentine suburb of Bertésina since it was built, the villa is still almost shockingly dominant (the Valmarana at Vigardolo is instead hemmed in by other buildings), and fanfares

Plate 65a
Drawing by Palladio of a villa, the design underlying the built villa Valmarana at Vigardolo (Royal Institute of British Architects). The gable and *serliana* are directly inspired by Roman baths. This is an early drawing and the vaulting systems are rather limited; the built villa has flat ceilings throughout, even in the *sala*.

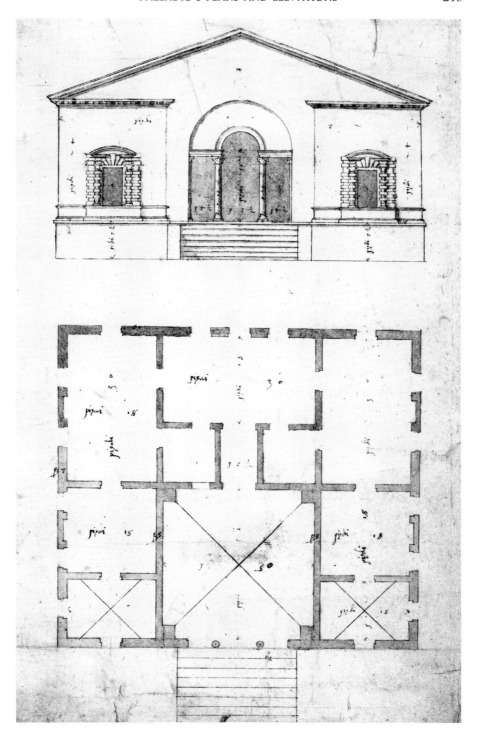

Plate 65b
Villa Valmarana, Vigardolo, Vicenza. The bulk of the villa, much taller than the
elevation in Palladio's drawing (though it has no basement), dwarfs the *serliana*
frontispiece. Also its bare wall surfaces are unenlivened by the rusticated window
jambs Palladio intended, and are rendered still barer by recent new plastering.
Its blank surfaces place it with the villa Godi as an early work by the architect —
though presumably he did not see through its execution.

its grand architecture in the way all Palladio's villas must once have done
in their original, humbler and much less competitive surroundings. Part of
that is sheer scale, in the way the house rises on its base, and in the
largeness of its apertures; partly its rustication, which helps to give the
building unity of mass. It is comparatively broad, according to the pattern
of the 1530s, and its interior distribution still simple.

The most interesting of these early designs (Plate 67a) is one which
later became the villa Pisani at Bagnolo or, rather, which the villa Pisani
nearly became. Though the family was Venetian, the property was near
Vicenza, and had been confiscated from the rebel Vicentine Nogarola
family shortly after the Wars; Giovanni Pisani had bought it from the State
at auction in 1523, shortly before he became *podestà* of Vicenza. This was
a large property, and had already had a '*palazzo*' on it, burnt out during
the Wars. But once again the decision to build, taken about 1540, was part

Plate 66
Villa Caldogno, Caldogno, Vicenza. This villa does not appear among Palladio's
drawings or in the *Four Books*, but its design can be attributed to him and dated
to the 1540s on the grounds of its resemblance to other villas of the period.
Not only the frontispiece but also the quoins of the basement are similar to
those of the villa Pisani at Bagnolo. There is a magnificent series of frescoes
inside (see Plate 5).

of a wider investment both in irrigation in order to plant rice and in the
provision of a waterway navigable back to Venice: another drawing by
Palladio, which presumably he made for Giovanni Pisani once his initial
design had attracted him, locates the villa directly beside the river on
which it still stands (Plate 67b). Unfortunately Pisani did not follow through
the original scheme, but halfway through the building declined its most
innovative (and probably expensive) feature, its semicircular 'exedra' front
(Plate 67c). He adopted instead a three-arched rusticated loggia (much like
that of the Caldogno), deriving from Palladio's designs but almost certainly
not executed by him, although Palladio accepts the modification in his
woodcut in the *Quattro Libri*. Giovanni's sons had called Palladio back to
the villa in the 1560s to build them *barchesse*, and the woodcut is surely
based on the building as it was then. However, though nothing is said in
the text, the woodcut literally turns its back on the bastardization, showing

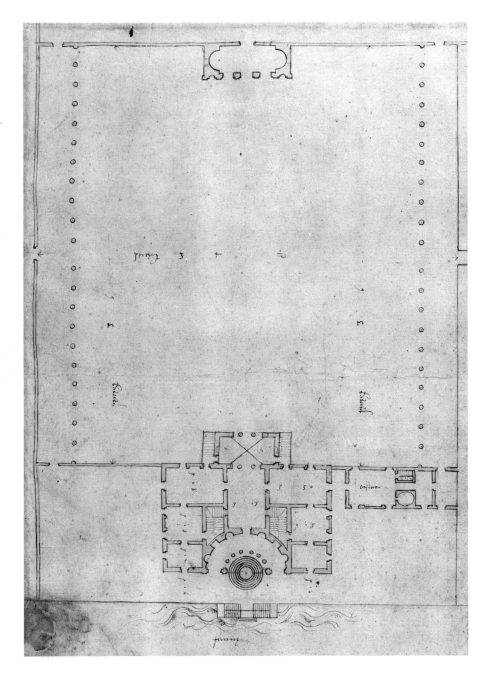

Plate 67a

Villa Pisani, Bagnolo, Vicenza. Drawing by Palladio for the villa and its *cortivo* (Royal Institute of British Architects). On this design the villa would have presented a still grander *sala* than that built. The pavilion that faces the house across the *cortivo* is also a grand idea – but so much for show and otherwise unnecessary that its chances of being built were particularly slim.

Plate 67b
The villa Pisani beside its river today: the colossal dykes now mask the front, which in Palladio's time gave directly on to the waterway and was clearly the main entrance. In the present *cortivo* the outbuildings run along one side only and do not extend out from the house as Palladio liked to have them.

the villa from what had been the garden front in the original scheme, now dressed up as if it were a façade with a temple front that was never built and even in the woodcut fits awkwardly to the thermal window that had been built (Plates 67d–f). Even the towers – which seem to have been provided for no other reason than to make a powerful, 'regal' framework for the exedra – remained stunted simulacra of themselves; no wonder Palladio hints darkly in the *Quattro Libri* at the trouble he has had with owners who will not follow the architect's recommendation (QL II, i).

The exedra and its convex and concave steps derived from Bramante's celebrated link between the Belvedere villa on the hill and the Vatican palace – that is, from one of the most ambitious architectural schemes then in circulation, although the idea must first have been transmitted to Palladio via Serlio, and Alvise Cornaro had already much more modestly installed

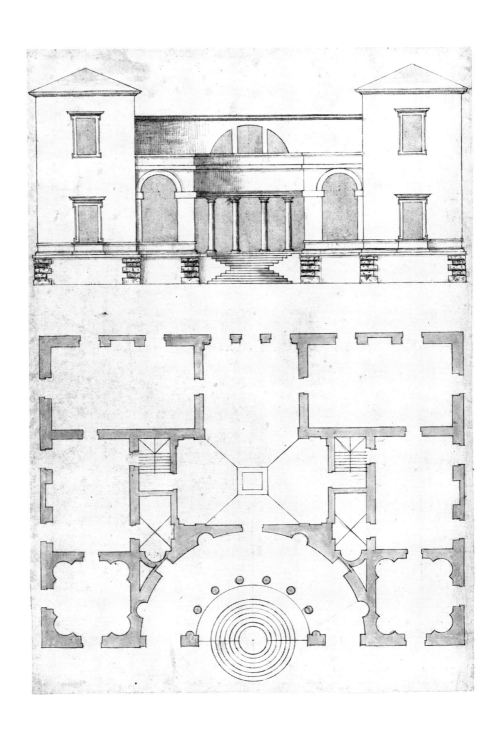

Plate 67c
Drawing by Palladio for the villa Pisani, closely corresponding to the plan on which it was started (Royal Institute of British Architects). However, in a change of plan at a late stage the magnificent exedra was replaced by a three-arched loggia perhaps adapted from Palladio's design for the pavilion across the *cortivo*. There are clear signs of improvisation at the roofline, for instance a second gable above the pediment of the loggia; it is likely that by this time Palladio was no longer supervising the execution of the building, although his drawings would still have been put to use.

Plate 67d
The villa from the court. The thermal window above the door was to have been matched by a similar one at the other end of the hall overlooking the exedra. It lights a vast hall rising two storeys in height, also inspired by Roman baths.

such steps at the entrance to his 'Odeon' in Padua. What a jewel it would have been had it been carried through, with that both bold and exquisite sense for perfect placement that characterizes Palladio's execution of a building – and by the absence of which his buildings are so easily marred. However that may be, these early drawings by Palladio show building design radically rethought and recast, both inside and out. It may even have been his desire to incorporate the exedra that led Palladio to break

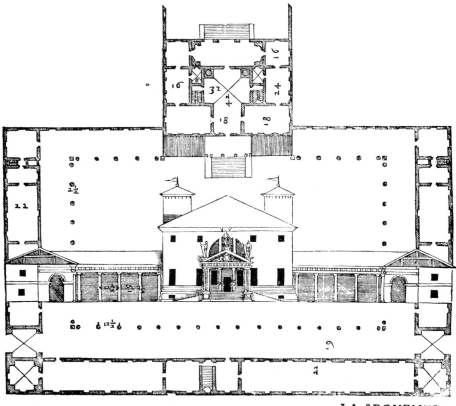

LA SEGVENTE

Plate 67e
Woodcut of the villa from the *Four Books* (II, xiv). Palladio shows the building
from the back, though he disguises the fact by providing a rather miniature
loggia and a system of steps. This was Palladio's first villa for a Venetian patron
and is the first of the villas for Venetian owners he shows in the *Four Books*. He
stresses its cardinal features, its linked outbuildings and their Doric order, its
piano nobile for the owner and its basement 'for the household', its *sala* rising to
the roof, its grand main steps and its hidden, but well placed and well lit
servants' stairs.

for the first time with the old tripartite regimentation: in two earlier
drawings (including his first quick sketch) he had retained partition walls
running the depth of the house, but in the later two and the executed
building the internal walls have a more complicated pattern.

The drawing in which Palladio figures the villa Pisani on its site, beside
its river, reveals that already at this time Palladio was also thinking about
the *cortivo*. It looks to have been entirely for 'representation', containing

no stalls for cattle or even stables for horses, merely two long porticoes; the pavilion facing the main house declares the nature of the space it surveys. Certainly this is not a farmyard, which would have adjoined, as it did in most cases, and as it is shown to do in the site plans for the villa Pojana. However, in these plans Palladio does not yet lead the porticoes directly off from the house, in the way he developed for villas of the 1550s and on which he insisted in the *Quattro Libri*, since he wished not only to provide a kind of umbrella or parasol for the owner on his circumambulations but also to 'sequentialize' these spaces as well: the porticoes serve to gather in the outbuildings and the *cortivo* and subordinate them to the hieratic block of the villa.

From the more experimental architecture of the 1540s the path leads directly to such classic successes of Palladio's maturity as the palazzo Chiericati in Vicenza, begun in 1551, which, because of its open site, naturally comes closer to his villas than do his other palaces in Vicenza. Ultimately one can derive the palazzo Chiericati, with its inversion of the

Plate 67f
The vaulted hall as built, with its *grottesche* decoration. In scale and amplitude it was even more impressive than the *entrata* and *sala* of the villa Porto at Thiene, for instance; it is itself outdone by the enormous *sala* of the villa Foscari at Malcontenta. The blocked-in window should have overlooked the exedra.

usual scheme of central aperture and corner solids, from an early 1540s drawing such as that in Plate 64, with its side entrances and the equal scansion of the broad front by three *serliane* beneath three gables — a scheme inspired once again by Palladio's study of Roman baths. The design for the palazzo Chiericati even retains some of the elements of that drawing's plan — the apsidal *entrata*, the coved domes in the square rooms — but that may be coincidence; Palladio had moved a long way in the interim (the staircase, in particular, of the drawing, though of a type he used in the villa Godi, is old fashioned). Then in the early to mid 1550s, with the country houses Pisani (at Montagnana), Cornaro, Badoer and Thiene (at Cicogna, rebuilt) and the town houses Antonini (in Udine), Garzadori (never built) and later Trissino (never built) Palladio introduced and subsequently established as it were his own stereotype, the temple-fronted palace or villa. The new format took hold perhaps the more definitively because in some ways it reverted to the 'Venetian house' type: it presented once again a central frontispiece and aperture and an obvious tripartition; however it included and continued Palladio's own earlier vestibule and hall system, and in the villas the *sala* usually rises behind the temple front above the other rooms to the roof.

The settled anatomy of Palladio's interior and exterior planning was codified in the *Quattro Libri*, published in 1570. In the basement, 'the lowest part of the building, which I make partly underground, go the wine cellars, the wood stores, the pantries, the kitchens, the servants' day-rooms, the washing-places, the ovens, and such things necessary for the daily round: from which there arise two conveniencies, one that the upper part is unencumbered, the other, no less important, that the upper part shall be safe, clean and healthy for habitation, since the floor will be removed from the damp of the ground, besides the fact that being raised up, it achieves greater beauty, both in the being looked upon and in the looking out.' This formula applied to town as well as to country houses, and its only major constraint was the level of the water table: thus the palazzo Chiericati has only a half basement, while the basements of Palladio's palaces on higher ground elsewhere in the town are more fully buried. Palladio also remarks (QL II, xiii) on the advantages of sloping floors for cleaning; these, together with shallow central conduits to collect water, can be seen for instance in the basement of the villa Cornaro at Piombino Dese.

Above the basement, Palladio in his maturity liked particularly to place a 'four-columned' hall, which on the one hand imitated the Roman atrium 'of four columns' described by Vitruvius and on the other served 'to proportion the width to the height, and to render the room above well founded' (QL II, viii; II, xiv). What exactly Palladio meant by that can be seen, for instance, in his own woodcut of the palazzo Iseppo Porto in

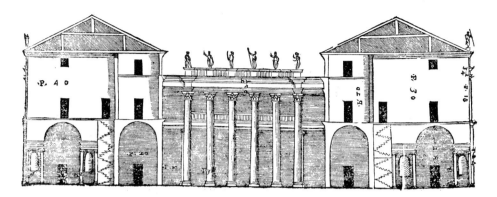

Plate 68

Palazzo Iseppo Porto, Vicenza, from the *Four Books* (II, iii). Neither the courtyard
nor the second, guest wing of the palace were ever built (see p. 34). 'Cube
rooms' have more to do with Inigo Jones and English Palladianism than Palladio
himself, who specifically required rooms to be higher than their shorter side,
that is, taller than a cube. Palladio's 'four columns' device enabled him to make
a long, low room seem taller, and to give form to a merely box-like space. At
the same time it recalled Vitruvius, who discusses a type of hall 'of four columns'
(see Plate 16).

Vicenza (Plate 68). It shows in section the *sala* above and *entrata* below
(and the same disposition mirrored in the guesthouse across the courtyard,
which was never built), the upper chamber with a flat ceiling and the
entrata with four columns which obviously strengthen the vault. One
cannot fail to notice that in section the four columns form a *serliana*, and
in a sense the four columns were a *serliana* in three dimensions: while the
whole *serliana* formed roughly a square, and was for that reason a convenient and satisfying building unit – witness the Basilica – the four
columns produced a cube, a convenient and satisfying spatial unit for the
'most beautiful part of the house'. On the other hand Palladio did not like
simple cubical rooms: he declares (QL I, xxiii) that the height of the vault
of square rooms should be a third more than their length or breadth. In
the classical orders, the height of the entablature over two columns will
be greater than the distance between them (except in the Tuscan order, in
which Palladio says the intercolumniation may vary) – usually much
greater, so that at least two bays are needed to produce a square; in the
Ionic order, as Palladio gives it, three. There were therefore in the 'eye' of
the architect two competing senses of proportion, that relating to the
classical orders and that of a simple geometry of whole number ratios.
Both the *serliana* and the four columns system were a means of reconciling

Plate 69
Villa Almerico (Rotonda), Vicenza: interior. The *sala* of the villa Rotonda is
rendered more dramatic by the rather narrow corridors approaching it. They
may be compared to the perspectival tunnels opening on to the proscenium
and spectators' *cavea* of the Teatro Olimpico in Vicenza (see Plate 3). The
painting was undertaken for the Capra family who bought the villa in the early
seventeenth century; the figures are gesticulatory and gigantesque and the
colours loud, compared to the 'school' of Veronese.

the two; one might think of it as if Palladio's buildings were composed in prefabricated classical-order units.

In the 1560s Palladio produced one more notable variation on the *sala*, the imitation of the interior of the Pantheon that is the kernel and perhaps also the *raison d'être* of the villa Rotonda. The villa is known above all from the outside, but it is likely that, as virtually throughout Palladio's work, it was the internal structure that dictated or informed the rest. The villa does not echo the Pantheon at all closely on the outside, since the dome is shallow and the mass and proportions of the villa quite different; but on the inside the imitation of the effect of standing beneath the dome of the Pantheon is real and striking (Plate 69) — both despite and thanks to the rather later and rather violently coloured illusionistic painted decoration. Despite the four equal temple fronts on the outside, the interior of the villa is symmetrical on each axis but not on both, a further sign that the villa had a practical destination and was not an abstract study for an ideal building.

The temple fronts of the Rotonda are no different from those of other buildings in belonging both to the inside and to the outside of the house, making both an appropriate frontispiece and a kind of antechamber or extension to the *sala*. Palladio (QL II, iii) explained of the villa that 'because it enjoys beautiful views in every direction ... loggias have been made on all four sides', and he says as much again for the projected villa Trissino at Meledo, which was to have had a similar plan: 'because each façade has beautiful views, four loggias in the Corinthian order go there'. Therefore the loggias of both these houses, set up on hills, served primarily the owner's desire to look out rather than the passer-by's interest in looking on, although Palladio was conscious of their external effect and gives quite a long description of the countryside in which the villa Rotonda is so well situated, borrowing, significantly, some of his vocabulary from Pliny's description of the site of one of his own villas: it was not only of very easy ascent, it was visible from all around from very pleasant hills 'which create the effect of a very large theatre'.

The use of other rooms would depend on the size and nature of the household in residence, and that might vary with each visit. It seems that any *stanza* could be or become a bedroom; many *stanze* would contain a bed without their being either anyone's bedroom in particular or for use specially as a bedroom, but could become so when necessary. It was probably more usual than not to have visitors, especially if the owner was a man of any importance; and it was not unusual for the owner to let a friend or friends stay for a time in his absence, whether they were his peers or his protégés. People carried with them most other furniture, and their personal possessions, and when the household had moved out the rooms were surely almost as bare as they are in Palladio's uninhabited villas today: there might remain only the bedsteads and the tables, perhaps also a few storage chests and a single writing desk. A sign that the villas remained generally empty are the frescoes that adorn the full length of walls sometimes of all the larger rooms. Smaller rooms, however, *camere* or *camerini*, were rather different: the owner might well choose one to be his *studiolo*, his private room, which would have a key, and he might keep in it permanently or during his absence possessions such as books, valuables (including works of art) and legal and other documents. Palladio also mentions the use of such smaller rooms not for habitation at all but as lumber-rooms (QL II, ii): 'The small *stanze* are to be divided [vertically] so as to create *camerini*, where one places *studioli* or libraries, or riding gear and other things of which we have need every day, and which it would not be well to keep in the rooms where one sleeps, eats or receives guests'.

It is perhaps remarkable that Palladio's villas were not (with one exception) divided into apartments, especially since he claims that the houses of the Greeks (QL II, xi) were divided into 'antechambers, chambers and postchambers', which would correspond to the unit called the *apartment* in France. In the exception mentioned, the rather mysterious villa Mocenigo (Plate 70) in the village of Marocco (unbuilt; even the intended site is not known), Palladio provided four apartments precisely of this kind, without saying whether he regarded them as Greek or French, or whether they were for four different people, or why he had provided them; but the unusual double stair of the Mocenigo, forming the centrepiece of the interior, each arm rising straight and parallel to create an X-profile, suggests more French influence than Greek revivalism. In most cases Palladio's system of sequential rooms produced only an 'antechamber' and 'chamber', in which the owner might create the equivalent of an apartment. It is difficult to see in a villa such as Mario Repeta's, a series of single-storey rooms round a court lacking any main block as such, any quarters strongly demarcated from any others, even though in this case Palladio speaks specifically of guest-rooms distinct from the owner's. Generally in his villas circulation on the 'noble' floor or floors is free; and Palladio's stated idea (QL II, ii) was that his large, medium-sized and small rooms could be used 'interchangeably'.

Lastly, the difference between the gentleman's floor or floors and the servants' rooms upstairs was almost as clear as the differentiation to the basement. It is much clearer than the difference between the servants' rooms, storage rooms, granaries or attics doubling as barns. Palladio calls *mezati* those rooms within the house that were not suitable for gentlemen – *mezati* meaning strictly mezzanine rooms above the smaller rooms on the 'noble' floor or floors which had lower vaults or ceilings in order to respect

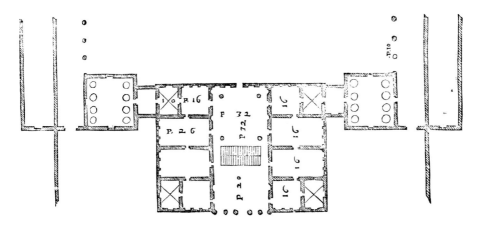

Plate 70
Villa Mocenigo, Marocco, Treviso, from the *Four Books* (II, xiv). The design,
dating to the early 1560s, reveals once again that there is no essential difference
between a town and a country house. Note the double basement, or ground
floor with mezzanine, which became almost standard in the last quarter of the
sixteenth century and then in the seventeenth: compare the palazzo Thiene al
Castello in Vicenza (see Plate 22) or villa Verlato, Villaverla (see Plate 9).

proportion. Rooms on the attic storey were also unsuitable — such as those
over the *stanze* in the wings of the villa Foscari, which Palladio equated
with *mezati* (QL II, xiv). It emerges that Palladio regarded any room under
eight Vicentine feet high (2·8 metres) as unsuitable for a gentleman's
habitation. Attic rooms, of under that height, he usually assigns to storage,
or else to servants' rooms, or once both; architecturally there seems to
have been very little difference. Servants not only had smaller rooms but

also smaller stairs, stairs of the kind that Palladio tucked away more or less invisibly ('secretly'); broader, and stone, stairs were required up to the *piano nobile* and also between the two 'noble' floors if there were two.

20

Conveniency

If, when one enters a Palladian villa, it seems surprisingly bare as well as airy and spacious, that is not a Palladian quality, but the norm in the Middle Ages and the Renaissance. Should one rent a house in a Muslim quarter of a Muslim country today it would not only be completely unfurnished but also completely uncharacterized, its rooms a series of undifferentiated vacant compartments. On the other hand already by the end of the eighteenth century Ottavio Bertotti Scamozzi was obliged to defend Palladio 'if in his buildings one cannot find those divisions and subdivisions of the parts that today's luxury has made obligatory'. Although in fact Palladio made some divisions of the parts, the use of rooms within them was not predetermined or fixed.

That was partly because much Renaissance furniture was not permanent but travelled with its owner from house to house, or at least might do so. Possessions were of two kinds, *móbili* and *immóbili*, movable and immovable goods: while houses and land belonged to the former category, their contents belonged to the latter. The *immobili* were patrimony (and commonly would continue long under joint ownership before one or another brother or cousin would buy or trade another out) but *mobili* were like cash, and on a man's death would be dispersed unless he made specific provision for them (for instance, for an art collection). While he was alive he would, within reason, carry his *mobili* around with him. Or, for the sake of a special occasion, such as a marriage, he would accumulate *mobili* from all possible sources — borrowing from relatives and friends, and if not directly hiring then buying with the intention of selling later or pawning. One would expect that Palladio's villas during the winter might stand almost as empty as they often are now; others, however, were so close to the owner's native city that he could make the journey within the day and therefore might keep both establishments running at the same time.

The standard storage unit, although there existed both cupboards and dressers in the Renaissance, was a chest, whether in the form of a *cassone* like those well known for their painted decoration or of squarer type, more like a strong-box (*forziere*). Their decoration was not only painted but often also carved or of leather. Chests served for the storage of clothes and linen and everything miscellaneous; dressers were for the display rather than the simple storage of plate and pottery, and cupboards were again primarily for utensils, for instance of glass – except that many were in effect strong-boxes mounted often detachably on a stand. Very little was 'built in', although in medieval buildings it is not uncommon to find niches in the wall resembling those for piscinae in a church. People therefore lived from day to day more or less ready, by today's standards, to move out instantly, bearing in mind that there were many things, such as trestle tables, ordinary benches or chairs, mattresses and common utensils, that it would be cheaper to buy than to transport. The general effect even in the grandest house would definitely be uncluttered: Palladio's provision of lumber-rooms reveals that unclutteredness was also the taste.

What are missing today from Palladio's houses are chiefly the textiles. Tapestries, which were anyway very expensive, or wall-hangings would seldom be used in a villa, not being needed to help retain the heat; they might well be hung in a town house, where accordingly one seldom sees the walls painted, but only a frieze and an elaborate ceiling (for instance in the southern wing, built in Palladio's time, of the palazzo Chiericati). Other fabrics in use included canopies for the four-poster beds, hangings of cloth across the doors, tablecloths (often more than one was laid) and sheets. Stores of sheets and tablecloths appear to have been considerable: 120 tablecloths and 150 sheets were recorded in the palazzo Barbarano in 1592. Similarly one would expect plentiful supplies of linen to wear: the standard undergarment for both men and women was the *camicia* or long shirt (of more or less refined materials from silk downwards), over which one would wear jackets, bodices, hose and overdresses, made of brocades and other materials. Linen was stored in portable chests severally disposed about the rooms of the house.

There would also have been all kinds of other objects now missing, even assuming that boots, riding gear, guns and other items for use outdoors had been put away, and that the maid had not left her brush and pan on the window-sill (as she has done, where they are immortalized in Veronese's fresco, in the eastern front room in the villa Barbaro): by the fire there would be fire-dogs, on the window-sill perhaps a flower-pot, on the tables and chests candlesticks, in the beds at night bed-warmers. On the walls there would be a few framed pictures, almost invariably either religious or portraits – much like those again that Veronese has painted illusionistically in the rooms of the villa Barbaro. And one would expect to find the most usual means of passing the time in those days, musical instruments – flutes, lutes, spinets – books and gaming boards.

In contrast to the general effect, the owner's study might be much more cluttered, dense and busy. It was anyway a small room, a kind of inhabitable safe, where not only books and papers but cash and documents were kept — anything precious, from small bronzes to ivory crucifixes, and anything private, from ivory crucifixes to *risqué* small bronzes. Several princely *studioli* have survived — such as Isabella d'Este's in the Ducal palace at Mantua, or Duke Francesco I's in the palazzo Vecchio in Florence; they seem now extremely cramped. After his death the famous *studiolo* of the Venetian connoisseur Gabriel Vendramín was locked and sealed, and there his collection, which he had forbidden to be sold, remained until any of his descendants should take an interest in it — but they seemed to have preferred whoring and gaming. Some such *studiolo* might come to contain an archive, like that from which Daniele Barbaro retrieved the papers of his great-uncle Ermolao, some of which he edited and published; the Barbaro archive containing Daniele's papers and many of his books is known to have survived into the eighteenth century. Other such private archives survived into the nineteenth century, eventually to pass into public institutions; the private Porto archive at the villa Porto in Thiene was known to few and unpublished until the 1980s. Logically, Palladio destined the *camerini* of his houses, the smaller rooms he set two to a floor, one above the other (opening off a staircase), indifferently to the functions of *studiolo*, library or storeroom.

Although a gentleman would usually carry all that he needed with him, there was room for variation depending on numerous factors — on the length of his stay (there are frequent mentions of people who find themselves forced to remain longer than they intended sending for a second instalment), or on the size of his immediate household: if he were travelling on business he would usually not take his wife with him, not least because she could usefully manage or monitor his affairs at home. It would depend also on his haste, or on the season, it being much more difficult to travel in winter, especially in a carriage: it was unusual if the roads became passable as early as March or remained so after November. The master would travel in a carriage, not necessarily together with his servants, some of whom it was usual to send ahead, but not alone: he would be driven; or he would ride his horse. Venetians travelling to and from the mainland would of course often do so in their own covered barge (there were also public services, notably the *burchiello* that travelled from Venice to Padua or vice versa within the day; one could go on by water to Vicenza, which had a port at the eastern end of the town). Most places on the plain were on a navigable river or canal or close to one. It was usual to draw carriages or barges either with horses or with mules, though these made slower progress.

When Giangiorgio Trissino set off down to Rome in 1545 he took with him not only Palladio and the painter Giambattista Maganza but also a cook and a number of other servants led by a majordomo, and a priest to say mass for them all; it was for a long stay. He went in a carriage drawn by mules, and there were also two mules saddled; it is not stated who rode them, but it is clear that some had to walk. The journey may have taken about three weeks. It emerges also that Trissino took with him all they needed for eating and sleeping, from linen and furniture to crockery, but when they arrived had to purchase mattresses, blankets, chairs, tables, stands and some other unspecified furniture. When Trissino went down again to Rome in 1550, probably not intending to stay so long, though in fact he died there, he went again in a similar carriage, but with much reduced entourage, and most of his possessions seem to have fitted into two trunks. Their contents were listed immediately after his death, and should serve to provide an idea of the kind of effects by which any of Palladio's patrons might have been surrounded.

One of the trunks contained mostly books, the other was mostly for clothes and stuffs, though neither was exclusively for either. Amongst these, amounting to a considerable library and to a considerable wardrobe, Trissino felt it desirable to carry with him table coverings of velvet, two copper pans for heating pies, a cuttlefish-bone which had been worked in Germany into a box which locked, four brass balls to go on the corners of a four-poster bed, naturally enough his own writings, both printed and his notes, kept in a small case, his keys, a portable altar and other instruments for the saying of mass, a perfume ball, an astrolabe, various little boxes or cases with various things in them, several bags or purses containing coins of various denominations, but amounting to 500 ducats or more, that is, a very bankable sum of money, rings, medals, spoons, knives, a mirror, a pair of spectacles, a clock with an embroidered hood, a tin flask, a small metal bell (probably for summoning servants), two salts of mother-of-pearl bound in silver, a silver basin and jug, a picture of Christ and two brass candlesticks.

Several portraits of the time show their sitters among some of the objects they most treasured, from clocks and statuettes to, of course, dogs. It was not, however, objects or even animals that contributed most to the 'ease' or 'conveniency' (*comodità*) of aristocratic Renaissance life, although animals and objects of all kinds (especially objects 'of *vertù*') were vital talking-points: if one visited, one would expect to be shown and discuss the owner's possessions. (Not by chance the Patriarchate Grimani, whose immense collection of antiques was the finest in Venice, inscribed messages celebrating friendship over the portals of their palace in campo Santa Maria Formosa.) Essentially, however, it was the attendance of servants that transformed a lowly life into an exalted one, making it part of the very definition of *civiltà* or nobility that one should not sully one's hands.

Correspondingly, the way in which Palladio's villas reflected and structured the relationship between the owner and his staff and tenants constituted, I believe, the essence of the *comodità* or conveniency to which he claimed his architecture was principally directed. By his provision of a basement below and an area of noble residence above (whether of one or of two *piani nóbili*) he distinguished owner's and servants' quarters architecturally, and much more clearly than had been done before; the same is true inside, where one part is narrow and cramped, the other high and airy (Palladio reckoned a gentleman needed rooms not less than ten feet high). The servants' stairs, linking ignoble basement and ignoble attic, are tucked away along with the lumber; where the owner must use the stairs, they are not only larger but also more prominent. Palladio then extended the principle to the outbuildings, using steps down from the house and porticoes to extend the hierarchy to the rest of the countryside station, so to call it. It is significant that while the agricultural manuals stress that porticoes are useful for storage and for keeping dry hay, threshing corn and so on – a point Palladio also makes – Palladio insists above all that they are for the owner's conveniency, to keep him dry. For him they had a ceremonial importance – consider the honour that devolved to Giangiorgio Trissino to have carried the Pope's train, or (still more appositely) to Marcantonio Barbaro to have borne Henri III's parasol.

Palladio's villas were designed therefore, from the beginning, to carry the kind of 'magnificence' that was made apparent above all by one's entourage, though he did not immediately evolve his most successful formulae. In my opinion, his villas are as a consequence less friendly and charming than their Early Renaissance predecessors, and I would say that Palladio himself was a pivot towards the trend that ensued, towards an ever greater frigidity. His villas retain, however, something of the charm of their predecessors, and also convey something of that flourishing *vertù* of the High Renaissance – connecting to a quality that Vanbrugh would later call the 'masculine'. It is a quality that conspicuously disappears after his death, for which the reason may well be, however, that the Venetians had lost their trousers.

Of all the various descriptions, poems, records and letters relating to Palladio's villas and villas of the period in general, few seem better to capture the tone of life within them and without them than the setting of the dialogues constituting Agostino Gallo's *Days of Agriculture* – originally, when first published in Brescia in 1556, *Ten Days* (*Le dieci giornate della vera agricoltura*), but then extended, due to demand, in successive reprints to *Fourteen* and *Twenty Days*. Gallo wrote as a nobleman for noblemen, while the authors of other manuals speak more as experienced factors, and are unable to convey the ease which, I think I have stressed enough, was essential to the villa. His interlocutors, moreover, were real figures in northern Italian society, Vincenzo Maggi and Giambattista Avogadro. Both were 'among those gentlemen who live [in the country] the greater part of the year to enjoy themselves in their honourable pleasures'. One day Vincenzo Maggio left his own villa to visit Giambattista Avogadro at his, and then, 'after they had strolled [*passeggiato*] for some time together, dispensing their discourse in praise of the good air and attractiveness of the villa, they sat down in the pretty garden [compare Plate 71] under a great bower, and after a certain silence, messer Vincenzo began ...'. Avogadro explains to him from the beginning where to buy a villa, how to tell good soil, and so on: he does not finish, and they agree to continue the next day. 'Messer Vincenzo Maggi, greatly desiring to fulfil the promise he had made to Avogadro, set off to his fine villa immediately after he had dined; and there, having dismounted, he found him in the very beautiful "little chapel" he had built at the top of the garden, looking west, and facing the long bower which divides it; and so, having greeted each other, first one and then the other, they took their seats. After they had discoursed some time of the beauty of the situation, and of the figures painted around [the "little chapel"], Maggi, so as not to waste time, began....'

'Come the third day, messer Vincenzo went at the accustomed hour to Avogadro's house, and found him taking the air [*passeggiare*] in his beautiful loggia, which looks west and out along a straight way bounded by two fine hedges of dogwood, dividing the garden from the houses of his labourers. After they had greeted each other, he was taken by the hand and led, step by step, to beneath a great chestnut, giving very dense shade, and which, since it gave coolth, had been provided with seats, and there they sat. And after they had talked of the wonderful attractiveness and delight of the various trees and shrubs and of the sweet singing of the birds all about, Maggi, placing his hand on his breast, said ...'. When the time came for him to depart, Avogadro accompanied him away 'for more than a mile, and invited him to dine with him the next day'; Maggi did not fail to appear, and 'when they had finished eating, they retired to a fresh, darker place to hear the sweet murmur of the water that runs westwards across the garden, and there, having had a chair brought for him to sit on, Maggi began ...'. 'Having returned on the fifth day at the accustomed hour to Avogadro's house, messer Vincenzo found him in the large room [*saletta*] of the fishpond under the central dovecot, where he took delight not only in looking out through the windows on to the long bower, the garden, the orchard and his fields to the east, but also in seeing an infinity of fish wandering and darting everywhere in the water. He greeted him, and having expressed his great admiration for such a beautiful prospect entered into their usual discussion . . .'. On another day they fed bread to the fish.

'Messer Vincenzo Maggi, wishing to return on the sixth day to messer Avogadro's house again at the usual hour, seeing that it was beginning to spot, and fearing more rain, mounted his leather-hooded coach; and when he got there, because of the rain which was beginning to fall heavily, they went into a fine room [*camerino*] off the great hall [*sala grande*], which looked east over the whole garden, adorned with many square tubs of cedars, lemon-trees, orange-trees, and with other fine round tubs full of different flowering plants, which rendered the place marvellously charming. And so, having first considered well the good order of all these things, Maggi began to say . . . Returning on the seventh day at the usual hour, Maggi found Avogadro just having dined in the middle of his very lovely bower, the better to enjoy a gentle breeze which all about was making tremble the branches of the trees of the garden, the varied flowers of the pleasant meadow, the shoots of the vines in the bower and the cedars, lemons and oranges of the pretty orchard; after they had greeted one another according to their custom, and seated themselves in that sweet freshness, Maggi, admiring the beauty of so many plants in their tubs loaded with fruit, resolved at last to turn to their discussion. . . .'

Among the variations that follow in the subsequent days, Avogadro is taking his ease (*passeggiare*) in his *sala grande*, and there when Maggi reaches him at their accustomed time his clock sounds the fifteenth hour (nine o'clock in the morning). On another day Maggi is led by a servant to find him in his 'little cave' (*grotticella*) formed by laurel and jasmine, and there they sit on some antique stonework, 'which was there for ornament'. On the eleventh day he finds Avogadro under his loggia, receiving rent from his herdsman for the second quarter, a cue for them to talk about cows that day. Because it rains, Maggi has to stay the night; the following morning, they go to Mass, and after Mass for a walk along the bank of a river. They return to find the herdsman beneath the loggia again, whom they invite to join them in their discussion of sheep — but there, beneath the loggia, not further inside or in the garden.

By the fourteenth day there are no more different places to sit, and variety is provided instead by a succession of other callers; Maggi finds the cue for another topic (particularly relevant to Palladio's villas), the growing of silk, having met on his journey to Avogadro a group of women carrying silk cocoons to sell in Brescia. Finally Maggi leaves, with Avogadro's permission, to take supper with his father-in-law at his villa, and then to go in the cool of the evening to another of his own *possessioni*.

Plate 71
Manuscript miniature showing a Venetian family in the garden of their villa
(Bibliothèque Nationale, Paris). The structure on the left is an open-air dining
room (compare Plates 40 and 41).

He therefore misses the excitement of the eighteenth day, when another
figure, Cornelio Ducco, drops in on Avogadro while on his way from one
of his *possessioni* to another, to find the house full of friends of his who
were hunting partridges with falcons; it is easy to find another place for
him at dinner, which is taken in the garden, and then after dinner Avogadro
and Ducco stay and talk, letting the rest go.

PART 5
Handlist of Villas

The following handlist is intended as a guide for use by visitors to Palladio's villas (and to a few others discussed at length in the book). It is arranged geographically, listing villas around Vicenza clockwise from the north, in groups it might be convenient to see in a day (within the groups listed from north to south). I have provided a note about condition and location, some rudimentary facts about the villas, and sometimes a translation of Palladio's remarks in the *Four Books*. I have given cross-references only to extended discussions in the text.

Few villas apart from the Rotonda can be reached by public transport. Several villas are open to the public on certain days in the summer months; the rest only by arrangement, which can be made by telephone, for the most part without difficulty. I have specified opening times and days (which, however, generally apply only between March and October) since they have remained unchanged now for some years, but I make the obvious proviso. The telephone numbers I have given are those of custodians, not of proprietors. For updated or further information or telephone numbers I have not given, one can apply to the Tourist Office of the capital of the relevant province (Vicenza, Verona, Padua, Treviso, Venice).

1.   Due north of Vicenza

Villa Caldogno, Caldogno

In the centre of the village of Caldogno. Owned by the municipality. Open Tuesday, Thursday, Saturday 9–12 a.m.; or by arrangement.

Not documented; not mentioned by Palladio in the *Four Books*. The design is datable to the 1540s (resemblances to the villa Pisani at Bagnolo) but the pediment bears the date of 1570. The extensive frescoes inside are of about the same date, by Giovanni Antonio Fasolo.

Villa Porto (Castello Porto-Colleoni), Thiene; now Thiene

In the centre of the town of Thiene. Imposing, archaic grandeur. Open Sunday 3–5 p.m.; tel. 0445–366015.

Built from about 1441 to 1453, architect unknown. Refurbished, heightened and decorated on the outside in the early 1520s; frescoes on the ground floor and perhaps also upstairs by Zelotti and Fasolo belong to the 1550s. (See pp. 32–4.)

Villa Godi, Lonedo di Lugo Vicentino; now Malinverni

Set among the foothills in a delightful spot, marred by industry in the river valley below; its interior is also today rather tatty and is shown badly lit. The nearby villa Piovene above it is highly Palladian but not by Palladio. Open Tuesday, Saturday, Sunday, public holidays 2–6 p.m. (3–7 p.m. June to August); tel. 0445–860561.

This is Palladio's earliest villa, begun about 1537 and completed by 1542. However, Palladio was called back at the end of the 1540s, and the lighting of the main room was altered (closing a semicircular upper window, opening the present *serliana*) when Zelotti undertook his frescoes there some time in the 1550s. The other frescoes, by Gualtiero Padovano, date not later than the early 1550s. Palladio seems also to have provided a design for some of the frescoed architecture, and for the wellhead in the garden. (See pp. 202–5.)

2.   North-east, near Castelfranco

Villa Barbaro, Maser, Treviso; now Luling Buschetti

This beautifully kept villa is outstanding both for the frescoes by Veronese inside and for its historical associations: Daniele and Marcantonio Barbaro were Palladio's most distinguished patrons, and he was to them 'our Palladio'. It is in beautiful country near Asolo, itself endowed with associations and with good restaurants. Open Tuesday, Saturday, Sunday, public holidays 3–6 p.m. (also through the winter 2–5 p.m.); tel. 0423–565002.

Probably Palladio's designs were carried out in the mid to later 1550s. Much has been made of the rather extraordinary fact that in the *Four Books* Palladio does not mention Veronese's frescoes done soon afterwards, even though he usually credits decorators and these are outright the finest murals in any of his villas. He chose instead to describe mainly the villa's waterworks. The chapel was added to the villa in 1580. (See pp. 90–100 for the brothers Barbaro; pp. 123–7 for the landscape frescoes; pp. 146–50 for the waterworks, grotto and gardens.)

Villa Emo, Fanzolo, Treviso

On the plain not far south of the villa Barbaro. Between the two one can visit the remains of the *barco* or park of Caterina Cornaro at Altivole (see p. 136). Open Saturday and Sunday, public holidays 3–6 p.m.; tel. 0423–487040.

Neither the villa, datable to the 1560s, nor the frescoes by Zelotti may seem quite to match the splendour or charm of the villa Barbaro. It is, however, a larger and grander establishment, still with its adjacent farm and park. Palladio described it as follows (QL II, xiv): 'At Fanzolo, an estate in the Trevigiano three miles from Castelfranco, is the building illustrated below of the Magnifico Signor Leonardo Emo. The cellars, granaries, stables and other functions "of villa" are on each side of the owner's house, and at their far ends are two dovecots, which both serve his needs and enhance the place, and one can pass everywhere under cover; which is one of the main things one wants in a house "of villa", as I have animadverted above. Behind the building is a garden in the form of a square extending 80 Trevisan *campi* [about 70 acres], through the middle of which runs a stream, making this a very fine and delightful site. The house is decorated with painting by Battista Venetiano [Zelotti].'

Villa Cornaro, Piombino Dese, Padua

In the centre of the village, through which rumble heavy lorries and much traffic; and modernity encroaches, now that the farm has gone (see the map on p. 104). Well kept by American owners, according to ideas resembling the National Trust's in England. Open Saturday 3.30–6 p.m.; tel. 049–9365017.

Giorgio Cornaro undertook the villa soon after inheriting from his father in 1551. The interior decoration is eighteenth-century, but hardly varies from sixteenth-century tradition. The villa has a magnificent 'four-columned' *sala*, of which Palladio said (QL II, xiv): 'The hall is placed in the very centre of the house, so that it is removed both from the heat and from the cold'. He then details some of the proportions of the house. Though the internal volume described by the columns is a cube, the room itself is not one (on this topic see further pp. 222–3).

3. Near Venice

Villa Giustinian, Roncade, Treviso; now Ciani-Bassetti

Very much the manor, or castle, of the village. Though the interior of the house is not open, the exterior and the court can be seen if you buy the excellent wine made here.

The villa was described as 'not yet finished' in 1514; it had been finished by 1529. The architect is not known. (See pp. 181–92.)

Villa Zen, Cessalto, Treviso

Deserted, abandoned, isolated in flat, featureless lagoon-side country. Probably the least visited of Palladio's villas. It looks too far gone now for restoration.

The design (no temple front, but a rusticated arcade at the rear, and a 'thermal' window) has much in common with villas of the 1540s; also

Palladio's description of it (QL II, xiv) stresses what were innovations then, but were no longer in the 1550s, to which it is usually dated. These novelties were the provision of a 'basement' or rather foundation (it has no rooms or space under the *piano nobile*, due to the soggy terrain); vaults rather than wooden ceilings; the different sizes and shapes of the rooms.

Villa Foscari, Malcontenta, Venezia

On the last limb of the Brenta river before Fusina and Venice, the villa can still be visited by boat (the 'Burchiello') from Venice. Open Tuesday, Saturday and first Sunday of the month 9–12 a.m.; tel. 041–969012.

The villa, for the brothers Foscari and therefore for two households, dates from the late 1550s, and the decoration of its magnificent *sala*, begun by Battista Franco and finished by Zelotti, to the early 1560s. Palladio's inspiration from Roman baths is nowhere more apparent. The house as built and as it survives (after restoration) corresponds particularly closely to the *Four Books* woodcut — even down to the detail of the balcony on the temple-front steps, a later addition now removed.

4.   Immediately outside Vicenza, on the eastern side

Villa Valmarana, Vigardolo; now Bressan

On first impression it might almost be an ordinary suburban house, though the villa is large. Newly restored and painted. One may call. (The refurbished remains of another villa Valmarana by Palladio (see p. 62) are close by at Lisiera by the river Astico near Bolzano Vicentino.)

One of Palladio's first villas, of the early 1540s. It has not gained by the alterations made to his original plan. (See p. 212.)

Villa Thiene, Quinto

Now the *municipio* of the village. Merely a relic or vestige of what it should have been, though large for one. Visible; open to callers most mornings; tel. 0444–365053.

The project dates from about 1545. (See pp. 41–3.)

Villa Trissino, Cricoli

On a roundabout on Vicenza's outer ring-road, though set back a little from it and still with country behind. Not open, but one may enter the grounds to see.

Designed by the owner himself, Giangiorgio Trissino, in the later 1530s. (See pp. 73–80, especially pp. 76–8.)

Villa Gazotti (Marcello), Bertesina

Set in a backwater village at the terminus of the no. 1 bus route from Vicenza. Run down but not entirely neglected. One may call.

Not in the *Four Books* but without doubt by Palladio. Of the early 1540s, it has one of his earliest cross-plan vaulted halls. (See p. 53.)

Villa Chiericati, Vancimuglio; now Rigo

In fairly ruinous, but very appealing condition in flat land settled with some beautiful hamlets. One is the next down the road, Sarmego; the villa Ferramosca (by Vincenzo Scamozzi) at the next after that, Barbano, should also be seen. Not open but visible from the road.

Still building in 1557. (See p. 59.)

Villa Almerico (Rotonda), now Valmarana

The villa still has a 'theatre' of hills around it, though the view across the river Bacchiglione is spoilt by modern urban sprawl. The house itself is now resplendently smart. Before or after one can also visit the villa Valmarana ai Nani close by, to see the frescoes by Tiepolo. To walk from the town takes perhaps 20 minutes. Alternatively take the no. 8 bus from the terminus outside piazza Castello, or a taxi; but getting back is more difficult. The road up to the villa is off the SS.247 to Noventa. Open Tuesday, Wednesday and Thursday 10–12 a.m., 3–6 p.m.; interior Wednesday by appointment only; tel. 0444–221793.

Built rapidly between 1566 and 1571; the interior decorations, save some chimneypieces, and most of the sculpture are of later date. Palladio remarked (QL II, iii): 'Among many honoured Vicentine gentlemen there is Monsignor Paolo Almerico, a man of the church, who was refendary of two Popes, Pius IV and Pius V, and who for his achievements won citizenship of Rome for himself and his family. This gentleman, after having travelled many years through desire for honour, finally, since all his family was dead, came home to his native city, and for his enjoyment retired to a house outside town on a hill, less than a quarter of a mile from the city. There he has built according to the following invention, which I did not think fit to place among the designs for villas because it is so close to the city that it is virtually in the city. The site is one of the most pleasant and delightful one could find, for it is atop a small hillock of easy ascent, and on one side is washed by the river Bacchiglione, on which boats may come, and on the other side it is surrounded by other most pleasant hills, which present the appearance of a vast theatre, and are all under cultivation, and abundant with the most excellent fruits and vines of the best quality.

Thus, because it enjoys in every direction beautiful views, of which some come to a point, others are more distant, and others extend to the horizon, loggias have been provided on all four fronts. Underneath these and the *sala* are the *stanze* for the "convenience" and use of the household. The *sala* is in the middle, and round, and takes its light from above. The *camerini* are mezzanined. Above the great *stanze*, which are vaulted according to the first method, and around the *sala* there is a place to walk $15\frac{1}{2}$ [Vicentine] feet broad [5·5 metres]. On the ends of the plinths that form a support to the stairs of the loggia are statues by Lorenzo Vicentino, a very excellent sculptor.' (See pp. 64–7 and 121–2.)

5.   South-east, in Paduan territory

Villa dei Vescovi, Luvigliano

A fine villa in a wonderful setting with excellent views. Not open.
    Built by Alvise Cornaro and his mason Andrea da Valle in the late 1530s. (See p. 169.)

Villa Garzoni, Pontecasale

An impressively large villa cropping up in a tiny village among vistaless fields. Custodian tel. 049–8803542.
    Built by Jacopo Sansovino it is thought in the late 1530s. (See pp. 160, 163, 200.)

6.   South and south-west

Villa Pisani, Bagnolo di Lonigo, Vicenza; now Ferri

The high dykes of the river Guà now mask the house, otherwise intact (though never built quite as it should have been) in an unspoilt landscape. Open Wednesday and Friday 9–11 a.m., 2–6 p.m.; tel. 0444–831104.
    An important and exceptionally well documented villa of the later 1540s. (See pp. 214–21.)

Villa Saraceno, Finale di Agugliaro, Vicenza

The villa had fallen into disrepair; it has now been bought by the Landmark Trust and is being restored. In the same village the villa 'delle Trombe' attributed groundlessly to Sanmicheli is also handsome. Visible but not open.
    The building dates to the later 1540s. (See p. 54.)

Villa Pojana, Pojana, Vicenza

To the south of the village, on the road to Montagnana. Owned by the
State, and not in wonderful repair. Tel. 0444–898554, or the custodian
may be at home.

  Datable to about 1550, and transitional between Palladio's early work
of the 1540s and his mature work of the 1550s (see p. 54). The central
arch's pierced archivolt is a motif first borrowed by Bramante from Early
Christian churches in Milan. The frescoes of the interior are very deliberately classical (see pp. 56–9). Palladio (QL II, xv) had this to say: 'In
Pogliana, an estate in the Vicentino, is the following building of the
Cavalier Pojana. Its rooms have been decorated with pictures and very
fine *stucchi* by the Veronese painters Bernardino India and Anselmo Canera
and by the Veronese sculptor Bartolomeo Ridolfi. The large rooms are a
square and two-thirds in length and are vaulted; the square rooms have
coves in the corners; there are mezzanines above the little rooms; the
height of the hall is one half more than its width, and at the apex is the
same height as the loggia; the vault of the hall springs from consoles, that
of the loggia is a groin vault; above all these rooms there is a granary,
and beneath them the cellars and the kitchen, for the floor of the *stanze*
rises five [Vicentine] feet above ground. On one side it has the yard, and
other places for "matters of villa"; on the other a garden corresponding
to the yard, and behind is the orchard and a fish-pond. So it is that this
gentleman, as he is magnificent, and of a very noble mind, has not neglected
to provide all those "ornaments" and "conveniencies" that are available
to render the site beautiful, delightful and "convenient".'

Villa Pisani, Montagnana, Padua; now Placco

The villa's position by a crossroads at the gate of the town (which has
spectacular walls) was once desirable but is now disastrous. The villa is
somewhat run down and its hall is permanently shuttered. Highly visible
but not open.

  Francesco Pisani was an early Venetian client (though not so early as
his namesake at Bagnolo): the house dates to the early 1550s. Palladio's
woodcut shows two service wings beside the house, reached over arches
spanning the road; one of them would have been contiguous with the
town's main barbican, making the house even more of a watchdog. Palladio
mentions the fine statues of the *Four Seasons* by Alessandro Vittoria in the
hall.

Villa Badoer, Fratta Polesine, Rovigo

The villa retains most of its grandeur, though its frescoes have suffered and it is rather distressingly bare. Owned by the municipality. Open daily 3.30–7 p.m., also 10–12 a.m. Sunday, Tuesday, Thursday; tel. 0425–68122.

The villa dates to the mid to later 1550s, a classic of Palladio's maturity, closely corresponding to his woodcut. Inigo Jones admired its 'circular logges'. (See pp. 170–2.)

7. Near Verona

Villa Sarego, Pedemonte; now Innocenti

The estate has been truncated but all that was ever built of the villa remains essentially unspoilt. One enters down a track by a garage. It can be reached by taxi or bus from Verona, having made an appointment. Tel. 045–7701345.

Though early enough to be included in the *Four Books* (1570), this is one of Palladio's last villas. (See p. 121.)

Bibliography

To date (1989) the literature on Palladio in English consists essentially of the following:

J. S. Ackerman, *Palladio*, Harmondsworth 1966 (and new edns)

J. S. Ackerman, *Palladio's Villas*, New York and Glückstadt 1967

H. Burns and others, *Andrea Palladio 1508–1580*, exhibition catalogue, Arts Council, London, 1975.

There are also C. Constant, *Palladio Guide*, Princeton 1986, and several picture books; and, in German, M. Wundram and T. Pape, *Andrea Palladio* (English edn 1989).

The documentation of Palladio's career was collected by G. G. Zorzi:

G. G. Zorzi, *Le opere pubbliche e i palazzi privati di Andrea Palladio*, Venice 1965

G. G. Zorzi, *Le chiese e i ponti di Andrea Palladio*, Venice 1966

G. G. Zorzi, *Le ville e i teatri di Andrea Palladio*, Venice 1968.

The standard *catalogue raisonné* is L. Puppi, *Andrea Palladio*, Milan 1973 (and new edns).

Numerous important articles (which I have not cited individually below) have appeared in the periodical *Bollettino del Centro Internazionale di Studi d'Architettura 'A. Palladio', Vicenza*. They represent probably the best introduction to a serious study of Palladio, and contain not least a wide bibliography. See also other architectural journals, and the periodical *Arte Veneta*, which contains an index of new publications.

The following may be mentioned as introductions to other aspects of this book beside Palladio's architecture:

D. R. Coffin, *The Villa in the Life of Renaissance Rome*, Princeton 1979

L. Crosato, *Gli affreschi nelle ville venete del '500*, Treviso 1962

G. Fragnito, *In museo e in villa: Saggi sul rinascimento perduto*, Venice 1988

P. F. Grendler, *Critics of the Italian world 1530–1560: Anton Francesco Doni, Niccolò Franco and Ortensio Lando*, Madison (Wisconsin) 1969

G. Mazzotti, *Ville Venete*, Rome 1963

P. Mometto, 'La vita in villa', in *Storia della cultura veneta* V, Vicenza 1976

A. Ventura, *Nobiltà e popolo nella società veneta del '400 e '500*, Bari 1964; this last is indispensable for the historical context of Palladio's villas.

These are the main sources I have used:
Annibale Caro, ed. A. Greco, *Lettere familiari*, Florence 1957–61
Anton Francesco Doni, *Le ville*, ed. U. Bellochi, Modena 1969
G. Falcone, *La nuova vaga et dilettevole villa*, Brescia 1559 (and other edns)
A. Gallo, *Le dieci giornate della vera agricoltura*, Venice 1565 (and subsequent and extended editions)
G. Marzari, *La historia di Vicenza*, Venice 1591
F. Monza, ed. D. Bortolan, *Cronaca*, Vicenza 1888
A. Palladio, *I quattro libri dell'architettura*, Venice 1570 (facsimile edition, Hoepli, Milan 1980)
A. Palladio, *Scritti minori*, ed. L. Puppi, Milan 1989
Bartolomeo Taegio, *La villa*, Milan 1559
Vitruvio, *I dieci libri dell'architettura, tradotti e commentati da Daniele Barbaro*, Venice 1556 and 1567 (the latter reprinted Il Polifilo, Milan 1987)
Also to the point is Carlo Goldoni's eighteenth-century *Trilogia della villeggiatura*, ed. G. Davico Bonino, Turin 1981 (or other edns).

Individual chapters are particularly indebted to the following works (among others):
Chapter 1: 'State, Sea and Land'
G. Cozzi, *Il Doge Niccolò Contarini. Ricerche sul patriziato veneziano agli inizi del '600*, Venice and Rome 1958 (and also other contributions by Cozzi)
Crisis and Change in the Venetian Economy, ed. B. Pullan, London 1968
Palladio e Verona, exhibition catalogue, Verona 1980

Chapter 2: 'Palladio's Early Career'
C. Bellinati, 'L'infanzia del Palladio a Padova fra Borgo Rogati e Borgo della Paglia', in *Alvise Cornaro e il suo tempo* (see Chapter 7)
F. Dupuigrenet Desroussilles, 'L'università di Padova dal 1405 al Concilio di Trento', in *Storia della cultura veneta*, III/ii, Vicenza 1981

Chapter 3: 'Several Gentlemen of Vicenza . . .'
D. Battilotti, *Vicenza al tempo di Palladio, attraverso il libro d'estimo del 1563–64*, Vicenza 1980
E. Franzina, *Vicenza, storia di una città*, Vicenza 1980
L. Puppi, *Scrittori vicentini d'architettura del secolo XVI*, Vicenza 1973

Chapter 4: 'The Public Worth of Private Houses'
U. Berger, *Palladios Frühwerk: Bauten und Zeichnungen*, Cologne and Vienna 1978 (also in *Arte Veneta* 1977)

M. Morresi, *La Villa Porto Colleoni a Thiene*, Milan 1988 (also in *Arte Veneta* 1985 and 1986)

Chapter 6: 'Giangiorgio Trissino'
B. Morsolin, *Giangiorgio Trissino*, Vicenza 1878
Atti del convegno di studi su Giangiorgio Trissino, Vicenza 1980

Chapter 7: 'Alvise Cornaro'
Ed. P. Carpeggiani, Alvise Cornaro, *Scritti sull'architettura*, Padua 1980
Alvise Cornaro e il suo tempo, exhibition catalogue, Padua 1980
Ed. G. Fiocco, *Alvise Cornaro, il suo tempo e le sue opere*, Vicenza 1965
E. Menegazzo, 'Alvise Cornaro: Un veneziano del Cinquecento nella Terraferma padovana', in *Storia della cultura veneta* III/ii, Vicenza 1981

Chapter 8: 'Daniele and Marcantonio Barbaro'
D. Battilotti, 'Villa Barbaro a Maser: un difficile cantiere', *Storia dell'Arte* liii, 1985, p. 33 (with references to previous articles)
B. Boucher, 'Last will of Daniele Barbaro', *Journal of the Warburg and Courtauld Institutes*, xlii, 1979, p. 272
P. J. Laven, *Daniele Barbaro, Patriarch Elect of Aquileia, with Special Reference to his Circle of Scholars and to his Literary Achievements*, Ph.D thesis, University of London, 1957
C. Yriarte, *La vie d'un patricien de Venise du 16ᵉ Siècle*, Paris 1874

Chapter 9: 'Matters of Villa'
J. Summerson, 'The idea of the villa', *Journal of the Royal Society of Arts*, cxvii, 1959, p. 570

Chapter 11: 'The Alchemy of Well-being'
F. E. Keller, *Zum Villenleben und Villenbau am Römischen Hof der Farnese. Kunstgeschichtliche Untersuchung bei Annibal Caro*, Berlin 1980

Chapter 12: 'Health and Fitness'
L. Comacchio, *Storia di Asolo, XVI: Il Barco della Regina Cornaro ad Altivole*, Asolo 1980
P. Holberton, 'The choice of texts for the Camerino pictures', in *Bacchanals by Titian and Rubens*, papers given at a symposium in the National-museum, Stockholm, ed. G. Cavalli-Björkman, Stockholm 1987

Chapter 13: 'Gardeners' Delights'
M. Azzi Visentini, *L'Orto Botanico di Padova e il giardino del Rinascimento*, Milan 1984
Ed. M. Azzi Visentini, *Il giardino veneto*, Milan 1988
J. Cartwright, *Italian Gardens of the Renaissance*, London 1914

Chapter 14: 'Farming Economics'
See also Chapter 1
A. Ventura, 'Considerazioni sull'agricoltura veneta e sull'accumulazione originaria del capitale nei secoli XVI e XVII', *Studi storici*, 1968, p. 674

Chapter 16: 'The Villa within the Villa'
P. Holberton, *Poetry and Painting in the time of Giorgione*, Ph.D. thesis, University of London, 1989

Chapter 17: 'The Anatomy of a Villa Farm'
C. Kolb Lewis, *The Villa Giustinian at Roncade*, New York and London 1977

Chapter 18: 'The Anatomy of a Villa House, before Palladio'
T. Carunchio, *Origini della villa rinascimentale. La ricerca di una tipologia*, Rome 1974
W. Prinz, *Studien zu den Anfängen des oberitalienischen Villenbaus*, Frankfurt n.d. [1973]
Ed. H. Wischermann, *Die Villa im Veneto (1444–1523) zum Stand der Forschung (Berichte und Forschungen zur Kunstgeschichte 1)*, Freiburg 1979

Acknowledgements

Accademia Carrara, Bergamo: Plate 41
Biblioteca Communale, Treviso: Plate 51
Bibliothèque Nationale, Paris: Plate 71 (= Cod. Maggi, Add. 134 rés., pp. 16–17)
British Library, London: Plate 58
Centro Internazionale di Studi d'Architettura 'A. Palladio', Vicenza: Plates 3, 12, 23, 35, 36, 69
Fitzwilliam Museum, Cambridge: Plate 45
Mansell Collection, London: Plate 47
Museo Civico, Padua: Plates 27, 28a and b
Museo Correr, Venice: Plate 57
Réunion des musées nationaux, Paris: Plates 25, 50
Rijksmuseum-Stichting, Amsterdam: Plate 29
Royal Institute of British Architects: Plates 43a, 63 (= RIBA V, 2), 64 (= RIBA XVII, 15), 65a (= RIBA XVII, 2r), 67a (= XVI, 7), 67c (= RIBA XVII, 17); also all photographs from the *Four Books* are from the RIBA's copy

Index

This is an index essentially of names and places, but special terms are also indexed to their explanation (but not other occurrence) in the text. Buildings are listed both under original proprietor (if private) and under town or village (unless homonymous with proprietor or not extant). Members of a family mentioned tangentially are subsumed under 'family' (e.g. Teódoro Thiene under Thiene family). For villas, the last reference (preceded by a semi-colon) is to the Handlist. Plate numbers are indicated in **bold**.